The Joy of
Well-Being

The Joy of Well-Being

A PRACTICAL GUIDE TO A HAPPY, HEALTHY, AND LONG LIFE

COLLEEN AND JASON WACHOB

balance

NEW YORK BOSTON

Balance
Hachette Book Group
1290 Avenue of the Americas, New York, NY 10104
grandcentralpublishing.com
twitter.com/grandcentralpub

First Edition: May 2023

Balance is an imprint of Grand Central Publishing. The Balance name and logo is a trademark of Hachette Book Group, Inc.

The publisher is not responsible for websites (or their content) that are not owned by the publisher.

The Hachette Speakers Bureau provides a wide range of authors for speaking events. To find out more, go to hachettespeakersbureau.com or email HachetteSpeakers@hbgusa.com.

Library of Congress Cataloging-in-Publication Data has been applied for.

ISBNs: 978-1-5387-2482-8 (hardcover), 978-1-5387-2484-2 (ebook)

Printed in the United States of America

LSC-C

Printing 1, 2023

Contents

*To Ellie and Grace, we hope that your journey
is filled with lots of joy and well-being.
We love you more than anything.*

Introduction:
We All Deserve the Joy of Well-Being

How do you know when it's time to change your life? Sometimes the realization is simply the slow accumulation of nagging voices inside your head. Sometimes that knowledge lands all at once, like a cosmic kick in the butt. Before mindbodygreen officially launched in 2009, we thought we were doing pretty okay. We were both deeply ensconced in the rise-and-grind lifestyle of early thirtysomethings with high-pressure jobs. Colleen had been working for years as an apparel executive for corporations like Gap, Walmart, and Amazon. Jason was flying one hundred thousand miles a year for business, often forgetting which time zone he was in, and constantly glued to his laptop. We worked hard, we packed intense workouts into our schedules when we could, we dabbled with trendy diets, and then... our bodies gave out.

Jason suffered debilitating sciatic back pain that made it difficult to walk, and then Colleen experienced a terrifying pulmonary embolism that took six months to recover from. These experiences spun us out and turned our world upside down. Before our bodies stopped us in our tracks, we thought we were doing pretty well, compared to other people we knew. Colleen went on multiple five-mile runs a week, and Jason would go to the gym for hours at a time. We knew we could do a little better in the eating department—Jason actually had his picture up on the wall at the Palm steakhouse in Midtown

Manhattan, next to those of Adam Sandler and Joe Namath, to commemorate his loyal patronage. Colleen enjoyed happy-hour drinks with her co-workers and friends most evenings. But during the week we always ate salad for lunch, so we figured it would come out in the wash, right? Not exactly.

It turns out that the grain-fed steak and sugar-laden margaritas weren't great for us, but the bigger problems were chronic stress and depletion. It's something that sneaks up on all of us at one time or another and can linger quietly for years, chipping away at sleep and energy levels, not to mention our overall well-being. Then, of course, there was the misalignment of our values and our jobs. Neither of us was sufficiently challenged or passionate enough about what we were doing in our working lives to feel that we were being fulfilled emotionally. More often than not we found ourselves doing what we thought we "should" do, instead of what we really wanted to do or what felt good for our bodies. But the body is wise. And it doesn't forget, even if we are in denial about what we are doing to it. Years and years of stress, dissatisfaction, and pressure don't dissipate— they accumulate. Sooner or later, your body demands your attention. Jason's body literally laid him out flat on the ground, not allowing him to move. Colleen's body landed her in a hospital bed, attended to by some very alarmed doctors who also wouldn't let her move. Eventually, we healed ourselves and changed our lives. But we had a lot to learn first.

Our bodies demanded we pay attention to well-being, and soon we learned that health and happiness are a virtuous circle. Your mental and emotional well-being drives your physical well-being and vice versa. Frequent margaritas and steaks might make us happy, but they don't make us healthy. Boutique fitness classes might make us healthy, but now, with two young children at home, contorting our schedules and blowing up our sleep just to fit it all in would definitely not make us happy. It's hard to make room for joy when you can barely keep your eyes open. When we first started on our well-being journey, we were shocked by the lack of clear-cut information about how to live a healthier life in a sustainable, low-cost way—so shocked, in fact, that we eventually decided to turn our quest for science-backed, holistic health and wellness information into a company that curates exactly that. That's how we started mindbodygreen. We figured that there were probably plenty of people out there like us who just wanted to feel better, people short on time who wanted a happier, healthier, and more joyful life but were not sure where to start.

We realized very quickly that we were not alone in our confusion. The current landscape of health and wellness, like many parts of our society, is full of discord. It's no wonder that so many of us are lost and overwhelmed when it comes to how to feel better in our lives. Fitness trends and nutrition brands are marketed to us like cultural identities. Are you keto or vegan? Do you fast intermittently or are you an intuitive eater? Have you tried the TikTok chlorophyll trend, or do you believe it's a scam? Is fruit hijacking your blood sugar, or is gluten the real culprit? Should you do F45 or sign up for Orangetheory Fitness? We are unable to reach consensus on a variety of hot-button health topics from the safety of sun exposure to optimal levels of protein intake, to whether you should salt your food, to whether you should avoid mouthwash (yes, that's a debate). Social media algorithms inadvertently encourage medical professionals who are on these platforms to have strong, polarizing points of view, because this approach will garner more views and engagement and enable more doctors to become "doc stars."

We all want to be happier and healthier, even if we can't agree on how to get there, and that desire, that *need* is more important than ever. In the wake of the COVID-19 pandemic, we have all had experiences navigating helplessness, confusion, and conflicting information about our health. We have lived through a collective trauma and are left to process it on increasingly depleted energy reserves.

Skyrocketing rates of anxiety, long COVID, and health fallout from years of chronic stress are all now piled upon the increasing rates of chronic illness, heart disease, diabetes, and mental illness that were there *before* the coronavirus upended our lives. Getting back to a baseline of health and happiness has never been more critical, and it has never felt more challenging.

Because crisis often amplifies what is already wrong in the world, we know that the hardship of the last few years has only deepened existing inequalities in health, stability, and well-being. The massive differences between our needs, our access, and our life circumstances have become more obvious than ever. And yet, we still find ourselves faced with advice that presumes we all have the same amount of time, money, and energy. In the current world of health and wellness, it can often seem like the brass ring of a happy, healthy, and long life is only for the people who have surplus of resources. The echo chamber of the internet and influencers have hijacked the concept of self-care. We feel like we are losing the self-care game if we aren't taking a nightly bath with sustainably sourced Epsom salts and keeping up with our daily gratitude journaling. Our social feeds have images of Kardashian-level wellness, filled with lymphatic drainage treatments, expensive vegan meal delivery, and workouts for a perkier posterior. In another corner of the wellness world are the elite longevity optimizers who are measuring their lactate after workouts and calculating their VO_2 max in a laboratory and wearing a continuous glucose monitoring device. These people offer great scientific insight, but at the same time they are bringing a technical intensity and rigidity to exercise and eating that sucks the fun right out of it.

We've got to face it: the internet does not get us closer to the work of understanding what will truly nurture our bodies and minds, nor does it help us understand what matters most in life. Some of us are hanging by a thread, others are taking it day by day, and many of us find ourselves in the position of making halting progress at best. We take a few steps forward; we take a few steps backward. Sometimes we have a hard time putting one foot in front of the other. We get on and off the wellness path, but we don't know for sure where it's even leading us.

The Joy of Well-Being is the title of this book, but we hope it's also a reawakening. We want you to look at your health and happiness through a completely different lens: well-being. It's a mindset shift that has the potential to change how you feel in your body, in your relationships, and in your life.

Wellness is about optimization and outcome. *Well-being* is about joy and journey.

You can dial in your VO$_2$ max, eliminate gluten, and stabilize your blood sugar all you want, but if your relationships are in shambles and you can't remember the last time you laughed, none of that matters. Better to go to a dance class, make some friends, and go out afterward for an old-fashioned full-fat ice cream. If you stress yourself out by spending too much time, money, and emotional energy trying to do everything you "should" do to be healthy or happy, it actually has the opposite effect. Your health will suffer right along with your quality of life. And that life is a long and winding road. When we reach for wellness, we're sprinting for goalposts, as if hitting a certain number on the scale or logging the right number of hours at the gym will unlock everlasting happiness. Life isn't about hitting your marks or avoiding pain and challenge. It's about engaging fully with *all* of your experiences and cultivating the small moments of joy along the way that bring the resilience we need to thrive through the struggle.

Using the word *well-being* instead of *wellness* is not just about swapping out one word for another. It is a fundamental frame shift that can reveal what's truly possible. Well-being is a state of being comfortable, healthy, and happy. It is not something we chase; it is something we weave together, day by day. Each day it looks different, asks something new of us, and provides fresh opportunities to find joy. Each person is the foundation of their own well-being. So, we must sit down, set our intentions, and try like hell to nourish ourselves in ways that support our bodies and sing to our souls. When we embrace the joy of well-being as our North Star, the cacophony of expert opinions dies away, the obsession with biometric data calms down, the confusion evaporates, and you are left with the only question that matters: will this next step support my health and bring me joy?

Of course, some steps are better than others. Some choices are wiser, more likely to bring you closer to well-being. After over a decade in the health space, we know that feeling better is easier to achieve than most people think, but we also know that there is a lot of noise out there. Which is why we are writing this book. *Our goal is to provide you with the raw material you need to weave well-being instead of chase wellness,* and to navigate the noise and integrate the goodness. Through our work at mindbodygreen, we have had the privilege of curating and sharing the best advice from all the most brilliant minds in holistic, science-based health. We are the product of our mentors—hundreds of the world's most brilliant well-being minds, PhDs, MDs, LAcs, therapists, movement specialists, spiritual leaders, and journalists. We've learned that doctors are people too (even though some have a God complex), and sometimes they can be driven to have a strong point of view and engage in tribalism to leverage social media algorithms or sell a book. Over the years we've developed a strong set of internal BS screeners that help us blend sources of information and listen for meaningful points of overlap in the chaos. We consider this act of discernment both an art and a science. This book is a distillation of almost fifteen years of experience on the forefront of the well-being conversation. In other words, we've done the legwork so you don't have to.

While this book won't tell you what adaptogen-laden beverage to buy at Erewhon, it will help you navigate the notoriously tricky wellness space by providing research-backed, agenda-free wisdom in fundamental areas of well-being: breath, sleep, nutrition, movement, stress, regeneration, social connection, and purpose. The first chapter of the book will explore what true well-being looks like, the challenges we face, and the mindsets we need to cultivate in order to live our best lives. The rest of the book dives into the heart of the matter and reveals how you can start feeling better, right now. We like to think about the subjects of the core eight chapters as *intentions* as much as practices—in fact, we'll use the words interchangeably throughout the book. Why? Because well-being is both ongoing choice and discrete actions. Intentions help you get into the mindset of meeting your commitment to well-being with determination and flexibility, every day. Likewise, we use the word *practice* because you must do the thing you set out to do, again and again, improving and reflecting on the process over time. Intentions help you see the big picture. Practices ground you in the moment.

Consider the following intentions:

- I will use my breath wisely.
- I will aim for deeper, more restful sleep.
- I will eat real food.
- I will move my body.
- I will teach my body resilience to stress.
- I will be a regenerative force in the world.
- I will cultivate meaningful connection.
- I will seek my purpose.

Each of these is important, useful, and potentially life-changing. The first five intentions focus on the changes we can make as individuals (breath, sleep, food, movement, resilience), and the last three concern our place in the world and our relationships with others (regeneration, connection, and purpose). Each of the practices we share to help you fulfill your intentions meet three criteria—they are easily accessible to everyone, they are science-backed, and they offer the possibility of joy. If it doesn't hit all three, it's not in the book. It's as simple as that.

No matter what intention or practice you are working on, we will teach you how to integrate these changes in a way that works for your life and brings you joy. Because health and happiness are so deeply connected, in the long term, you can't succeed at one without the other. Leave out the joy and you won't be happy, and then those new healthy habits? Kiss them goodbye. We have seen it over and over again in listening to thousands of people talk about their own struggles and journeys. People who are physically fit but can't sleep at night because of anxiety. People who are disciplined about their diet but lack meaning in life. People who are thriving at work but lack real connections with humans. By now we know that the all-or-nothing, "Try this! And this! And this!" approach to health and happiness doesn't work. Worse? It's exhausting. The opposite of joyful.

Choosing to support your well-being every day is far from impossible; moving the needle on all the markers of health is not hard when you have solid information, listen to your body, and use joy as a barometer for bringing new habits into your life. For some people, that might be by simply walking up a hill to work every day, and for others, it might be a yoga nidra class before bedtime. The secret is to develop the ability to listen to your body and be intentional about incorporating well-being into your life. These choices add up over time to improve your well-being status and become the lifestyle design elements that will change your life. By wisely weaving healthier habits and behaviors into your day, you can get to 80 percent of your maximum well-being—we promise. And we're talking about minutes a day, not hours, and all that's asked of you is integrating small moves that give you the biggest possible return on your investment.

But before you can do any of that, you have to take control. We call it being the CEO of your own health. Through a series of health issues that fell outside the ability of Western medicine to heal and alternative medicine to grasp, we have learned the importance of advocating for ourselves. There's nothing worse than suffering and relying on professional help that ultimately does more harm than good. You have to know yourself, be able to call bullshit, and listen to your intuition. The best place to begin is by figuring out what gives you joy, how you feel in your body now, and how you want to feel tomorrow and next week, and when you are seventy-five years old. These questions are fundamental to well-being, ones we will come back to again and again in this book.

Whatever you are bringing to the table in terms of time, energy, and money, this book will help you feel better by working with what you already have, from where you already are. It will prompt you to ask the questions that will help identify your growth edges: Where could you bring more attention to your health? What doors to joy could be unlocked? We also want you to dream big: How do you want to feel in your body in ten, twenty, thirty years? If you are twenty-five or over, it's probably time to start laying the foundation for sustainable well-being. We have both experienced the power of taking control of your own health and happiness, and we can't wait to share what we've learned with you.

Ultimately, when life is going fine, you don't invite radical change into your world, even though it might be exactly what you need. But when there are truly terrifying circumstances afoot, radical life change becomes a necessity. Our hope for you is that you don't have to wait until there's an emergency to make changes in your life. It's time for us all to recognize the stakes of well-being. Health and happiness are not frivolous nice-to-haves; they are essential to making the most of our time on earth. We all deserve the joy of well-being.

HOW TO USE THIS BOOK

This book is a guide, and you are on a journey.

In the pages that follow, we will step away from the "do this, then do that" paradigm so that each person can uncover their own personal path to well-being. We will dive deep into changing out your wellness lens for a well-being lens, and then walk you through the practices that will help you feel better now. Once you're done reading the book, which practices you choose to try first will be based on your reflections, your needs, and your excitement. Can you work on your sleep before you've conquered breathing? Of course! We know that not everyone will feel moved to focus on all eight areas, and honestly, you don't need to. Even if you decide to focus on four now and tackle the next four at a later date, you will be making huge strides. The beauty of these practices is that they are timeless. As your desires, needs, and challenges shift over the years, you might find yourself remembering a chapter that you didn't focus on before but that you really need in the moment. Our greatest hope for this book is that it becomes a well-being 101 reference text (one that's actually fun to read) that you can come back to again and again for ideas and inspiration.

The Joy of
Well-Being

Chapter One

What Well-Being Looks Like

Our time on this beautiful blue and green orb is full of difficulties, but if you live in the Barbagia region of Sardinia, Italy, and your name is Giuseppe, living a long, healthy life is not one of them.

For most of his life, Giuseppe lived much as his ancestors had for thousands of years. In this hardscrabble mountainous region of central Sardinia, the traditional way of life—farming and sheep herding, living in multigenerational homes, and matching daily routines with the seasons—has not changed very much. For most of his 102 years Giuseppe spent his days tilling the earth or herding sheep. He'd break for lunch and grab a nap before heading to the town square for a few hours to spend time with his friends, sharing wine and sardonic jokes in the soft afternoon light. Before the sun went down, he'd head back to the fields and work until it got dark. His wife would cook dinner for Giuseppe and their family, usually fava beans, hard cheese, and homemade bread. He'd drink at least a bottle of Sardinian wine a day, and when it was festival time, Giuseppe was reported to be a real party animal. As he got older Giuseppe slowed down, spending more time sitting and less time with the sheep. He lived with his daughter Maria and her family, who took good care of him, though he was expected to contribute to the household, doing chores and helping with childcare. He was surrounded by his grandchildren, engaged with their upbringing, and felt a sense of purpose and connection.[1]

When our friend Dan Buettner, a writer and researcher, went to interview the centenarians of Sardinia in 2004 for his bestselling book *The Blue Zones*, he talked to many people like Giuseppe who seemed to have found the secret to health, happiness, and longevity. Their lives weren't easy—just try tilling a field for twelve hours a day—but they were full of movement, purpose, family, and good, simple food. There was wine, there was laughter ringing off the cobblestones in the narrow village streets, and there was often a long climb back up to whitewashed houses hanging on a hill. Most centenarians were free of heart disease and cancer, and remained cognitively clear throughout their lives. When they died, they were often surrounded by family in the houses where they raised their children. No one's life is perfect, but the centenarians in Buettner's book found theirs to be full of meaning and good health. And it was as simple as moving every day, eating the foods that their families had been making for generations, sleeping with the sun, and regularly gathering with lifelong friends.

The research in *The Blue Zones* revealed that the keys to the good life were not held by Sardinians alone, but in fact were shared by multiple zones in disparate parts of the globe. These Blue Zones include Ikaria, Greece; Okinawa, Japan; Loma Linda, California; and Nicoya, Costa Rica. When you look closely at the stories of centenarians in these places, patterns in culture, cuisine, and behavior emerge. Buettner's work for the last two decades has been about mining the longevity lessons that can be found across Blue Zones. What these folks can teach us about avoiding disease, relating to one another, eating healthfully, and living with purpose is immense, and we will touch on Buettner's findings throughout this book.

But to us, what is most shocking about Dan's research is not the data—it's how it made us feel when we first read it.

Our first reaction was a little bit of grief and a nagging feeling that *that* is how life should be, *that* is well-being. This was followed quickly by a desire to sell all our belongings and move our family to a mountaintop in Italy.

It's safe to say that for most of us, the lives of the Blue Zone centenarians do sound a lot like fantasy, or at least life from a bygone era: rising with the sun, working with your hands toward a tangible result (Meat you can eat! Wool you can sell!), eating fish that you caught, drinking wine that your cousin made, playing games in the twilight with your grandchildren as the neighbors play music, and then crawling into bed for a restful eight to ten hours of sleep.

It's not just the locales that make this description feel so dreamy (though they are); it's the whole package—the low-stress life of eating good food, working hard, and making merry. To many of us, that kind of life feels utterly out of reach.

And friends, that is the problem.

ROADBLOCKS TO WELL-BEING

It says a lot about our reality that the pace of our lives, the quality of what we put into our bodies, and the rhythms of our social connection are so vastly different from those of the healthiest people on earth. It's shocking that for most people living in the United States, one of the richest countries in the world, that what it *really* takes to be happy and healthy seems so beyond reach. After all, while some of us might want to quit our lives and move to a Blue Zone, that isn't a possibility for most of us, and for many of us it's not a solution—we want to keep our current lives, just be a little bit happier and healthier in them.

Often, bridging the divide between the ideal and the real can feel impossible. Many of us live in densely populated cities, rarely interact with neighbors, and find it hard to integrate community into our lives. Others live in rural or suburban areas that are physically distant from extended family and friend groups. Regardless of our geography, we are mostly sedentary creatures, sitting at our desks for eight hours a day under artificial lights. Our front stoops and backyards are not spontaneous meeting places for members of the community—they are highly private spaces that may be safe but often feel lonely. We work long hours at stressful jobs, counting down the days until the weekend. Even though we might not love our jobs, we need them to pay for the many aspects of our lives—food, housing, medical bills. At night, we're exhausted, but we scramble to make dinner that seems "healthy" according to all the media we consume telling us what's good for us and what isn't. We get through the day, sometimes without being present or experiencing joy. Our commitment to our phones brings us more loneliness and stress than connection. We struggle to fall asleep, because our brains are already buzzing with tomorrow's to-do list, and we inevitably wake up feeling behind.

That is life in this modern world.

It's what we have to work with, and compared to the sun-soaked agrarian Mediterranean lifestyle, it does not always feel like we're living our best lives. And sometimes that's okay, and sometimes it just makes us sick and sad.

People who live in the Blue Zones are not more virtuous, they don't have more grit, and they are not genetically superior. But they did win the geographic lottery. They were born into a culture and environment that was intrinsically supportive of health and happiness. The rhythm and shape of life in the Blue Zones just happens to match up with what the human body and spirit need to live a long, healthy life. We need access to healthy food, we need to move our bodies regularly, we need real-life social connection, and we need our lives to be full of ease and sleep, not full of stress. And yet so many of us are not getting these needs met. This is the state of well-being for millions of us.

We Are Not Breathing Properly.

Despite the fact that our bodies were designed to breathe primarily through our noses, half of the population is breathing habitually through their mouths, which has real consequences for our sleep, not to mention our respiratory and dental health.[2] According to James Nestor, author of *Breath: The New Science of a Lost Art*, "Ninety percent of children have acquired some degree of deformity in their mouths and noses. Forty-five percent of adults snore occasionally, and a quarter of the population snores constantly."[3]

We Are in the Midst of a Sleep Crisis.

According to the US Centers for Disease Control and Prevention (CDC), about one-third of the population is getting insufficient sleep, which is correlated to chronic diseases like type 2 diabetes, heart disease, obesity, and depression.[4] This is probably why the CDC and other sleep experts have called sleep deprivation in the US a public health epidemic.[5]

We Are Not Eating to Support Health.

In the United States, 39.5 million people live in a place where there is limited access to supermarkets, and 19 million people live in what is considered a "food desert"—meaning their ability to get to a supermarket and buy food is severely compromised.[6] According to the US Census Bureau, the poverty rate is 13.4 percent, which is the equivalent of over 42 million people.[7] In 2018, Americans spent $931 billion on eating away from home—restaurants, dining halls, schools, and airplanes.[8] Only about one-third of Americans in 2020 reported cooking at home every day.[9] And this was during the first year of the pandemic, when most of us were shut-ins with extra time on our hands! The consequences of not eating real food are dire—one study from France showed that a 10 percent increase in consumption of highly processed food led to a 14 percent increased risk of death.[10] The bad news is that in the United States, two-thirds of all the calories consumed by kids come from highly processed foods.[11] Outrageously, our government uses taxpayer dollars to disproportionately subsidize crops, like corn and soybeans, that are used to make the foods that are so damaging to our health.[12]

We Move Our Bodies Less Than Ever.

Twenty-five percent of Americans sit more than eight hours a day.[13] James Levine, MD, of the Mayo Clinic, was so alarmed by the emerging research on the health effects of our sedentary lifestyles that in an interview with the *Los Angeles Times* he said, "Sitting is more dangerous than smoking, kills more people than HIV, and is more treacherous than parachuting. We are sitting ourselves to death."[14] And with the onset of the coronavirus pandemic in 2020, more able-bodied people than ever are working from home, which means they are not even getting the minimal exercise of getting in the car each morning, or walking to the subway.

We Are Chronically Stressed.

Since 2007, the American Psychological Association has done a survey all about stress in America and "its sources; its intensity; and how people are responding to stressors, both mentally and physically." Since the beginning, the rates of chronic stress that the report revealed have been high, but in 2020, eight of ten Americans were reporting increased levels of stress because of the pandemic, prompting the APA to "sound the alarm" on the state of mental health in the US.[15]

We Are Removed from Nature.

Despite living for millions of years in close connection with the land, most of us are living farther apart from nature than ever before. We live in cities made of brick and stone and glass, eat food that came from halfway across the world, and sit inside all day under artificial lights. Our modernized world has pulled us out of physical contact with the natural world, and this distance has even been reflected in our cultural conversations. The Greater Good Science Center at the University of California Berkeley did a study of references to nature in popular culture and found that "Nature features significantly less in popular culture today than it did in the first half of the 20th century, with a steady decline after the 1950s."[16] Is it a coincidence that our move away from nature has occurred in the same timeframe as an unprecedented rise in man-made carbon emissions, extinction events, sea level, and global warming? We think not.

Social Disconnection Is at an All-Time High.

The isolation of working and living in your home is not only bad news for your health, but it has led to a deepening mental health crisis that was burgeoning well before the word *isolation* took on a totally different meaning. In fact, a 2019 study from Cigna reported that "Only around half of Americans say they have meaningful, daily face-to-face social interactions."[17] Can you imagine what that statistic is now?

We Lack an Understanding of Our Own Purpose.

Having a sense of purpose, an understanding and sense of what makes your life meaningful, is linked to better health and a longer life. An eleven-year study led by Robert Butler, MD, and funded by the NIH showed that people between the ages of sixty-five and ninety-two who had clear goals and purpose lived longer and had a better quality of life than those who didn't.[18] And yet, according to an article in the *New York Times*, only a quarter of Americans understand their own purpose.[19]

None of this is our idea of a life well lived.

And yet, most of us know these things are bad. Chronic stress. Lack of sleep. Financial insecurity. Aimlessness. Loneliness. They are all well-documented barriers to well-being that we as a society have totally failed to address on a community, state, and national level. And that is unacceptable. Let us be clear: while this book is largely about how you as an individual can help yourself feel better, the institutions and systems that are putting us in this position in the first place are ultimately to blame for the majority of the hurdles to well-being that we face. It should not be expensive or difficult to navigate a healthcare system. No one should be forced to buy fast food simply because it is the only thing they can afford to eat or access.

And while we keep fighting for systemic change, *we also deserve to thrive.* Even though there is a lot you cannot control—a major lesson of the pandemic for us all—we want you to know that *what you can control is more than enough to help you live a better life and transform your well-being.* And it all starts with putting a different lens on health and wellness by using well-being—what brings you health *and* joy—as your North Star.

Acknowledging and accounting for the personal hurdles to well-being that you have in front of you is a necessary precursor to finding a way around them. In every chapter of this book, we lay out the ways in which the solutions we're discussing—how to breathe, sleep, and eat better—can still be accessed despite common barriers, and we provide strategies for integrating the micro changes that can tip the scales with minimal effort, time, and money. While not everyone has the resources or the knowledge to navigate around these challenges on their own, everyone deserves to be happier and healthier.

We'll say it again because it's so important: You deserve joy. You deserve to be healthy. You deserve to live a long life. You deserve more.

Spoiler alert: improving your well-being is not as hard as you think. But you've got to take the wheel.

APPOINT YOURSELF CEO

Here's a riddle: how does a man who is six foot seven fit into an economy class airline seat? Answer: not well.

Okay, so that's not exactly a riddle, but it was Jason's reality for the better part of 2009. After the stock market crashed in 2008, Jason saw the funding for his start-up (Crummy Brothers Organic Cookies) dry up and blow away. The next year, he flew over 125,000 miles traveling to different Whole Foods Markets all over the country, trying to scare up funding and hawk extra delicious, undercapitalized organic chocolate chip cookies. The stress of start-up life combined with the literal contortions of jamming himself into a small space for hundreds of hours eventually caught up with him in the form of two extruded disks and a fiery sciatic nerve. Toward the end of the year, the pain in his back became excruciating, to the point where he could barely walk even a few steps at a time. Eventually it got so bad he was bedridden, left to lie and stare at the ceiling, stressing about money and the imminent collapse of the company he had co-founded. By then he had tried cortisone shots (no dice), and multiple specialists told him that back surgery was his only option.

The only problem was that Jason's gut told him, very calmly, "Nope."

It was a small but strong voice, telling him there had to be another way. And it was surprising, because it's not like he was against surgery or that he thought it wouldn't help—it's just that it felt extreme. And although he couldn't explain why, it didn't feel right for him. So, when one of his doctors made a throwaway comment as he was walking out the door—"Yoga might help"—Jason latched on. Despite not identifying as a yoga guy, he threw himself into learning the poses that a physical therapist taught him, and he did them every morning and evening. And little by little, they helped. Slowly he got out of bed and could walk, and then finally he could get back on a plane. Sure, he had to do some downward dog at the gate in his suit and tie like a total goober, but at least he could sit for more than ten minutes at a time. Over the course of six months, his back fully healed, and over a decade later, he still hasn't had surgery. He is officially a former basketball-playing jock turned full-blown yoga aficionado.

To this day, Jason isn't sure what possessed him to say no to surgery and yes to yoga, to go against what multiple professionals and doctors assured him was the only option. But whatever it was, it taught him a life-changing lesson: you are the one who has to live with the consequences of your health decisions, so *you* have to be the one to call the shots. This isn't about not listening to your doctors—you should always take what doctors say very seriously. This isn't about discarding science—science should always inform your decisions. This is about getting all the information, deeply reflecting on the options in front of you, and *listening* to your whole self. This is your life, and as we tell our daughters, *you are the boss of your body.*

Once Jason got a taste of how wonderful it felt to find the right answer to a difficult health question and find greater happiness as a result, he was hooked. He started wondering what other parts of his life had been on autopilot and, like his back, were a disaster waiting to happen. Realizing that cookies weren't his passion, he got the idea to start mindbodygreen with the goal of making wellness accessible to the masses. He quickly realized that he wasn't the only one having a difficult time navigating past the status quo and making sense of the conflicting advice about health and wellness. The mission of mindbodygreen to bring no-agenda clarity to the confusion has resonated with more people than we could have imagined back in 2009, and today it resonates more than ever.

Why? Because our healthcare system isn't set up to focus on prevention. Its sweet spot is intervention—and even in that, the gold standards of treatment can often feel inadequate, even to doctors.

If you have a chronic condition that needs to be managed, you are often told that your first stop is the pharmacy, not the supermarket or the gym. There are plenty of people living with conditions that are hard to diagnose because their symptoms are so generalized— fatigue, headaches, low energy—that what ails them could be almost anything. And if you don't have a diagnosis in our healthcare system, it's impossible to get help from medical doctors, which means many people are left hopeless, frustrated, and unhealed. About a decade ago, Jason was plagued by anxiety, fatigue, and a strange tingling in his legs. He went to a handful of doctors who ran all sorts of tests, but ultimately looked at him and said, "There's nothing wrong with you." Having learned a thing or two about following his gut, eventually he went to a functional medicine doctor, Frank Lipman, MD, and found out that he wasn't crazy ("Are you sure you aren't just stressed?" one of the previous doctors had said); he had a parasite. After a few weeks on medication to eradicate the parasite and months of supplementation, his symptoms disappeared, but his memory of medical gaslighting remained.

Holistic and alternative medicine modalities are becoming more mainstream, but some of the wonderful solutions they have to offer are still accessible to only the most privileged and well resourced among us. Even if we can access them, it is hard to identify the legit practitioners from the charlatans who are looking to cash in on our desperation. After her pulmonary embolism and at the beginning of our fertility struggle, Colleen went to an energy worker who did an assessment of her and then bluntly delivered the news that she was "only at about 1 percent of health." There to be helped and healed, Colleen instead walked away feeling both devastated and angry. She didn't know what the energy worker was trying to sell her by diagnosing her as almost hopeless, but Colleen knew her body and her health were not that far gone. She later learned that her experience wasn't unique; this celebrity healer was "working through his own shit," and it had affected other patients as well.

With experiences like these, it's no wonder that more and more, people are taking their health and happiness into their own hands. But being the CEO of your own health and happiness is not just about making the right call; it's about advocating for yourself, being flexible and open to change, and most importantly becoming a better listener when it comes to your own needs and desires. And we're not saying this is easy. We're saying it's important. Because who knows just how disruptive surgery will be to your life? Who knows that treadmills make you groan, but a walk with a good friend makes your heart sing? Who knows that fasting in the evening would actually be a relief, not a challenge? Who knows? You do. Learning how to truly take care of your own well-being will be one of life's most meaningful journeys. If you're going to be healthier, you've got to take into consideration what will make *you* happier. Not your doctor, or your partner, or your friends on Instagram. Getting healthier can't begin with the word *should*, and feeling better doesn't result from restriction, deprivation, or "no pain, no gain." That's toxic, self-defeating rhetoric. Real well-being is when your mind, body, and spirit are aligned with your values and with how you want to live your most authentic life.

As the CEO of your own well-being journey you have to take stock and determine what will matter most to your happiness and health, and bring you joy.

To get started with that, we suggest taking a look at your well-being baseline. In other words, where are you right now in your journey? Here are some questions to get you started:

▪ What about your life feels sweet and fulfilling?
▪ What about your life feels rushed and chaotic?
▪ How does your body feel?

- Are there any health issues that you are working with?
- What could feel better: energy levels, sleep?
- How about that big brain of yours? Are you challenged and engaged? Or are you on intellectual autopilot?
- Would you say that your days are filled with purpose? How does that manifest for you?
- Have you acknowledged, processed, or healed your trauma? (We all have some.)
- What would you like more of in your life—love, time, connection, movement, meaning?
- What are your wildest dreams for your life?

Answering these questions isn't a one-and-done task. You should periodically check in with yourself by posing these questions when life feels challenging, when there's a major transition, and when you're feeling your best. You will gain valuable information that will help you identify what is always a struggle, what patterns seem to persist, and what you can lean into that consistently brings you joy. We recommend setting aside some time during your day—maybe a brisk walk, maybe some early morning journaling, maybe just some cogitating in the shower—to think about the answers to these questions. Feel free to pause here and reflect—we'll wait.

THE HEALTH PILEUP

Our friend Martha used to be a runner.

When she was in her late twenties, she loved to put on her headphones, slip an iPod Shuffle (remember those?) in her back pocket, and race through Golden Gate Park in San Francisco, trying to reach the ocean before the sun dipped below the horizon. Then one day during a waitressing shift she felt a searing pain in her left heel, one that felt like she was stepping on a giant nail with every footfall.

This went on for a year, and some days she couldn't walk at all. She quit waitressing and joked that she started a new profession— patient. Cortisone shots, physical therapy, surgery. Three years later, it got better; she could walk again, just not very far, and no running allowed. Not long after, she developed pain in her left hip, then her lower back, then her glutes. An orthopedic surgeon confirmed that she had torn cartilage in her hip, and the option was more physical therapy or surgery. She did physical therapy for years and found she could manage the pain and occasional flare-ups. But she had stopped moving as much, started drinking a lot more, and found herself more tired and less happy. She gained twenty pounds and wondered if she'd ever be able to run again. One day, ten years after it began, she woke up and realized that she had high cholesterol, she was tired all the time, she was in therapy for anxiety, and she had no idea how to untangle the web of unhappiness that she found herself in. All her life she had been fit, healthy, and happy, but in the last decade things had gone completely off the rails. How did this happen?

We call this the Health Pileup, and it's what happens when your health in one area—physical, emotional, or spiritual—is compromised and creates a domino effect in all the other areas. For Martha, a physical injury led to more physical problems, but also emotional and psychological issues. For others, it's chronic stress that leads to health problems like high blood pressure, heart disease, and substance abuse. Sometimes people just feel spiritually adrift—maybe they've lost a job that they cared about, which can lead to a crisis of identity that brings on depression. At mindbodygreen, and in our own lives, we've seen a million different permutations of the same fundamental truth—that each aspect of our health and happiness is intricately connected and integrated, for better or worse. You can't ignore your anxiety and be healthy. You can't ignore an autoimmune disorder and be happy.

The good news is that the flip side of the Health Pileup is the

Well-Being Wave—when you make one positive change and the other aspects of your well-being rise as well. Take sleep. Is there anything in your life that is not improved by a deep, restful, rejuvenating night of sleep? As people who are regularly woken up at three a.m. by the pitter patter of little feet asking for yet another glass of water, we feel this deep in our weary parent bones. We are happier, more energized, and in an altogether different mindset when we get enough sleep. Same goes for exercise, eating well, and getting out into nature with friends and family.

What the Well-Being Wave means is that we don't have to change everything at once. We don't have to treat feeling better like every day is New Year's and we've got to do all the things at once. In fact, definitely don't do all the things in this book at once. We want you to take stock of what you need the most and start there. What will have the maximum impact on your well-being status? This book is dedicated to the micro moments of health and happiness, because we know that they can have an outsized impact over time and across the different areas your life. And once that Well-Being Wave starts to swell, you'll get better and better at learning to ride it.

Recognizing the interconnected nature of health and happiness is one of the most important steps to learning how to flip the script and turn a Health Pileup into a Well-Being Wave. It helps you understand that small moves have a ripple effect. As you're reading this book, you'll start to connect dots that you've never noticed before. Maybe you never realized how much going to sleep on an overstuffed stomach could impact your slumber, or the impact that physical fitness can have on your mental fitness. Or maybe you didn't know that *how* you eat may be just as important as *what* you eat. Giuseppe from Sardinia ate a simple meal of home-cooked whole foods every day, and that's important. But he also shared those meals with his family in a joyful and relaxed way. We know that social connection and interaction can help soothe the stress response, helping to keep us happy and even improving our gut health and digestion.[20] And that's just one example of the interconnectedness of well-being. You'll notice as you read on that this book is full of them.

DO WHAT BRINGS YOU JOY

If you only remember one sentence from this book, let it be this one: *Any healthy change you make has to be a joyful one.* What do we mean by joyful? Changes that bring you pleasure, delight, or satisfaction and just plain make your days better. When we think of joy in this context, we think about our daughter when she gets out of karate class—grinning ear to ear, bouncing on her toes, and just generally excited to be alive. We don't expect every adult to be able to bring that level of enthusiasm to the table (even if they do manage to break a piece of plywood in half with one chop), but each choice we make should be a step toward that feeling. There is so much value for our well-being in pursuing things that make us feel happy and fulfilled.

How you feel about a behavior change and how it fits into your life (or not) directly affects both how effective that change will be in helping you feel better and whether or not you'll be able to stick with it. If your day leaves you depleted and you are managing to get through it only with multiple shots of espresso, then chances are adding in an hour of exercise a day is an unrealistic goal. If you love, love, love to eat meat, switching to a vegetarian diet is not going to last long, despite your best intentions. And if you can't imagine your life without television before bedtime, vowing to eliminate screens two hours before going to bed is probably going to lead to some serious grumpiness. Why won't any of these perfectly reasonable, healthy-seeming changes work for you when they work for thousands of other people and are recommended by a bazillion experts? Because you won't be happy. Worse than not inviting joy, you might even be killing it. Life is way too short for that, especially when there are plenty of alternative solutions that can improve your health. So, whether or not it's good for you, or you should do it to model good behavior for your kids matters very little. You've got to get real with yourself if it's just not for you.

But admitting to ourselves that something that works for others won't work for us is surprisingly difficult. We all want to believe we've got the willpower, the motivation, the *grit* to overcome challenges and win the day. Our bootstrapping, suck-it-up, and side-hustle culture of rugged individualism can often mean that we see failure where there is none. That's the first challenge, but there are more. For starters, it can be difficult to really tune in to what we need *right now*—not what we needed ten years ago or what we think we will want in six months, but what feels good for our life in its current configuration. So often, major life shifts happen (kids, job change, moving across the country, going through menopause) and we forget to adjust and evolve our health habits so they work for the new chapter of life we find ourselves in.

It can be hard to stop spinning long enough to take stock of where we are in the first place and where we really want to be. We forget to ask what would really make us healthy *and* happy. When Colleen had a pulmonary embolism at the ripe old age of thirty-two, she had been living life with the volume turned up to ten. Sixty-hour workweeks, power yoga classes, and five-mile runs. Lattes, margarita dinners, and late nights falling asleep with her laptop on her stomach. Then one day, she wasn't able to walk, never mind run, without shortness of breath. In the six months it took her to recover, diminished oxygen levels and a medical mess-up with her medication led to a crushing fatigue that had her taking naps for the first time since she was a toddler. She found herself wanting to stay in and go to bed well before her friends had even made it home from happy hour. Her body had sidelined her from the life she was living at high speed, forcing her to reflect on all the ways that that life had actually compromised her health. But even more interesting was the fact that when she did stop and take stock, she realized that what she had been doing wasn't actually making her all that happy in the first place. The reason she needed all those lattes was because she was staying up late working on presentations, and the five-mile runs had been leaving her feeling pretty depleted whereas once they had been energizing. In those days we were beginning to talk about starting a family, and Colleen found herself getting more excited about slowing down and getting comfortable with life at home. What had started as a health disaster forced her to take a good look at what was working and what wasn't, and what made sense for life *now*. What that began to look like was slow-flow yoga, the stirrings of a career change, and ditching the lattes for a good night's sleep. Fortunately, you don't need a pulmonary embolism to take a beat and reflect on where you are in life and what will bring you joy.

HOW TO GET TO 80 PERCENT OF MAXIMUM WELL-BEING

mindbodygreen has a reputation as being the United Nations of health. We love hearing this, because that is 100 percent by design. We have some guardrails around what we share with our audience (no conspiracy theories allowed, we focus on cutting-edge science and holistic modalities), and we might not ultimately decide to endorse any one point of view, but we are always open to listening. Over the years this has proven to be our biggest asset, as it allows us to focus on the commonalities between all the disparate and sometimes contentious voices in the wellness space. In the algorithmic driven echo-chambers in which we live, mindbodygreen is one of the few sanctuaries within well-being which welcomes multiple points of view. Strangely enough, that alone is considered a somewhat contrarian stance. Needless to say, when it comes to advice for living a healthier, happier life, we have heard it all. In the past fourteen years we have published over one hundred thousand articles by over five thousand contributors and interviewed over four hundred expert guests on our podcast. Click around our website and you will find the opinions and research of practitioners of Traditional Chinese Medicine and Ayurveda alongside that of Western-trained medical doctors, nutritionists, journalists, healthcare entrepreneurs, and research scientists. On our media platform, we take it all in and curate and share only what is relevant and of interest to our audience. But because a book does not have the infinite content capabilities of the internet, we have to be more discerning here. At first this felt like a major challenge, but then we realized that all that listening set us up really well to share the points of connection between all those different voices. There are some basic universal truths that hold up no matter if you're talking to an acupuncturist or an endocrinologist. We have been around for all the trends and tried most of them ourselves. Anytime a new trend in health and wellness breaks through, we dive deep into the research and, with help from our team of over twenty editors, road test it and canvass our network of first adopters to see how it holds up. Did we try raw veganism in 2010 so you wouldn't have to? Yes, we did. And it was super unsatisfying for us, but if it has worked for you, keep doing it!

We know by now that well-being is not a one-size-fits-all endeavor, but by filtering out the noise, we have found eight practices that are time tested, science backed, and agreed on by almost every single expert we talk to as excellent ways to improve your overall well-being. Even more exciting, what we've found is that by exploring and experimenting and integrating these practices into your life, you can achieve 80 percent of your maximum health and well-being. And you can do it without wildly changing your diet, buying an expensive piece of gym equipment, or moving to Italy. It doesn't take as much money, time, or effort as you might think because it's all about making tiny, strategic changes that you can easily incorporate into your day and creating habits that amplify the Well-Being Wave.

What do we mean by 80 percent of maximum well-being? Using

percentages as a mental model as opposed to a peer-reviewed statistical analysis has helped us to get an idea where our well-being baseline actually is—what it looks and feels like. And as for how we define health, we think about it like this: *health is more than the absence of disease; it is the state of mental, physical, spiritual, emotional, and environmental well-being.* It is waking up and feeling good in your body and energized for the day, having moments that bring you joy, and knowing you're able to spend time on the things that engage and challenge you, that you have meaningful relationships and purpose, and that you can move with ease through your day knowing that you are connected to the world.

It would be pretty hard to attain and sustain 100 percent maximum health 100 percent of the time—even Giuseppe was probably only consistently at 90 percent. If you are disease-free and living like a typical American, you're probably at about 50 percent on average (again, roll with us on the guesstimate). Chances are you're not getting enough sleep, you are overly stressed, and you're not moving your body as much as you need to or eating in a way that makes you feel good. You might wish that you had more time for friends, family, and self-care. Maybe you are dealing with a chronic condition or an injury, and your percentage is even lower than 50 percent. Maybe you're doing pretty well with the things we've listed but would love to feel just 10 percent better overall. The point is, we all could use a tune-up at minimum and an overhaul at maximum. But setting your goal at 80 percent of your "best life" and achieving that is eminently doable. From a health span and well-being standpoint, it is actually a huge achievement, and it means a healthier, happier, longer life.

Every once in a while, you might have the time and energy to shoot the moon and go for that extra 20 percent. What that might look like is diving into the technical details of health and tracking your biometrics with blood tests or fitness trackers. Optimizing, as they say in Silicon Valley. However, not everyone wants or needs to do that. Colleen, for instance, is not an optimizer. She frankly doesn't have the time or inclination—but she has figured out what her 80 percent looks like, and she's able to achieve that benchmark about 80 percent of the time (are you sensing that this is a magic number for us?). She doesn't ever experiment with the latest cleanse, or make it to boutique fitness classes, or put $300 organic oils on her face. What her well-being requires is expressing what she's grateful for each morning, taking in the sunrise outside, walking to get coffee every day, lifting weights a few times week, eating with an attention to her protein intake, and watching television to help unwind her brain before bed. Family trips to the beach and going on walks with a friend after her children are in bed also bring her a lot of joy. For her, these are the sustainable choices that also make her happy—no optimization required.

Jason, on the other hand, loves information. He's had good luck with using data from his fitness trackers to tweak small things here and there that really make a difference. He gets no less than twenty-eight vials of blood drawn every six months so he can stay on top of all his different levels, from vitamin D to homocysteine, to his ApoB. (Don't worry, he's a big guy. Lots of blood.) A driving motivator for Jason is his struggle with the poor longevity track record among the men in his family—his dad died of a heart attack at forty-seven, a year younger than Jason is now, and both of his grandfathers died in their forties, one from a heart attack and one from cancer. Jason doesn't believe that genes are destiny and plans on thriving well into his nineties. As a result, he's decided to take a more active role in monitoring his health. This history ends with him. On a lighter note, the tinkering makes him happy. It doesn't stress him out. He's naturally curious and finds the act of experimenting to be creative and joyful.

Just remember that the name of the game is discernment. Sometimes you might only want to reach for 80 percent; other times, you might be looking to go the extra mile. Reflect and tune in to your body's needs and who you are. If your heart rate variability app makes you feel worried and stressed, *please* delete it. If it helps keep you motivated and energized and you are delighted to check in with the app at the end of the day, go for it. For some people, reaching for that extra 20 percent might mean signing up for a meditation retreat, joining a book club, or training for a 10K. Because we know there are people out there who want to go the extra mile, at the end of each chapter we've included a section with ideas for how to get that extra 20 percent in each practice area. It's all about that self-knowledge.

The next eight chapters of this book each cover an area of well-being that is crucial to getting to your own personal 80 percent. Within these chapters are the most time-tested, science-backed tools that will bring more well-being into your life. Our suggestions are based on years of filtering through the noise to find the signal of health and happiness. Probably the most interesting, satisfying realization we've had about well-being over the course of the last decade is that all the things that work—like really, truly *work*—are all the things that most everyone agrees on, and they happen to be the simplest and oldest approaches to living well.

In the next chapter we'll talk about something so fundamental, so obvious, that if we're lucky, we take it for granted each and every day: breath. Respiration is no less than the foundation of life, which is why we chose this as our first practice. How well you are breathing and using oxygen affects literally every cell in your body, every minute of every day. It affects how you sleep, how you move, how you digest your food, how your brain works, how your heart pumps, and everything in between. And even though our bodies do a wonderful job of self-regulating breath, recent changes to the way we live have created a few undermining cracks in the foundation. We'll share one shockingly easy way to help fill them in.

In chapter 3, we'll talk about sleep, because the science behind it is loud and unimpeachable: sleep is foundational to our well-being, and most of us are way too in our heads about it. This is an area in which we can all use some help, and like with breathing, a little change can go a long way. Not-so-fun fact: if you don't sleep for five days, you may have to go to the emergency room, whereas missing the gym or your vegetables for five days won't have such a profound impact. We'll dispel some major misconceptions about sleep—is it really true that you've got to get eight hours a night every night?—and talk to experts about how a good night's sleep actually starts in the morning.

In chapter 4 we'll focus on what might be the most confusing and frustrating wellness topic out there: food. We have had literally hundreds of experts on our podcast talking about food and have read hundreds of books, and as a result, we can relate to anyone who feels absolutely flooded with confusion. Everyone has a well-meaning hot take on what the real problem is with what we are eating and how we can fix it. Often, the science is not fully baked around these ideas— pun intended. So maybe they're right; maybe they're wrong. For the purposes of this book, we're not really interested in what *might* work; we're interested in what experts can agree is a sure thing, because that will give you the biggest return on your investment. We chose to tackle this three-hundred-pound gorilla because in this area more than any other, we know you need a voice of simplicity and calm. In this chapter, we help you cut through the noise, ignore the hot-button issues, and find a way to eat that is joyful, evidence-based, and doable.

Chapter 5 is all about moving your body. There is no greater joy than moving your body and feeling it grow stronger every day, yet joy is an aspect of exercise that is rarely discussed. This is another trend-driven area of overwhelm for people, but maintaining strength and some element of movement is critical to well-being now and far into the future. We will show you how to reframe how you think about exercise. When you put the well-being lens on movement, you see that integrating shorter bursts of movement into your day, finding activities that are actually fun, and rethinking your ideas about resistance training are all you really need.

In chapter 6, we'll talk about the age-old practice of cold exposure and its ability to teach the body resilience through *good* stress. While the science is young, we chose to include cold therapy because every day new studies come out that confirm the benefits of short bursts of healthy stress (like cold-water plunges) to help improve immune response and increase resilience to stress and anxiety. While a cold shower might sound like hell, it might just be one of the cheapest, easiest ways to increase your health and happiness—another reason we chose to cover it.

In chapter 7 we tackle an important part of well-being that is often overlooked: environment. Even though it might feel like it sometimes, we are not all walking around in our own tiny bubbles—we live in the world. The air, the dirt, the sun, the pollen, the animals, the rising sea levels, the extreme weather events, all of it. Though we have largely separated ourselves from nature by building climate-controlled dwellings inside metal boxes and by driving on paved roads, we evolved *with* nature, not outside of it. We have spent decades ignoring our impact on the world in terms of climate change and environmental toxins, and now we are paying the price. We chose to include this chapter because of how deeply it is connected to all the other practice areas—for instance, breathing through your nose is great, but there's only so much it can help if the air is polluted. This chapter will look at the different ways we can improve our health and happiness by waking up to the world around us, understanding how it impacts us, and working toward a more regenerative future.

In chapter 8 we look at the impact social connection can make in our lives. Human-to-human connection is vital to our health and happiness, yet the simple act of meaningful social interaction always seems to be at the bottom of everyone's wellness to-do list. In this chapter we dive into the evidence that social connection is powerful medicine, not just for mental and emotional health but also for your physical health. While there are many structural and cultural obstacles to real-life connection in the digital age, we'll look at what experts have to say about how to connect with others skillfully and intentionally. At the end of the chapter, we'll talk about how to reach out and engage in ways that fill you up and contribute unexpectedly to your health and well-being.

The final chapter is by far the most existential: purpose. What is it, and do you have it? We are on earth for a short amount of time, and how we spend that time and why we bother putting our feet on the ground every morning matters. And whether or not we wake up every day feeling like we have a meaningful existence, feeling like we are a part of something greater, and believing that we belong here matters greatly to our health and happiness. Here we'll look at some of the latest brain science on how spirituality is protective against depression and talk about the many different paths to purpose and well-being and how they evolve over one's life. We chose to include this chapter in part because of what a powerful variable purpose is in the well-being equation—humans have been seeking out the answers to big questions from day one, after all—and how dangerously close we are to forgetting about it.

Part of our own purpose at mindbodygreen, and what helps keep us healthy and happy as people, is sharing what we have been lucky enough to learn about well-being over the years. We believe everyone should have access to information—from the age-old to the brand-new—that can help them flourish with what they've got. The modern world may not be intrinsically supportive of our health and happiness, but it does provide us with an abundance of scientific insight and discovery. In the pages to come we will navigate the chaos and help you integrate that abundance into your life by curating the best of what we have learned from the most knowledgeable experts in the world on health and happiness. It's time to start living the good life. So where do we begin? As any good well-being book does: by taking a deep breath (through your nose).

Chapter Two

Breathe

You don't know what you've got till it's gone.

Wrapped inside every cliché is a shimmering kernel of truth—and this one Colleen felt right square in her chest the moment she lost her breath and collapsed on the dirty, crusty escalator stairs of the High Street A-train subway stop. On the train her chest had felt tight, almost like someone tied her a little too tightly in a corset. But the second she started walking, making her way through the human scrum toward the station exit, she felt dizzy and seriously breathless. It wasn't an unfamiliar feeling—after all, she was a runner and would often push herself to the point of losing her breath—but feeling this way when simply walking? Never. The confusion of the moment left her brain grasping for plausible explanations. She had just come from Tara Stiles's Saturday morning yoga class, and the subway was stuffy in the May heat, so maybe she was just overheated. Never mind that she took the same yoga class and the same train almost every weekend, even when it was broiling in August. By the time she reached the stairs and the promise of light and fresh air, she thought she was in the clear, but instead, she collapsed. For Colleen, the experience was characterized more by denial than anything. She called her doctor at Jason's urging but was dismissive of her own symptoms, telling them that it was possible she was just dehydrated given the heat.

For the next twenty-four hours she told herself stories that she was fine. But by Sunday night, Jason insisted that she go to the doctor in the morning. When she called him from the doctor's office on Monday and told him she was being sent to the ER immediately, Jason was gripped by fear. He had lost his grandmother to cancer the previous month, and the grief was still fresh. He knew that one day people you loved were healthy and whole, and the next, they were just gone.

When Colleen arrived at the ER, doctors told her that she had "showers" of blood clots in her lungs and that she was lucky to be alive. The clots had wended their way from a mysteriously swollen ankle (which she had dismissed as a TRX injury) into her lungs, making it harder and harder to breathe. Luckily, it was caught early, and she was prescribed blood thinners and monitored carefully by good doctors. But for the next six months she struggled with her breath; while the clots were slowly dissipating, they were still causing trouble. Jason spent those weeks in a state of hypervigilance, watching Colleen to make sure she wasn't pushing herself and that she was healing. The doctors were pretty clear about what a near miss the first go-around had been, and Jason couldn't shake the feeling that it wasn't over. Colleen spent those months more fatigued than ever, dealing with headaches and shortness of breath upon even minor exertion. Though she would never choose to repeat that experience, it did leave a lingering gift: never again would she take for granted the simple act of an easy, full breath.

Until then, like most of us, Colleen hadn't thought much about breath. After all, breathing is the most fundamental, boring thing we do, right? Humans breathe between 17,000 and 30,000 times a day.[1] If you live to be eighty years old, that works out to between 400 and 800 million breaths in a lifetime. It's a vital bodily function that is unique because we can both consciously control it and take our hands off the wheel and let our brains regulate it. But most of the time, we just forget about breathing altogether. Until very recently, most of the medical establishment in the Western World has completely ignored the various impacts of breath. Most people don't worry about breath at all, until it's suddenly lost or severely compromised.

Spoiler alert: we should.

BREATH IS LIFE

There's a good reason that we chose breath as the first focus in a book about well-being: Breath is the foundation of physical and mental health. The air we breathe represents our deepest connection to our environment, our spirituality, and ourselves. And despite it being the most natural thing in the world, most of us are not breathing in a way that supports our overall health and happiness. In fact, some experts estimate that around 50 to 80 percent[2] of adults exhibit what they call "dysfunctional breathing patterns," and if you suffer from anxiety, allergies, or sleep apnea, or if you snore (yes, even a little), there's a good chance your breathing patterns are to blame or are making the situation worse.

What exactly does it mean to have a dysfunctional breathing pattern? Put simply, it's whenever you are breathing too hard, too fast, or primarily through your mouth.

What causes our breathing patterns to get off track? That's a more complicated question because breathing is multidimensional— meaning there are biochemical, biomechanical, and psychophysiological components of breathing.[3] For instance, the level of carbon dioxide in your body affects the pH level in your blood, which directly controls respiration rate; how well your diaphragm is engaging to help pump air in and out of your lungs impacts the efficiency of your breathing; and how well your nervous system is regulating your emotional state impacts everything. If any one of these elements gets out of whack, it can lead to a dysfunctional pattern. These patterns can be short lived, like Colleen's experience with pulmonary embolism, or they can be chronic, which often happens when someone has an anxiety disorder or sleep apnea.

If you've ever been in a car accident, run a really intense road race, or even just had a blowout fight with someone, you've experienced the ill effects of not-great breathing in action, if only for a little while. When your fight-or-flight response is triggered, or when your adrenaline is high because of exertion, your breathing pattern becomes temporarily dysfunctional. When people are stressed, they breathe faster. They take harder breaths and often breathe with their upper chests and through their mouths. In this case, blood chemistry has changed your breathing pattern. For short bursts of time, this is fine, or even good. After all, our bodies evolved the fight-or-flight response for a reason: we needed to pull in extra oxygen for short bursts of time to get away from all those lions and bears. The problem is that many of us are breathing harder and faster, and with our mouths open, almost every minute of every day. It may not be as obvious as it is when you are sucking wind at the finish line, but the same processes are at play. When you are overbreathing—subtly and chronically or obviously and temporarily—your nervous system is in a state of physiological stress brought on by the fight-or-flight mode. If you are always breathing that way, the ill effects on the body are very much like what happens when the body is exposed to long-term chronic stress—fatigue, inflammation, cardiovascular wear and tear, and hormonal dysfunction.

For those whose breathing is chronically dysfunctional, the impacts on well-being are immense. Why? It is as simple and profound as this: in order to function, every single cell in your body needs to receive adequate oxygen and dispose of carbon dioxide. Anything that compromises the ability of the lungs to do their job— replenish the oxygen and expel the CO_2—will have cascading effects on our health and mental state. Dysfunctional breathing changes our blood chemistry, which, over time, can create deficiencies that interfere with the healthy functioning of the nervous, cardiovascular, and digestive systems. This could mean your hands and feet are always cold, or maybe you have brain fog and headaches, or even chest pains and heart palpitations.[4] Even more obvious, dysfunctional breathing patterns can make it harder for your red blood cells to release oxygen to all your other cells, which is exactly as bad as it sounds.[5]

Just one example of the sneaky and insidious effects of poor breathing is how it torpedoes sleep. Some sleep experts believe that the cause of sleep apnea and insomnia can be traced back to dysfunctional breathing patterns. Sleep apnea occurs when breathing stops and starts, interrupting sleep, and insomnia is a sleep disorder in which people find it difficult to get to sleep, stay asleep, or get back to sleep after waking up. Both of these disorders are disastrous for health. The long-term effects of chronic sleep disruptions increase the risk of hypertension, cardiovascular disease, weight gain, diabetes, and cancer. (More on this in the next chapter.) And in many cases, how we're breathing contributes to whether or not we're waking up during the nighttime. We interviewed Patrick McKeown, one of the world's foremost breathing experts and bestselling author of *The Oxygen Advantage*, and he explained how this happens. During the daytime, your breathing patterns lock into place. If you're chronically breathing through your mouth at a rate that is too fast, that becomes your norm. When you go to sleep at night, that pattern holds. And when you are breathing hard and fast during sleep, the reptilian brain gets nervous. It has evolved to arouse you from sleep when you are overbreathing for a good reason: it thinks we're in danger.[6] Maybe there's a bear in the cave that your body senses, or maybe you're overcome by food poisoning and your body needs to purge safely. Both things require you to be awake, right? So, when your breathing pattern is dysfunctional, your brain can interpret that data as a warning signal—one you need to wake up to deal with.[7] Of course, if you wake up in the middle of the night, safe in your comfy bed, you will have no idea why you woke up. In this way, the connection between breathing rate and sleep disorders is impossible to pick up on outside of a sleep lab. As a result, most people struggling with insomnia or sleep apnea due to dysfunctional breathing don't know just how high the deck is stacked against them. They turn to exercise, weight loss programs, or pharmaceuticals to help them sleep, not realizing that the answer could be as simple as breath.

It's becoming more and more widely recognized that cultivating functional breathing patterns could be the solution to a mind-blowing array of problems, from controlling inflammation to balancing our nervous system, managing anxiety, and healing our microbiome. On a certain level, this shouldn't be a shock. After all, cellular respiration is how we evolved to climb out of the primordial goo millions of years ago, so it makes sense that we might want to prioritize its good functioning. And yet, we haven't.

Why has our breathing gotten so wildly off track? How did we evolve into a species of mouth breathers who can't sleep even though there aren't any bears in our caves?

Simple answer: we stopped breathing through our noses.

MOUTH BREATHING

James Nestor's bestseller *Breath: The New Science of a Lost Art* has done more than just about any other book to bring greater awareness to the importance of everyday respiration. As part of research for his book, Nestor went on a journalistic scavenger hunt that took him all over the world, from dental offices to look at kids' X-rays to the Paris catacombs to study skulls. What he found was shocking. Around the early nineteenth century, humans' skulls started to look different from the ones that came before. Modern skulls are characterized by narrow faces and crooked teeth, whereas our ancient, hunter-gatherer forebears had the kind of straight teeth that would put orthodontists permanently out of business. The human jaw itself is gradually becoming smaller. These anatomical changes to our bones (smaller nasal openings, crowded teeth, bone loss) naturally have an impact on our soft tissue structures as well—smaller airways, narrow V-shaped arches in the roof of our mouths, and other changes to musculature. Smaller faces and smaller nasal passages make it harder to get air through our noses, so now we have to open our mouths and breathe harder and faster to get the same amount of oxygen.[8]

What accounts for this change? According to Nestor and other experts, the answer is food. With the advent of agriculture, the kind of food we ate began to change, slowly at first and then drastically. We went from chewing for hours upon hours to barely chewing at all. After all, noshing on roots to extract the starch takes time. But if you've ever watched kids eat breakfast, you know it takes mere seconds for humans to gobble up squishy, soft oatmeal. From around the early nineteenth century, industrialized, highly processed food became the norm, and so did the changes in our faces and mouths. Nestor and others mark the lack of chewing, and the impact that it has on bone structure, as the smoking gun when it comes to why such a drastic change in such a basic life function happened in the first place.

How we ended up here is fascinating. But we're more interested in how we can use this knowledge to get back to breathing in a way that better supports health—no matter how small our heads are. One of our favorite takeaways from Nestor's book is right there in the subtitle: breathing is a lost art. Which means that once upon a time, we knew exactly what we were doing, and for those of us who are off track, there is a roadmap back. In some parts of the world and in certain cultures, people have always prioritized breath (see: yogis and Buddhist monks). Nestor tells an instructive story about George

Catlin, a prolific chronicler of Native American life in the early nineteenth century. In his life he visited over fifty Native American tribes, like the Crow and the Osage, and took hundreds of pages of notes on the different cultures and lifestyles, even painting portraits of his subjects. Catlin documented what Nestor calls almost "superhuman physical characteristics"[9] of the native peoples—they had straight teeth, broad shoulders, and beautiful faces, and they were remarkably healthy. He also reported on their strong beliefs and practices around breath. They believed that "breath inhaled through the mouth sapped the body of strength, deformed the face, and caused stress and disease."[10] They went to great lengths to teach their children how to breathe properly through their noses and even minimized smiling and talking so as to not excessively breathe through the mouth. After extending his anthropological scope and traveling to live with native peoples in South America, Catlin found similar approaches to nasal breathing and himself became an evangelist of the practice, overcoming a debilitating respiratory disease and living a long life.

So how can we be more like George Catlin and the native peoples he devoted his life to?

By keeping our mouths closed.

ZIP IT

There are many ancient and modern breathing practices that can improve our health and happiness by helping to foster healthier respiration patterns. Breathwork can help you breathe slower and lighter. It can help you improve your lung capacity and your tolerance to carbon dioxide. There is the kind of Tummo breathing that is utilized in the Wim Hof Method, there is pranayama (yogic breathing), Buteyko, box breathing, resonant breathing, basic breath holds, Sudarshan Kriya, Holotropic Breathwork, and Andrew Weil's 4-7-8 technique. All are practiced across the world by hundreds of thousands of people to powerful effect, helping people control anxiety, improve blood chemistry, and tune up the immune system. These are all wonderful techniques to practice, and we're sure at least one of them could change your life.

But here's the straight talk: We've tried just about every technique out there and have our favorites (you'll find some at the end of the chapter), but from what we've seen, tried, and learned, you can improve your breathing patterns and get to 80 percent of where you want to be by doing only one thing: breathing through your nose.

This requires you to keep your mouth closed, of course. Consider this your small contribution to turning down the volume in a very, very noisy world. In fact, we want you to do it right now. See? So easy. If you have allergies, or asthma, or chronic sinusitis, this will be an absolute game changer for you. If you have sleep apnea, or insomnia—it's a must-try. And the beautiful part? It's free, it's easy, and breathing is something you have to do anyway. Of all the health-boosting practices in this book, breathing through your nose is by far the most accessible—no external barriers to be found.

There are three main underlying reasons why breathing through your nose is the most important thing you can do right now to start breathing better. Each one feeds into a downstream benefit like better respiratory health, nervous system resilience, and hormonal balance—which we'll get into a bit later in the chapter.

First, if you're not breathing through your nose, you're missing out on the benefits of the world's most intricate and well-designed filtration system. Inside our sinus cavity is a seashell-like structure; the air entering our noses has to make its way through many twists and turns before it gets to the lungs.[11] This gives the air time to heat up and become moisturized. It also gives the millions of cilia (tiny hairs) in our nasal passages time to collect all the nasty germs and particulate that might be in the air we're breathing. This is what our lungs function optimally with—highly conditioned and clean air. Breathing through your nose also creates negative pressure in and positive pressure out, which helps tone the soft tissue in our nasal passages and throat, pulling it back and opening the airway up even further. This guards against the muscle and soft tissue atrophy that can lead straight to obstructive sleep apnea.[12] On the other hand, when you open your mouth and inhale, there is no filter between what comes in and your lungs, and no negative/positive pressure being created. It's straight-up throat and trachea, and those are short tubes compared to the sophisticated labyrinth of your nasal cavity. In a world where forest fires, pollution, and airborne viruses are becoming increasingly commonplace, our nose is truly our first line of defense.[13]

The second reason to breathe through your nose is because it increases your CO_2 tolerance, which increases your oxygen absorption and your physiological resilience. We all know that oxygen is important, but the real invisible hero of functional breathing is carbon dioxide. And we all need more of it for optimal breathing. Blood chemistry is all about balance. It's not as simple as oxygen = good and CO_2 = bad. Oxygen is what our cells use for fuel, but in order to make the best use of that fuel, we need the right amount of carbon dioxide in our bloodstream to make that oxygen bioavailable to our cells. For most people, the solution isn't breathing more to get more oxygen; it's breathing less and more slowly to build up CO_2 in the bloodstream so you can make better use of the oxygen you've got.[14] If your mouth is an oxygen superhighway, your nose is a two-lane scenic route. Breathing through your nose immediately slows you down and helps you build up a tolerance to CO_2, which helps your cells and body tissues better absorb the oxygen they so desperately want.

The third reason breathing through your nose gives you the most bang for your buck is nitric oxide. This wonder molecule is a biological messenger that is created in the sinus tissues when you breathe through your nose—but not your mouth. Nitric oxide increases vasodilation (circulation) helping to keep smooth muscles like your heart and arteries healthy, and it aids in delivery and absorption of oxygen to your cells.[15] It's a little like adding the world's best immune booster to your air smoothie. New studies show that nitric oxide may also help respiratory infections by "inactivating viruses and inhibiting their replication." There are even clinical trials underway to study the effects of nitric oxide in COVID-19 patients.[16]

So now you're reading along, and you're breathing through your nose. Check in with yourself. How does it feel? Is it hard because you're stuffed up? Does it feel strange because you're used to breathing primarily through your mouth? Or is it easy? This is good information to have, and it's the first place to start. Check in with your breath throughout the day, notice how hard and fast you're breathing when at rest as opposed to when walking up the stairs. Because we're all about baby steps, challenge yourself to finish this chapter without breathing through your mouth even once. In the following sections, we'll explore some areas where keeping your mouth closed and your nose open is a real benefit. By the way, did you make it this far breathing through your nose? If not, that's okay; just zip your lips and begin again.

ALLERGIES, ASTHMA, AND IMMUNITY

Many of the experts we've talked to over the years have seen powerful and profound changes in their own health simply by breathing through their noses. In fact, that's often what makes them such passionate practitioners and researchers—they've felt the transformation and they want to help others too.

Patrick McKeown knows what it's like to breathe primarily through your mouth. As a child Patrick suffered from severe asthma and allergies, which affected far more than his ability to take part in athletics. Due to his chronically stuffy nose, he was a mouth breather—which, as we learned, can have significant downstream effects. When you're breathing primarily through your nose, your blood chemistry is off—you're losing too much carbon dioxide through the lungs. When that happens, your blood pH decreases and hemoglobin, which is the main carrier of oxygen, doesn't release oxygen as readily. If you've ever seen someone have a panic attack and breathe into a paper bag, it's the same idea—in a panic attack, they are overoxygenating because they're breathing too fast (which makes them dizzy, panicky, and woozy), but by breathing into the bag, they are increasing their carbon dioxide levels, which restores balance.

According to Patrick, the other problem with mouth breathing is that "it activates a greater amplitude of the upper chest and less amplitude of the diaphragm. So, it's not recruiting the main breathing muscles to the same extent, which activates the fight-or-flight response. If you're breathing hard and fast all the time, this information feeds back from the body to the brain."[17] What that meant for Patrick was that his body was in a state of chronic stress and that for him, sleep and cognition were the biggest problems. He remembers having to drag himself out of bed before high school because he never felt rested. This impacted his ability to concentrate on his schoolwork, which meant he had to work harder and longer hours just to make up for his inability to focus.

It wasn't until years later, after several failed nose and throat surgeries, that Patrick began intentionally breathing from his nose. Now he's known as "the patron saint of nasal breathing," but at first, it was hard. He would breathe through his nose and feel like he was suffocating. After a few minutes he'd have to open his mouth and take big gulps of air. But he stuck with it, using Breathe Right strips to sleep at night, and eventually he woke up one morning feeling better than he had in fifteen years. He realized he had finally slept through the night, and it wasn't long before he noticed the increased warmth of his feet and hands. The wheezing from his asthma decreased by about 50 percent in a few short weeks, and he was able to focus and concentrate at a level he'd never imagined.

Breathing through your nose as much as possible may improve conditions like asthma, and allergies, which we know are intimately connected. Many experts believe that because allergic rhinitis (that's medical speak for allergies) makes it difficult to breathe through the nose, the unconditioned, unfiltered air that comes from mouth breathing exacerbates asthma symptoms.[18] If it sounds daunting to try to breathe through your nose when it is clogged, remember that nasal breathing begets nasal breathing. The more and longer you are able to do it, the more improvement you will see.

Beyond improving conditions like allergies and asthma, breathing through your nose can help improve immune functioning for everyone. Many people who are mouth breathers find themselves constantly sick with colds, sinus infections, and other respiratory ailments.[19] We talked earlier in the chapter about the nasal cavity being an important filter, but it does more than humidify air for your lungs. The nasal passages and the mucous membranes that line them are the greatest opportunity for filtering bacteria and viruses out of the air. After all, there are as many hair follicles inside your nose as on your head.[20] Working in concert with mucus, these defenders help launch an immediate immune reaction when bacteria or virus is picked up. In the era of constantly evolving COVID-19 viruses, breathing through your nose has never looked better.

SOOTHING STRESS AND ANXIETY

In 2019, when Brian Mackenzie started running a breathwork for stress relief program at San Quentin State Prison, the first thing he told the men in front of him was that they needed to trust him. He said that each and every one of them could feel better and would be impacted in profound ways if they just did what he advised and went with the program—not a small ask of men who survived time in a maximum-security prison by being very conservative with their trust. Most of the inmates in front of Brian that day were doing hard time for a range of serious crimes. Brian knew he and his team had their work cut out for them, because most of these men lived in a well-earned state of hypervigilance. They survived by erecting walls within walls, fight-or-flight response always at the ready.

On that first day and in the weeks that followed, Brian noticed that the most curious and the most skeptical of them all was a man named Rauch. He was tall and serious, and despite Rauch's relatively low-key demeanor, Brian could tell that he commanded the respect of the group. He'd often scoff or crack jokes when Brian presented the group exercises, making everyone laugh. But every single time, he'd do them anyway. For four weeks, Rauch showed up and did the work—groaning a little less each day.

One day, about four weeks into the program, Rauch pulled Brian aside in the yard and said he wanted to talk. He reminded Brian of what he'd said at the beginning of the program—that it would change him in unexpected ways—and told him a story. A fellow inmate had tried to start a fight with Rauch in the yard. This was someone Rauch felt confident he could kill, or at the very least beat the crap out of, and normally he might have. But this time, Rauch paused. He did what Brian told him to do, and then he smiled because he knew he didn't need to touch the guy. For the first time in his life, Rauch walked away from a fight.

What did he do?

He just shut his mouth and took a breath. And then he did it again, and again.

By breathing slowly through his nose, he triggered a release of nitric oxide and elevated the oxygen availability to critical parts of his brain. In the span of seconds, he was able to disrupt the normal escalation of his fight-or-flight response and engage his prefrontal cortex (the part of the brain responsible for overriding our emotions with reason).

Over the course of the next few weeks, Rauch would continue to report amazing instances of self-control and good decision-making, impressing Brian and surprising even himself. This was a pretty remarkable outcome considering Brian Mackenzie's program wasn't anger management or group therapy. It was simply learning how to hack your nervous system by harnessing the power of nasal breathing.

Mackenzie had been practicing, teaching, and researching breath-work for over ten years before he set foot in San Quentin. As one of the world's leading experts on how breath can be used to optimize health and performance, he trains Olympic athletes, top executives, and elite members of the military. He's also the first one to tell you that you're not going to de-stress your life and control your anxiety by changing the world around you. Rauch wasn't getting out of prison anytime soon, and San Quentin wasn't going to be a kinder, gentler place, no matter what he did. All he could do was learn how to manage what was coming at him. Whether you are a lead singer in a world-famous band, a three-time gold medalist, or just an average person, stress is unavoidable. Mackenzie tries to help clients understand that they are not going to remove stress, but they can use their breath to change their physiological response to it. He believes that simply by breathing through the nose and using certain techniques to downshift in moments of high stress, everyone can learn to gain greater control over their physiology.

Anxiety disorders—including generalized anxiety disorder, panic disorder, obsessive compulsive disorder (OCD), post-traumatic stress disorder (PTSD), and phobias—affect forty million adults in the US, yet only 36.9 percent of those people get treatment.[21] Over 25 percent of children in the US have an anxiety disorder, which is related to higher instances of depression, eating disorders, and attention-deficit/hyperactivity disorder (ADHD).[22] And that doesn't include the hundreds of millions of people who are living day-to-day with high levels of chronic stress that threaten their health and happiness. Therapy and prescription medications to treat anxiety and stress aren't always effective or accessible; breathing is both.

When you understand how your nervous system works and the positive impact your breath has on that system, you can change the way you react to stress. We talked about how breathing influences the fight-or-flight mechanism, otherwise known as the sympathetic branch of our nervous system, but respiration also influences the parasympathetic branch of the nervous system, known as "rest and digest."[23] Fast breathing through your mouth can act as a trigger for the sympathetic nervous system, heightening or even causing anxiety. Elissa Epel, PhD, a psychologist and professor at the University of California San Francisco, says, "The rate and depth we breathe at is a huge determinant of our mental state."[24] So if we can learn to breathe consistently through our noses, we can potentially teach the body to better engage the parasympathetic nervous system (rest and digest). When we experience a stressful event, that "rest and digest" pathway is more accessible to us and we find greater resilience. We can move through our stress response more quickly and naturally, make better choices, and get to the other side. Maybe that means walking away from a fight or waiting twenty-four hours before sending email composed in anger or choosing to take a walk after a tough day instead of heading straight to happy hour.

If you find yourself breathing faster or harder in a stressful situation or when you're on the verge of a panic attack, the first and best thing you can do is breathe through your nose. It might not resolve everything, but it will help. When you're in the middle of a crisis, it can be hard to think clearly—everyone's been there—but we've found that the one thing we can always remember is this: just shut your mouth.

LEVEL UP YOUR FITNESS

If you have ever been to an exercise class—spin, cardio kickboxing—you've probably been told to breathe out of your mouth. (We're still not sure about the logic behind this advice.) So, what if you didn't? Patrick McKeown and Brian Mackenzie both tell their clients to nasal breathe even during exercise, primarily because of the enhanced benefits of nitric oxide and oxygen absorption that you get only when breathing through your nose.[25]

So why is it that when you do physical exercise with your mouth shut, it's tough at first? Well, naturally, your nose is a physically smaller threshold through which oxygen and CO_2 can pass. So, while carbon dioxide is being generated at a higher rate in your muscles, it's got a smaller exit. As CO_2 builds up in your body you will feel the urge to breathe and gasp, and it will probably be uncomfortable. But stick with it as long as you can—your blood vessels will begin to dilate and the increased nitric oxide in your system will help you more readily absorb the oxygen being delivered to your tissues.[26] If you continue exercising this way for a few weeks, you'll see that the "air hunger" diminishes and your body now has a higher CO_2 tolerance. You'll experience less breathlessness during physical activity and more efficiency in your workouts.

In 2018, a study by George Dallam, PhD, a sports scientist at Colorado State University, worked to prove how nasal breathing during exercise can enhance performance. In this small but illuminating study, Dallam gathered ten athletes and asked them to breathe through their noses every time they exercised for six months. He measured their performance at the beginning of the study (when they weren't exclusively nasal breathing) and again after six months of nasal breathing. The study found that the athletes were able to retain 100 percent of their baseline work rate and intensity even while breathing exclusively through their noses. But the exciting part is that they had 22 percent less ventilation—in layman's terms, 22 percent less breathlessness. This study serves as a strong data point to support what McKeown and others believe—that we should all keep our mouths closed while working out, because it saves energy. There is an energy cost associated with breathing, and you could very well direct it elsewhere. You use 2 to 3 percent of your oxygen consumption to support your breathing muscles when just sitting at your desk. If you're walking, it might be 5 to 6 percent, and if you are doing high-intensity exercise, it could be 14 to 15 percent. Brian Mackenzie works with professional athletes whose energy expenditures need to be meticulously dialed in. At the professional level, an extra couple of seconds of gas in the tank means the difference between winning or not. Even if you're not an elite athlete, the energy you gain by breathing through your nose during your morning walk could be just enough to get you motivated to tag an extra five minutes on, and then five more. No matter what kind of movement you're doing, nasal breathing will also just simply help you feel better by increasing blood flow to the brain and other tissues.[27]

SUPPORTING HORMONAL BALANCE

Many women are aware that perimenopause and menopause can bring about insomnia, hot flashes, fatigue, and headaches. But, according to Patrick McKeown, many people don't know that the hormonal shifts that come with aging may also come with changes to breathing patterns.[28]

Before health researcher Tanya Bentley, PhD, co-founded the Health and Human Performance Foundation with Brian Mackenzie, she was a working mom trying to fit it all in. In her early forties, she was an accomplished health researcher working for a private health services research firm in Beverly Hills, California. She had a job she loved and a family with two healthy kids, and she had even managed to negotiate two days a week of working from home, which back in 2010 was a real coup. Mostly she felt pretty good with the exception of the general life stress of juggling a family and a big job, so when the hot flashes began, she almost didn't notice them. When she began having more and more combined with some night sweats, it dawned on her that she was experiencing perimenopause. The hot flashes erupted from within a handful of times a week, and although hers were pretty mild compared to some women's, they would occasionally make her feel like she was about to "explode with heat."[29] Some nights, she would wake up with her pajamas soaked and damp bedsheets. Thinking it was just something she had to get through, Tanya went about her life.

In the meantime, Tanya participated in a CrossFit class that incorporated breathwork. After the first class she was intrigued, so she signed up for a few more classes. By the third class of superventilation (fast breathing), breath holds, and deep relaxation breathing, she was hooked. She started practicing some of the techniques she learned in class on the two days a week that she worked from home. The kids were in school, so she could just lay on her fuzzy blue carpet and breathe. Even now, Tanya gets emotional talking about those simple breathing sessions—she felt overwhelmed by a strange sense of peace and was so moved by it she'd often find herself in tears, glad that no one was there to see her crying on the floor just because she was breathing. Tanya may have chalked that up to the salubrious effects of a busy woman finally carving out some me time, but within only a couple of weeks she noticed more long-lasting benefits. She felt less stressed, had more energy, and, during her group runs, she realized she was suddenly keeping up with people who used to leave her in their dust. One surprising benefit was the effect on her perimenopause symptoms—a few weeks into the breathwork journey, she felt a cool breeze come in through the window of her office and shivered. Something about the rapid temperature change reminded her that she hadn't had a single hot flash or night sweat in over a week. The only thing that had really changed in her life was the breathwork, so she remembers thinking, *Wow, really?* Both symptoms disappeared, and she no longer had to order her life around them by opening windows and sleeping on a beach towel at night.

By the time Tanya met Brian about a year later, she had realized the unique healing capacity of breath and was ready to devote her research career to the science of this powerful practice. Years after quitting her day job to start the foundation with Brian, Tanya is no longer surprised by what she experienced. She is the first one to acknowledge that the research is in early stages when it comes to the impact on breath and hormonal shifts, stress, and overall well-being, and this is one of the reasons Tanya and Brian wanted to start a dedicated research foundation in the first place. Early though it may be, the promise of this line of research is clear: in some of the individual case studies Tanya has conducted, she has seen the potential of breathwork to help women in all sorts of ways. In one case, a woman's severe night sweats (four or five per night) went from crippling to gone, thanks to breathwork. Another woman with a decades-long struggle with migraines was able to reduce her stress and end her headaches by doing a mere ten minutes of intentional breathing a day.[30]

What's going on here? How might hormones be related to breathing?

According to Tanya, her stress levels at the time are the key to understanding how breathing might have impacted her hot flashes and night sweats. She says, "We don't know the mechanism of action per se for exactly how breathing practices reduce vasomotor symptoms of perimenopause/menopause, but since most likely it's related to the balance of our sympathetic and parasympathetic nervous system, it's intimately intertwined with stress and stress response."[31] The massive relief and downshifting of her nervous system when she began doing breathwork speaks to this theory, since the first, most noticeable impact on her well-being was stress reduction.

Patrick McKeown has another, related take on how breathwork might shift what's happening with hormones on the level of blood chemistry. He points out that there is a lot we don't know, but we do know that men and women breathe differently, and it all comes down to sex hormones. As estrogen and progesterone levels fluctuate throughout a woman's menstrual cycle and throughout her lifetime, so too does her breathing.[32] Why? Progesterone is a respiratory stimulant, which unconsciously quickens the pace of breathing, which means the chest becomes more involved—which causes carbon dioxide levels to drop, sometimes by as much as 25 percent.[33] Depleted oxygen absorption affects blood circulation (are your hands and feet always cold?) and perceptions of pain, and can exacerbate panic, fatigue, and anxiety. Interestingly, these are all symptoms of premenstrual syndrome, premenstrual dysphoric disorder, and perimenopause.

Let's be clear: the connection between hormonal fluctuations and dysfunctional breathing patterns and how they play into this life-altering array of symptoms is completely underresearched. Fun fact: most research on breathing (and just about everything else) has been done on men, not women. Why? In part because the hormonal changes in their monthly cycles would "complicate the analysis." Between 1977 and 1993, the Food and Drug Administration excluded premenopausal women from *all* of their clinical trials for this reason.[34] The research that has been done and is still in progress points to breathing as a major source of insight into what is at the root of so many women's health problems and how women like Tanya might finally get some relief. For now, we know that progesterone is a respiratory stimulant, and we know that overbreathing can cause a cascade of ill effects, including exacerbating stress. If you're dealing with major symptoms of perimenopause, the first stop is, of course, your doctor's office. Everybody is different, so naturally every solution will be different. But given what we know about the power of breath, breathing through your nose is an absolutely safe, easy practice to experiment with for improved overall health and well-being. If there's an ancillary benefit of fewer night sweats, we'd say that's a win.

For those of you who skimmed the science a little (no shame, folks), we want to be loud and clear. If you read only one sentence of this chapter, let it be this:

Breathe through your nose.

INTEGRATE: NASAL BREATHING AND YOUR LIFE

When we moved mindbodygreen out of our apartment and into a real-deal office, we were really invested in making the space work for the health and well-being of our employees. Very earnestly, and very on brand, we built a meditation room out of a space that once held a copy machine. We redecorated with a beautiful handwoven rug, comfy cushions, and a giant Himalayan salt lamp, with the help of our feng shui consultant. Despite our best efforts, that space probably got infinitely more action in its former life as a copy room. Our employees simply found it too difficult to step away from work long enough to meditate. In hindsight, we can't help but laugh at our well-meaning younger selves. When we started there was a lot we didn't understand about how habits and change work in reality. We were long on ambition and short on practicality, which is where most people go wrong in trying to create healthy change. Now we know that small changes wisely woven into your day get you where you want to go faster than big, showy, inconvenient Change with a capital C.

Breathing through your nose is the easiest change you can make to start feeling better right now. Even more important, it's vital to setting yourself up for success in the chapters to come and helping you get to 80 percent of your maximum well-being. But when it comes to improving your breathing patterns, you don't need a twenty-minute breathwork session or a meditation room. In fact, you shouldn't think about your breathwork practice as something that you have to "add in" at all. It takes exactly *zero* extra time. Breathing is something you already do every day, something that gets done no matter what. It's kind of like choosing to put your pants on before your shirt instead of the other way around. Either way, you're getting dressed. All you're doing by incorporating nasal breathing and slow breathing techniques is changing the *way* you are breathing. Once you make the switch and lock it in, then breathing through your nose will become your default—something you do without thinking. To get to that sweet spot, here are some tricks and tips for increasing the amount of time you breathe through your nose and integrating it into your day:

■ Start by finding chunks of time when it's easy to breathe through your nose. Identify three things that you do in your day no matter what. And then, whether you're doing the dishes, checking email, making breakfast, or driving, make a conscious effort to practice breathing through your nose.

■ If you find you're having a hard time remembering to nasal breathe, try setting a reminder on your phone that will prompt you a few times a day.

■ Is there anyone in your life who you need to listen to more? Your kids? Your employees? Your spouse? Active listening skills are in short supply in the world, and we can all do better in this regard. Here's an opportunity to kill two birds with one stone. Make it a point to do more listening and less talking. (And, of course, while you're not talking, breathe through your nose.)

■ After you've mastered daytime nasal breathing, it's time to try it at night. If you're someone who snores or wakes up with a dry mouth and clogged sinuses, you probably need some assistance. Might we suggest taping your mouth shut?[35] This may seem crazy, but it's as simple as putting some soft tape horizontally on your lips. Mouth taping is great for people who persistently mouth breathe because it ensures seven to eight solid hours of nose breathing, without much work. As we know, the more you breathe through your nose, the more you are toning your soft tissue and increasing CO_2 capacity. Think about it as passively training yourself to breathe the way nature intended.

FINAL THOUGHTS

If your breathing patterns are healthy, moving the needle on everything else will be that much easier. Why? Because everything is connected. We call this the Well-Being Constellation—where each point of light (breath, sleep, nutrition, movement, resilience, environment, relationships, purpose) is critical to the beauty and fullness of the big picture. In the next chapter we dive deep into sleep and talk about how it intersects with the ways we are breathing, eating, moving, connecting, and living.

THAT EXTRA 20 PERCENT

We mentioned earlier that there are a lot of breathing practices and techniques out there. They are becoming more and more accessible, but some people still find them intimidating. We tell everyone to start with nasal breathing, but for those who want to take a shot at the extra 20 percent, here are some breathing practices we recommend.

THE 4-7-8 BREATH

Otherwise known as the relaxing breath, this exercise is borrowed from Andrew Weil, MD. It's a good one to pull out when you are feeling extra keyed up. It will help you slow your heart rate, soothe the nervous system, and create some space between the inhale and the exhale. Here's how you do it:

■ Empty your lungs of air. Inhale for four seconds, hold your breath for seven seconds, and then exhale out of your mouth for eight seconds. Repeat this sequence four times.

THE 4-4-4-4 BREATH

This technique is known as box breathing, and it's often associated with the Navy SEALs. It's a performance and energy booster that will sharpen your focus and reduce stress. It's a good one to use if you find yourself in an afternoon slump or before an important call or meeting.

■ Empty your lungs of air. At the bottom of your breath, hold for a count of four, then inhale for four seconds, hold your breath at the top for four seconds, and finally exhale out of the nose for four seconds. Repeat this sequence for five minutes to feel the maximum effects.

COHERENT BREATHING

Sometimes called the 5-5 breath, this technique really helps us slow down our rate of breathing. It will help you find a sense of calm throughout the day.

■ Breathe normally for a few minutes, and then for one minute, breathe in for four seconds and breathe out for four seconds.
■ Repeat by inhaling for five seconds and then exhaling for five seconds for another minute.
■ You can keep repeating and expanding by moving on to six seconds and then seven seconds, all the way to ten seconds as your CO_2 tolerance grows.

THE EASIEST BREATH

■ Inhale for a count of two and exhale for a count of four. Do this as many times as you need to!

Chapter Three

Sleep: A Vital Sign

Colleen is no stranger to sleep problems. They started early in life. She remembers being unable to sleep the night before she ran her first marathon with her best friend from growing up. They had driven a few hours north to Sacramento for the race and were planning to stay in a hotel room the night before the seven a.m. start time. While Colleen's friend fell asleep quickly, Colleen couldn't seem to drop off. Eventually, she went down to the hotel lobby for some Tylenol PM, which seemed like a good idea at the time and did help her fall asleep. She had to compensate for the grogginess with multiple cups of coffee in the morning. Luckily, at the age of twenty-one, her body took this poor care in stride (literally), and she ran a faster than expected first marathon of three hours and forty-nine minutes.

A few years later, the sleep anxiety struck again in a major way while she was in her first real job. Colleen had her final project in her rotational training program, where you are grilled by senior executives for thirty minutes. The project determined her final job placement and where she would start her career. In the nights leading up to the presentation, her anxiety increased. Was the final project and placement important? Sure, but the perceived impact to her career was spiraling out of control in her brain. At this point in time, Colleen did not have a therapist or psychiatrist to help her with solutions to her insomnia. After four nights of lots of Tylenol PM and little sleep, she went to the ER and was quickly prescribed some Xanax. There was no mention of other ways to help control her thoughts, anxiety, and sleep, or how her massive caffeine intake was working at odds with her sleep goals. Worse still, she didn't feel like she could talk about any of this with her colleagues, who were all caring people. Unfortunately, in 2002 mental health conversations in the workplace were still taboo and a potential career killer. The secrecy around what she was going through naturally made things so much worse. Ultimately, she managed to get through the presentation, but it marked the beginning of a lifelong struggle.

The kind of trouble that Colleen has experienced with sleep is common. Some people go through bouts of insomnia or struggle with sleep off and on throughout their lives. Often, we muddle through and do our best, not knowing how to fix it and just wanting it to curb the damage in the short term. But even for those of us who are minorly but chronically sleep deprived, there are invisible ill effects on our well-being. Sometimes by looking at the obvious catastrophes of extreme cases, we can see the hidden damage of the every day. Which is where Shelby Harris, PsyD, CBSM, comes in.

Harris is a behavioral psychologist and sleep specialist. She sees patients all the time who suffer from bad dreams that destroy their sleep, first by waking them up and then by making them too fearful to fall asleep in the first place. Most of us get nightmares occasionally, but when we think about people haunted by their dreams on a regular basis, we usually think about little kids and people suffering from PTSD. We don't usually think about people like Jamie, a thirty-eight-year-old stay-at-home mom of bright-eyed three-year-old twins. But before she went to see Harris, every night for weeks, Jamie was haunted by a series of nightmares that woke her sometimes two or three times a night. She had no history of trauma, and the dreams were never the same. Sometimes they were realistic, like the time she dreamed she was trapped outside a burning building, her family inside, just out of reach. Other times they were more surreally terrifying, like the one where a floating heart was barreling toward her but she couldn't run because her feet were stuck to the ground. No matter what kind of nightmare it was, the waking up part was always the same: Jamie would find herself beside her sleeping husband, gasping for breath and with tears streaming down her face, alone in her fear of falling back to sleep.

After a few months, Jamie's nightmares were compounded by full-blown insomnia at night and painful flare-ups of fibromyalgia during the day. Completely out of gas by lunchtime, she would have to guzzle coffee to make it to twelve thirty p.m., when she could collapse on the couch while her twins napped. Eventually, Jamie's fatigue and pain reached a high-water mark. There were days when she had to call her mother-in-law to come watch the kids because she couldn't get out of bed. By the time she was referred to Harris, then director of the Behavioral Sleep Medicine Program at Montefiore Medical Center, Jamie was in the midst of a full-blown depression.

Luckily, Jamie got the help she needed. Instead of going into intensive psychotherapy, which is what her primary care physician thought she'd have to do, Harris started working with her on something called imagery rehearsal therapy to get at the root of the problem. Over the course of half a dozen sessions, Jamie would rescript the nightmares she'd had the night before. She'd visualize changing the dream without analyzing the initial nightmare. The goal of this type of evidence-based cognitive behavioral therapy is to lessen the intensity and frequency of the bad dreams, and it has been proven to lead to better sleep.[1] For Jamie, image rehearsal therapy worked fast—she started having fewer bad dreams and felt less stressed about them when they did happen, because she knew she could rescript them and regain a sense of control. As her nightmares got better, Jamie's sleep improved dramatically. Once that changed, everything else followed. Her pain tolerance got better, so the fibromyalgia inter- fered less with her life. Her energy levels improved, so she was able to take her kids to the park and the grocery store, little things that she had missed and that had made her feel terrible when she couldn't do them because of fatigue. For the first few weeks that she was feeling better and getting good sleep, Jamie couldn't believe just how much her life had changed—not only in terms of what she was able to do, but *how* she was able to do it: with joy, energy, and gratitude for just how much her body was capable of healing itself when given half a chance.

According to Harris, Jamie's case was dramatic, but not uncom- mon. Sleep is often the linchpin of health and happiness. When it goes missing, everything falls apart. Whether the cause is insomnia, anxiety, stress, sleep apnea, or chronic nightmares, inadequate sleep has cascading negative effects on our well-being, to the point where sometimes it becomes difficult to figure out what came first, smoke or fire? Bad sleep or depression? Sleep specialists point out that peo- ple often underestimate just how profoundly sleep impacts other conditions. If someone walks into a doctor's office and complains of depression and bad sleep, likely the doctor will tell them that when they treat the depression their sleep will improve, but many of the experts we have talked to say that sometimes it's wiser and more effective to treat the lack of sleep first, or at least in parallel. Harris says, "What we actually find in the research, and what I see with patients, is that when people sleep better, they actually engage more in therapy, and they're able to do more in their lives that makes them feel good. And guess what, you get better outcomes."[2] According to her, the same goes for other medical issues like fibromyalgia, chronic pain, cancer treatments, and anxiety. If there's something wrong with your sleep, chances are it's affecting something else, causing weight gain or brain fog, or worsening a chronic disease. Put simply: when people sleep better, it helps every single part of their life improve.

THE NEW VITAL SIGN

In the world of health and wellness, doctors and health practitioners can find a lot to disagree about, but the importance of sleep is without debate. And while you may be able to go longer without sleep than you can without breath, sleep is just as critical to your well-being. It touches every part of our lives and our world. We strongly agree with experts who argue that sleep is just as important as nutrition, exercise, and mindfulness. And yet, according to the CDC, more than one-third of Americans don't get enough sleep.[3] The outcomes of this chronic lack of sleep are devastating; it is making us overweight, sick, inflamed, and imbalanced. Over time, depriving your body of the sleep it needs is just as harmful as drunk driving, chronically overeating, or not exercising, and the consequences are much more serious than next-day drowsiness. As much as we'd like to believe in the superpowers of resistance training, vegetables, and meditation, none of it will make up for lost shut-eye.

Over the years, as we've done a deep dive into the research, we have learned that long-term sleep deprivation can lead to increased risk of diabetes, obesity, heart disease, and stroke.[4] It can contribute to an increase in mood swings, headaches, sexual dysfunction, and performance deficits at work and school. It greatly decreases your quality of life, as well as your attention span and memory. On a macro level, lack of sleep is associated with a decrease in public health and an increase in clinical burnout and utilization of healthcare.

Not to mention it can make it impossible to feel good. You are getting through the days, not thriving through them.

If you are lucky enough to be unfamiliar with this particular feeling, we suggest volunteering to spend a few nights babysitting a couple kids under the age of five. That will give you the full experience.

One of our favorite sleep experts, Michael Breus, PhD—aka the Sleep Doctor—is fond of saying that sleep should be considered the new vital sign. Why? Because it is a critical nervous system function and basic survival need for most mammals, and definitely for humans. Like your respiration rate or your pulse, if something is out of whack with your sleep, critical body functions are in play and you can count on a constellation of symptoms to follow.

Have you ever stopped to think about why we spend so much time sleeping? After all, we're talking about a third of our lives if we're getting a good seven hours a night. What exactly is going on in there while we're drooling on our pillow? A lot of critical biological processes, it turns out. When you're in the land of Nod, your body is getting down to business repairing the wear and tear on your DNA, cells, tissues, and organs. It is removing toxins, regulating your metabolism, and restoring energy. Your body is literally growing muscles and consolidating memories. It is regulating your blood sugar and cholesterol and restoring endocrine homeostasis. And so much more. So, if in a fit of productivity, you find yourself resentful of how much time you have to commit to sleeping, remember that your body is not just wasting time in dreamland—it is getting some serious heavy lifting done when it comes to repair and restoration. With that in mind, it's easy to see why shorting ourselves on those precious hours can wreak havoc on our health over time.[5]

Even if you are not included in that one-third of Americans who are chronically bleary-eyed, chances are you could be getting better sleep. We live in a world filled with screens, electric lights, and stress, which is enough to make even the Sandman feel wired every now and again. And much of the time, sleep is the last thing we prioritize on our endless list of to-dos. We often try to make up for sleep on the weekend (80 percent of adults worldwide do this[6]) or tough it out and load up on caffeine. Then, in order to wind down before bed we have to drink a couple of glasses of wine, which greatly disrupts the quality of our sleep (more on that soon.) Even when we do make it to bed, it seems like there is always something that gets in the way—a pressing deadline, an urgent email that needs to be answered, a kid who needs attention. Then, despite knowing better, when we wake up in the middle of the night, we grab our phones and start scrolling until the sun comes up.

Life is all about ebbs and flows, and as a result, most of us have struggled with sleep at one point or another. Sleep disturbances often occur around major life transitions like parenthood, moving, changing jobs, and the loss of a loved one. They can also come out of nowhere and surprise us when there are natural shifts in our hormones. Throughout their lives women especially are in a constant struggle with their hormones, and their bodies are constantly trying to recalibrate. When major hormonal shifts occur—think pregnancy, perimenopause, menopause—sleep is always affected, and it will differ wildly from person to person.

We could all use some additional help when sleep feels impossible, elusive, or just not as easy as we'd like it to be. Because the holistic importance of sleep can't be underestimated, we are putting this chapter front and center so that you can begin to make the small changes that will support the sleep that is critical to every other part of your health and happiness. While there is going to be a lot of important information in this chapter, the biggest takeaway is this: your body knows how to get the sleep it needs; you just have to get out of its way. As you'll see in the following sections about circadian rhythms, every part of us is built to move inexorably toward sweet, sweet slumber. Our bodies know what to do and how to do it, so getting better sleep is less about adding in a bunch of life hacks to help you sleep and more about removing the points of friction between you and a good night's sleep. Once you know how sleep works, it's easy to start smoothing the path with small changes. But the biggest change of all is so easy you could do it in two seconds, and simultaneously so hard it takes some folks a lifetime: you've got to chill out about sleep. This might seem counterintuitive, considering we're about to go deep into how important it is and how you can make it better, but the truth is that the biggest obstacle to sleep is anxiety about sleep.

The amount of media attention sleep has gotten in the last few years is great. People are starting to pay attention and realize that shut-eye is not optional, and there's no gold medal for the person who can get by on the least sleep, there's only a shortened life span. But all the attention has had the negative effect of simultaneously freaking people out and attracting their inner overachiever. For readers like you who care about your health and stay informed and diligent about it, sleep can feel like the next thing you have to fix right away. While it's good to be aware of how well you're sleeping, too much attention to it is actually going to make it worse. Finding this balance between awareness and anxiety isn't as hard as it sounds, but it does require us to listen to our bodies and to trust them. Listen to your body when it's asking for more rest, and when it's struggling to find that rest, trust in your body's ability to find its way. The beautiful thing about sleep is that if you have a bad night, there's always tomorrow night, and the next night, and the next night—in other words, there are plenty of opportunities begin again.

THE BASICS: HOW MANY Z'S DO YOU NEED AND WHAT KIND?

You're probably wondering, *How do I know if I'm getting enough sleep?*

This question gets right to the heart of the first level of anxiety that people come up against when it comes to sleep. So, we're going to bust up a key myth right out of the gate. Most people have heard that eight hours of sleep is optimal for everyone and the ultimate brass ring. But sleep experts agree that it simply isn't true. According to the American Academy of Sleep Medicine, the Sleep Research Society, and the National Sleep Foundation, the answer is seven to nine hours for the average adult. That two-hour range is a big one, and many people's sleep baseline falls on the lower end of the spectrum—those people are called short sleepers, which just means that their bodies naturally require less sleep than long sleepers, who need to clock in something closer to nine hours. According to sleep expert Michael Breus, PhD, the problem with the eight-hour myth isn't that it's bad to shoot for eight hours of sleep; it's that for short sleepers who don't need that much, the anxiety of trying to reach that unrealistic goal can make everything worse. Instead of going to bed when they're actually sleepy, some people will jump into bed early in order to "get in their eight." The problem then is that they aren't able to fall asleep when they want to, which makes them anxious, which arouses their sympathetic nervous system (stress response), which makes it hard to sleep. "What happens is that it triggers a washing machine of anxiety that comes through because of this expectation," says Breus. To make the eight-hour-myth even more problematic, experts remind us that everybody's sleep needs change throughout their lives, and even from season to season. For women, sleep needs can be hooked to monthly menstrual cycles, meaning that some women might need more sleep before their periods and less sleep after their periods. You're probably noticing by now that trying to pin down exactly how much sleep you need is more art than science. The only hard and fast rule is getting at least seven hours of sleep; beyond that, play around within that two-hour range and see what feels good.

There's one more problem with focusing too heavily on the number of hours you get: it ignores the importance of *good* sleep, or the *quality* of those hours. All sleep is not created equal. There are different stages of sleep, and all of them are essential to the different biological processes that occur during sleep. But some stages are more prone to disruption than others. The internal pattern of your sleep cycles is called your sleep architecture. Sounds important, right? It is. The continuity and depth of your sleep depends on that solid foundation. The average human will run through five ninety-minute cycles a night, which each include two main types of sleep: Rapid eye movement (REM) and non-REM (NREM). These types of sleep occur in four distinct stages of sleep (each with differences in brain wave activity and eye movements).

- **Stage 1:** You're slowing down and dozing off. This stage lasts from one to five minutes and opens the door to unconsciousness. It's kind of like the waiting room for sleep. You've got to do your time here to get to the next stage, but at least there isn't any terrible soft jazz playing in the background.
- **Stage 2:** For the next ten to sixty minutes, your body is fully relaxed and it's harder to be woken up. In this stage, your body is actively preparing for deep sleep by relaxing your muscles, slowing your heart rate, and lowering your core temperature.
- **Stage 3:** This is the deep sleep that is critical to biological processes, and it lasts between twenty and forty minutes, usually at the beginning of the night. This is where the magic happens. Your body emits large amounts of human growth factor, which is critical for repairing your cells while you rest. It's also when your brain's glymphatic system gets to work clearing metabolic waste products from the brain through what scientists call a pseudo-lymphatic network. We think about it as a team of night janitors for your brain. When the night janitors can't do their work, metabolic waste builds up and the consequence can be neurodegenerative diseases like Alzheimer's and dementia.[7]
- **Stage 4:** This is REM sleep, the stage where we have our most vivid and memorable dreams. Which makes it even more amazing that at the same time our brains are dreaming, they are also processing information and knitting together long-term memories. When we don't get enough REM sleep, it can affect both our concentration and mood.[8]

Each stage is important and unique, but deep sleep and REM sleep are the most easily disrupted, and those disruptions are the most acutely felt.

HOW DO YOU KNOW WHERE YOU STAND WITH SLEEP?

How do you know if you are getting enough time in each sleep stage? How do you know if the quality of your sleep is good enough to keep your body's trains running on time? According to Shelby Harris, it's as simple as being aware of how you feel during the day. Understanding your own norms—what does a good day feel like in terms of energy and alertness throughout the day? After you wake up, how long does it take you to get to your highest energy zone of the day—is it an hour after you wake up, two hours, three? Harris cautions that it's unrealistic to expect yourself to bound out of bed like a kid on Christmas morning. Something called sleep inertia gets in the way of us being that excited to wake up. Generally, it takes between two and three hours to feel fully alert (taking caffeine out of the equation). So, if you typically wake up at seven a.m. and you're still yawning on the conference call at eleven a.m., that might be a sign that you're not getting the amount or quality of sleep that your body needs. Same goes for prolonged periods of sleepiness or fatigue. Harris says that "it's normal to have moments of being sleepy, those dips in your circadian rhythm throughout the day, like after lunch or after dinner." Sleepiness, fatigue, and even naps are fine as long as they are every once in a while, but if you find yourself consistently relying on caffeine in the afternoon to stay awake, it's important to look more closely at your sleep quality and quantity.

Here are a couple not-so-obvious signs that you might not be maximizing your time between the sheets.

Warning Flag #1: One sign that you might not be getting enough sleep is if you rely on the weekends to catch up. Many people will clock in around six hours of sleep during weeknights and then sleep like teenagers on the weekend. Experts agree that sleep debt is real, and just like the kind that goes on your credit card, too much is bad news. Unfortunately, sleep debt is even harder to pay off because you only have so many hours in the weekend. If your baseline is eight, but you're getting six hours of sleep five nights a week in the middle of the week, you're missing out on ten hours. Even if you sleep an extra two hours on Saturday and Sunday, you're still in the hole by six hours. Over time, it accumulates, and the next thing you know, you're chronically sleep deprived.

Warning Flag #2: Many people turn to sleep aids when they find themselves struggling to sleep. Often this is something you might dip into if you are going through a stressful moment in your life, but stop using them as soon as you can. Sleep experts say using sleep aids occasionally is not necessarily a sign that you aren't getting healthy sleep, as long as it's temporary. But we all know someone who takes Benadryl every night just to get some shut-eye. And that, friends, is a red flag. Going back to first principles: your body knows how to sleep, and if you can't sleep without pharmaceuticals, that is something to look at more closely.

Big Takeaway: If you feel tired all the time, you're probably not getting the sleep you need. If you're relying on coffee to keep you awake in the afternoon and sleep aids to get a minimum amount of sleep at night, you're probably stuck in a vicious cycle.

INSOMNIA AND THE ENDLESS NIGHT

There are over one hundred distinct sleep disorders that affect the quality, timing, and duration of sleep, for example sleep apnea (periodic interruptions in sleep and breathing), narcolepsy (excessive sleepiness during the day), restless leg syndrome, and sleepwalking.

Between 50 and 70 million US adults have a sleep disorder, but insomnia is by far the most common at about 30 percent.[9] Insomnia is a disorder of sleep, but experts like Shelby Harris often say that it's really a disorder of perception. You can't sleep because you are so focused on sleep. It's a vicious cycle where you look at the clock and count the minutes you have left until your alarm goes off, and then as a result of the pressure you're putting on yourself to make the best use of those minutes, now you really can't sleep. When you have multiple nights of this for more than three weeks, it's called insomnia. And boy, does it suck. But luckily, sleep loss and sleep disorders are treatable problems. You *can* learn how to manage it, and for most people it is truly a short-term problem. For people like Colleen who have long-term issues, where sleep really ebbs and flows, insomnia is something you might have to live with but not suffer from. It's possible to learn your triggers, remove barriers to sleep, and set yourself up for a good night's rest. Insomnia is a bad night's sleep on steroids, but it's still just a bad night's sleep—the fundamentals of your circadian rhythms, and tools that you can use to support them, are the same no matter how many bad nights you've had. Inspired by the rigor that she puts into her own children's bedtime routines, Colleen likes to call this sleep retraining. Where do we start? Sleep cycles of course.

GET WITH THE RHYTHM

If you ever want to experience the power of nature, you should go camping. Not to bathe in the quiet of the forest or observe the spectacle of a squirrel making off with your tuna sandwich, but because of how quickly greater exposure to natural light will literally change your body chemistry. In an experiment done at the University of Colorado Boulder, researchers wanted to know more about the inner workings of our internal clocks, so they tracked eight adults over the course of a week. The amount of artificial and natural light the subjects got was measured, as were their melatonin levels (the sleep hormone) throughout the day. After a week of observing the participants' normal routines of work, school, and sleep, the researchers took these lucky folks camping for a week in the Rockies and measured all of the same things—melatonin, amount of sleep, and so on. The researchers found that after seven days of sunshine, sunsets, and the gentle glow of the campfire, the subjects' internal clocks recalibrated quickly.

Every human being is subject to the powerful cycles of light and darkness. The sleep-wake cycle, aka your circadian rhythm, coordinates critical biological processes throughout the body, from the digestive system to the endocrine system. Our master clock is located in our brain's hypothalamus and sends signals from there to *all* of our cells via "clock genes," which regulate numerous physiological activities. This master clock is highly influenced by external cues like light and temperature (but especially light) and is tied to the cycle of day and night. In our ordinary lives, since the 1930s, we have been subject to more and more artificial light as we spend more and more of our time indoors. But when we're out in nature, like the campers in the study, daylight hits specific cells in our eyes called melanopsin retinal ganglion cells. This tells the melatonin faucet in the brain to turn off—perking you up naturally and getting your body ready for the day. Once that happens, the master clock sets its timer for fourteen to sixteen hours later, when it will start to turn the melatonin faucet back on to get the body ready for sleep.

Back at the campsite, without their blackout shades, the study's participants were waking up earlier, which meant that their melatonin faucets were getting turned off earlier as well. The researchers estimate that the sun was four times as intense as the light that the subjects experienced indoors, where of course it was filtering through windows and doors. But in the great outdoors, there's no escaping that sweet, sweet sunshine. For the campers, this change in light exposure shifted the onset of melatonin to two hours earlier, which impacted their bedtime by shifting it to an hour earlier as well.[10] Besides being a really cool way to be more in sync with nature, this study highlights a smart strategy for using our body's master clock to get a better night's sleep. Every sleep expert we talk to has slightly different takeaways for how to boost your slumber, but they are all rooted in supporting your circadian rhythms. Remember, the best way to get better sleep is to remove the barriers to sleep and embrace what your body already knows how to do. Our bodies know how to use the light and the darkness to help us get the best sleep possible, so why not use that to our advantage?

A GOOD NIGHT'S SLEEP IS AN ALL-DAY AFFAIR

If you've heard anything about how to improve your sleep, it probably revolved around bedtime. Blackout shades. No phones in the bedroom. Turn down the temperature. Sleep naked. Do some gentle yoga. And while these sleep retraining activities are important, they're only about a third of the story. For those of us who have the hardest time sleeping, sneaking in ways to smooth the path to bedtime actually starts the moment you wake up. If you're trying to maximize high-quality sleep, you need to incorporate healthy sleep-promoting behaviors all day long. The following recommendations are those with the most solid backing in the evidence and the ones that all of our sleep experts are on board with. Aside from the tip to buy comfy pajamas, each and every one of these sleep practices are free and accessible to everyone. In fact, if you cut out alcohol and caffeine, you will even save money. It may take time to integrate these changes into your life, and it should. Remember, by seamlessly integrating the shifts that feel good and easy, you're more likely to find long-term success moving the needle on sleep.

In the sections below, we've broken down your sleep training best practices by time of day—morning, noon, and night. Within each section you'll find a couple of rules to live by and accompanying integration tips to help make these changes as easy and joyful as possible.

Morning Sleep Training

Get at least fifteen minutes of natural light as soon as you can upon waking.

According to Andrew Huberman, PhD, a neuroscientist and host of *The Huberman Lab*, a well-respected podcast about science-based tools for living a better life, "25+ quality papers & reviews converge on the fact that increasing natural light exposure (especially in the first 1–3 hours of the day) + limiting bright artificial light 10pm–4am can improve mood, offset myopia [nearsightedness], improve glucose tolerance, testosterone, estrogen and melatonin profiles."[11] Huberman also points out that it is a low-effort practice that has outsized benefits. Because sunlight syncs your circadian rhythms, this is a gentle, natural way to shut down your melatonin faucet and stimulate cortisol (a hormone that rises in the morning to stimulate waking up) so you can be alert and at your best. It also starts the timer on your fourteen- to sixteen-hour cycle, setting your body up to turn on the melatonin at the right time.[12] Think about your daily sun exposure as winding your internal watch, a daily, simple practice to help keep your body's processes running on time. Not only does a nicely synced circadian rhythm help keep your sleep on track so your body can repair itself, but it can also help digestion and immune function throughout the day. We can also say from experience that welcoming the morning outside and listening to the sounds of the world waking up is an incredibly joyful way to start the day.

INTEGRATION TIPS:

- Before you lunge for the coffee maker, try grabbing some water and your sneakers. If you exercise in the morning anyway, try lining it up with getting some natural light first thing when you wake up. If you have a dog to walk, this is a natural motivator for getting out there.
- When the temperature is right, take your coffee or tea outside and enjoy it on the patio or your front steps. If it's too cold for that, you can always pull a chair up to a sunny window spot. You won't get quite the same amount of light, but some is better than none.
- If the sun doesn't rise before you do, that's okay—just get out there as soon as Mother Nature allows.
- Don't let the perfect be the enemy of the good—work in some sunlight in the morning however you can. For instance, we don't always get out there within an hour of waking like the experts suggest, but we do go for a walk as soon as we drop our kids off at school, around eight o'clock, and for us, that's good enough.

Always wake up at the same time. Yes, even on weekends. (Sorry.)

Why shouldn't you sleep in on the weekends? Again, it's all about that master clock. If you usually get up at seven a.m. and go to bed at eleven p.m., and then on the weekends you wake up at nine a.m. and go to bed at one a.m., you may be getting the same amount of sleep, but you're throwing off your circadian rhythms. So, what is going to happen on Sunday night when you try to go to bed at eleven p.m.? Maybe you'll get to sleep on time, but likely, you won't. Then come Monday morning you're having a very unpleasant time dragging your butt out of bed for that eight a.m. conference call. So, what do you do? You brew an extra cup of coffee to perk up, and then maybe another one to make up for the fact that you got less sleep last night. I think you see where we're going with this. We mess up our master clock enough by staying up too late, working on screens late at night, rarely getting outdoors, going on drinking and food binges in the wee hours, and consuming way too much caffeine. In other words, we're doing enough to disrupt our circadian rhythms already. Getting up at the same time every morning is not only the least we can do; it is critical to helping us right the ship. And while sleeping in on the weekends might feel great temporarily, it's one of those short-term gain, long-term pain situations. Better to avoid the social jet lag altogether (another term for the vicious cycle), get the shut-eye you need during the week, and spend more of your weekend doing fun stuff. Like camping.

One exception to the rule: According to Michael Breus, "You never want to get less than five hours of sleep. Period. End of story." Less than five hours is when physiological reaction time begins to slow, which can lead to accidents, particularly for those who drive. So, if you had a truly sleepless night, stay in bed and away from heavy machinery.

INTEGRATION TIPS:

- Prepare for the transition. If you're used to capitalizing on the weekend to make up for sleep debt, the first week or two of getting up at a consistent time might make you feel sleepier because you are indeed getting less sleep. Soon this will normalize, thanks to the sleep drive that is building up and the compounding motivation to go to bed earlier, which will ultimately lead to you sleeping deeper, better, and more consistently.

- Reward yourself for good behavior. If motivation for this new routine is tricky, treat yourself to something a little extra upon waking. You could buy yourself a delicious coffee at the café down the street, or a smoothie loaded with nut butter on your way to an earlier yoga class—whatever floats your sleep boat.

▪ Skip the melatonin. Since melatonin is so important to our sleep-wake cycle, you might be wondering, *Hey, why not just pop some melatonin supplements and call it a day?* First of all, melatonin might help you get to sleep, but it doesn't help you stay asleep or improve the quality of your sleep cycles. Your body also starts to build up a tolerance to it, which means you have to take more and more to get the same effect. Most experts will tell you to use melatonin only to "reset" your sleep-wake cycle if you get wildly off track—for instance, because of jet lag or shift work. Bottom line: it's a crutch you don't need and one that could do more harm than good. Stick to good old-fashioned sunlight to get your melatonin flowing.

Daytime Sleep Training

Exercise for a better night's sleep.

This one is as dead simple and commonsensical as it gets: tire yourself out physically and you'll sleep better. Michael Breus puts it this way, "Sleep is recovery. If you haven't done anything you need to recover from, you're not going to sleep particularly well."[13] The mutually beneficial relationship between exercise and sleep has been heavily researched over the years, and according to the Sleep Foundation, "moderate-to-vigorous exercise can increase sleep quality for adults by reducing sleep onset—or the time it takes to fall asleep—and decrease the amount of time they lie awake in bed during the night. Additionally, physical activity can help alleviate daytime sleepiness and, for some people, reduce the need for sleep medications."[14] For those dealing with sleep disorders like anxiety and obstructive sleep apnea, exercising is even more beneficial. According to a meta-analysis of nineteen studies, researchers found that for women with insomnia, practicing yoga significantly improved their sleep quality.[15] In another study, when people with obstructive sleep apnea did regular aerobic activity, their symptoms were reduced regardless of weight loss.[16]

INTEGRATION TIPS:

- Double your pleasure and your sleep benefits by walking outside when you first wake up.
- You don't have to run a marathon; just aim for twenty minutes of moderate exercise a day: walking, lifting weights, yoga, whatever works. And by the way, you can break it up. If it works better for your schedule and your life to take five-minute walks four times a day, knock yourself out. The cumulative effect is the same: better sleep.
- Don't exercise too close to bedtime if you can help it. Give your body's core temperature a chance to cool down by cutting out exercise three or four hours before bedtime. Light stretching is okay, but in order for your melatonin faucet to start opening up in earnest, you don't want your core temperature to be too elevated.[17]

Commit to a caffeine curfew.

This is no one's favorite thing to hear, but the half-life of caffeine is between six and eight hours for the average Joe. (Get it? Cup of Joe? No? Okay, okay.) In practical terms, this means your two o'clock cup of coffee may leave caffeine in your bloodstream at your nine or ten o'clock bedtime. Caffeine is a stimulant no matter how you slice it, and that means it is public enemy number one when it comes to sleep quality. Notice we said *quality*. Some people—maybe you—might object to this and remind us that they can have a cup of coffee at dinner and still fall asleep just fine, thank you very much. We believe you! But if we put you in a sleep lab, chances are we would pick up on disrupted sleep quality after an evening cup of coffee. Caffeine actually hinders your ability to get into deep sleep cycles, which you'll remember is the stage that is critical to physical restoration and absolutely vital to our overall health and happiness. Most experts agree that you should stop drinking all caffeine by two o'clock in the afternoon, but some go even further and say you should stop by nine a.m.

This is where we call on you to check in with yourself and experiment. The good news is that you don't need a sophisticated blood test to tell you how well you metabolize caffeine. Some of us are just biochemically sensitive, and there's no shame in that—though maybe there's a little less fun. For instance, Colleen knows she can't even look at a cup of decaf past noon or she's in for a bad night. Jason, however, can have an espresso at dinner and fall asleep without a problem. But because he knows how it messes with his deep sleep, Jason stops caffeine at two p.m. Colleen is even more disciplined about adhering to a caffeine curfew, stopping well before lunch. When it comes to caffeine, it's one of those parts of life where you play the cards you're dealt. What can we say?

INTEGRATION TIPS:

- Experiment with slowly moving back the timing of your last caffeinated beverage. If you're used to having a cup of coffee at three p.m. to get you through the afternoon slump, try moving it back by an hour, then another, and another.
- Have your coffee outside, or near a window, so that you are starting your day with sun exposure.
- If you are caffeine sensitive, beware of overdoing it on the dark chocolate late at night. Chocolate is a sneaky source of caffeine.

Nighttime Sleep Training

Stop drinking alcohol three hours before bedtime.

We know! This one hurts. And obviously it's not always tenable. If you're on vacation or at a holiday party, you're not going to be checking your watch. And you shouldn't—remember, we're shooting for balance, not perfection, so don't call the joy police on us. But facts are facts, and alcohol is a well-documented disruptor of stage 3 deep sleep. Many people who struggle with sleep turn to alcohol, a depressant, to help nudge them over into dreamland. And while alcohol might help you fall asleep, you almost never wake up feeling rested because of the havoc it's wreaking on deep sleep. Think about it: You're putting a literal toxin into your body, which then disrupts the entire restoration process for...cleaning up toxins.[18] Not great! To make things worse, one review of the science literature about alcohol use found that "Chronic alcohol exposure damages nerve cells and fibers, reducing the likelihood of synchronized neuronal firing across the cortex, which is necessary for slow wave sleep. With prolonged use, neurotransmitter systems adapt and modulate their release, which can increase sleep disruption and change sleep architecture, sometimes permanently."[19] As if that wasn't bad enough, alcohol is also a diuretic, which means that it increases the water and salt that is lost from the body, turning it more quickly into urine. Translation: If you're up peeing all night, you're not sleeping.

INTEGRATION TIPS:

- If you usually have a glass of wine or beer after dinner, try having it with dinner, and then, if you can, move it to before dinner. Maybe there's a reason happy hour traditionally starts at five p.m.?
- If you can, stop drinking all fluids at least two hours before bed. Jason's technique is front-loading his water during the first half of the day, so even if he stops by seven p.m., he's still adequately hydrated.
- And, of course, if you don't drink alcohol, you probably shouldn't start.

Put yourself to bed like a three-year-old.

As anyone with small children knows, it's all about the bedtime routine. Every desperately underrested parent who has stumbled bleary-eyed into the pediatrician's office has heard the same spiel—you've got to construct a consistent, predictable bedtime ritual for your kid. For instance, brushing teeth, reading books, story time, song time, say-goodnight-to-every-animal-in-the-house time, and finally lights out. When you think of it from the kid's perspective (and not the adult *Go the Fuck to Sleep* perspective), it actually sounds kind of...great. You take a nice warm bath, you get a mini massage post-bath with your nice-smelling lotion, you get a story, someone sings you a song, and then it's lights out. We're here to say that a cozy bedtime routine is just as important for you as it is for your kids. Think of all the work you did today, all the caring, all the responsibilities! You definitely deserve it. Beyond that, it is sleep retraining 101, and experts across the board recommended establishing a routine in order to get a good night's sleep. What does this mean? Have a consistent bedtime. Wind down at least thirty minutes before bed (this means no screens for many people). Only use the bed for sleep. Keep the bedroom dark and cool. Make it smell nice where you sleep. Have a cozy, comfy bed. And minimize noise pollution with a white noise machine or earplugs. Doesn't that sound nice?

INTEGRATION TIPS:

- Reframe it. The minute we started thinking about a bedtime routine as "putting ourselves to bed" like a cherished child, it feels a lot less like a bunch of extra stuff we have to do and more like taking care of ourselves in a way that feels good. It's a small frame shift, but it really helps. And if you have a question about what you should or shouldn't do for yourself before bedtime, just ask: *Would I let a three-year-old do it?* As in, *Would I let a three-year-old eat a half a chocolate bar an hour before bed?* Or, *Would I let a three-year-old go to bed an hour later than usual?* No matter how old we are, we thrive with nurturing and boundaries—even if we have to do it ourselves.

- Use your senses to help craft your routine. Smell: find an amazing-smelling essential oil spray for your sheets and pajamas that brings you joy or just dab the essential oil on your wrists. Touch: invest in some comfy pajamas and a kick-ass pillow. Sound: if you're into music, you could listen to a few of your favorite songs before bedtime. Sight: make sure your shades are robust and that there isn't any light pollution in your bedroom.

- Keep it cool. Think about how nice it feels to get all cozy in the wintertime in your bed—ideal sleeping conditions, if you ask us. And the experts agree—you should shoot for temperatures in the mid-sixties Fahrenheit to keep your core temperature down and the melatonin flowing. If you want some more temperature-related tips from Jason, your resident quantified-self expert, check out thejoyofwellbeing.com/sleep.

- If you want to help signal to your body to fall asleep, there's value in taking a bath to help modulate your body temperature. Make it a little more joyful by burning a candle or scent that helps you relax.

- If you respond to yoga nidra, work it into your evening routine to give yourself the ultimate spiritual wind-down.

- If you're familiar with sleep hygiene at all, it won't sound bonkers for us to suggest you remove your cell phone from the bedroom. Believe it or not, there is some research behind removing your alarm clock as well. One study found that clock monitoring (aka rolling over and saying to yourself *How the heck am I still awake at 12:35?*) resulted in pre-sleep worry, exacerbating sleep issues.[20] Consider covering your clock with a pillowcase or face your clock away from view, that way you still have alarm capabilities without the pre-sleep disturbance.

Avoid anxiety triggers.

We talked about how anxiety is the enemy of sleep. As the fuel for insomnia, it's a major barrier to our bodies achieving the parasympathetic state of "rest and digest" that we need to do just that. When you can, intentionally remove major or minor sources of stress from the hours approaching bedtime. Look for sources both externally and internally. Triggers can come in various shapes and sizes. You will have to learn to listen to your body's cues: the dread before you pick up the phone, the anxiety before you see a work email, the text from a family member that can cause your blood pressure to rise. We need to get better at understanding our triggers so we can work on silencing them at bedtime. While some stressful intrusions are unavoidable, in this modern life there are many external sources of stress that we absolutely have the power to avoid.

Internal sources of stress and anxiety related to bedtime are a battle some of us have to fight. Sometimes it's a laundry list of daily worries and stresses that march through our brains just when we're trying to get to sleep. And sometimes it's the stories we tell ourselves about how well we sleep, how much sleep we need, how much we don't think we'll be able to get it if we don't do everything perfectly. Both kinds of internal stress can be devastating to our sleep. In the first case, whatever you can do during the day to downshift your stress level will be helpful—meditation, breathing exercises, therapy—so do what you can to turn down the noise in general. As for the second kind of stress, this is going to make you want to throw the book at us after a whole chapter, but here's a secret that applies to the sleep-anxious among us: if you just chill out about sleep, you probably don't need to do anything else. Truly. Trust in your body's ability to sleep. You're built for it. Of course, don't do boneheaded things like drink coffee at night or take your computer to bed with you, but otherwise, try to relax. The worst thing you can do for your sleep is to try to perfect it. Michael Breus put it best: "Sleep is a lot like love. The less you look for it, the more it shows up."[21] It's maddening to the control freaks among us, but so, so true.

INTEGRATION TIPS:

- If you're prone to taking your worries to bed with you, we suggest keeping a worry journal on your bedside table. If something pops up and keeps spinning, into the worry journal it goes. If you respond to meditation, that's another tool that can help get you out of the worry cycle.
- If you can, set some boundaries around phone notifications a couple hours before bed. This will help filter out everything from stressful work emails to bad news about the world, and we guarantee it will help you sleep better. Better yet, keep the phone out of the bedroom altogether.
- Identify your stress triggers and systematically eliminate them from your evening.

FINAL THOUGHTS

Be kind to yourself about sleep. How easy or hard it is to sleep is not about the content of your character, and it's not something you can change through sheer willpower. It's like the tide: it will come and go and come back again. Colleen still has times when she has to call her doctor for a short-term prescription sleep aid in order to make it through a rough patch. Sleep will never be "fixed" for many people, but a bad night's sleep doesn't always need to feel like an emergency. If you listen to your body and prioritize making the lead-up to bedtime a little more joyful, you'll eventually figure it out. Approaching sleep with as much patience and curiosity as she could was the only thing that really helped Colleen. She had to experiment with what helped *her* and what didn't. For instance, we watch TV right before bedtime (with light blocking glasses, of course). We know. The screens! The blue light! The horror! But sometimes the right thing for everyone else is the wrong thing for you. Turning off Colleen's brain is not easy, and for some reason, television helps her zone out and wind down. So that's what we do, and it helps her sleep. If you find something that works for you, throw the rulebook out the window. If we say it once we'll say it a thousand times: it's all about what brings you joy, because that will be what actually works.

THAT EXTRA 20 PERCENT

If you're someone who likes to go the extra mile when it comes to optimization, you're in luck—there's a slew of sleep trackers on the market that can help you figure out how much sleep you're getting and what kind of quality sleep you're able to achieve. You can see pretty clearly how a night of drinking or a stressful couple of days affects your sleep by tracking patterns over time. For some of us (like Jason), this is really helpful, because you can identify what kinds of foods, beverages, and lifestyle choices impact sleep and then eliminate or reduce them. On the other hand, sometimes things don't affect you as much as you thought, and you can keep enjoying them worry-free.

A big, big warning flag here for anyone who has struggled with sleep and is looking for sleep trackers to help them shore up their slumber: there is a fine line between optimization and obsession. While sleep trackers can be illuminating, they can cause even more trouble for people who are prone to performance anxiety. This gamification of slumber can cause orthosomnia, which is another way of saying that you're taking the tracking too far, and it's making your insomnia worse. It's also important to note that many sleep trackers are still in early development stages, and no tracker will ever be a substitute for how you feel.

ESTABLISH YOUR BASELINE

At the beginning of the chapter, we mentioned that when it comes to the ideal sleep duration, there's a large window (seven to nine hours). If you're having trouble figuring out if you're a short sleeper or a long sleeper, or if you're just wanting to dial it in, Shelby Harris gave us a protocol for figuring it out. She warns that it's not an exact science, but it will give you a pretty good idea of where you land on the spectrum. Here's what you do (if you can find the time off): Take a week and go to bed when you naturally feel sleepy. Don't set the alarm in the morning. Then simply track how many hours of sleep you're getting each night. When you have a week's worth of data, take the average of nights 4 through 7. The first few days you're probably paying off sleep debt, so you eliminate those from the equation. What you are left with is probably your baseline sleep need.

Chapter Four

Eat Real Food

It may seem like Americans and Italians don't have a lot in common except pizza and pasta. But in the early twentieth century, we had another *P* in common: pellagra.

If you've never heard of it, consider yourself lucky. Pellagra is a disease that caused a brutal epidemic, killing hundreds of thousands of people beginning in the late eighteenth century. In the early 1900s pellagra spread to the Southeastern United States. Its victims were afflicted with scaly dark spots all over their bodies, teeth that fell out, bloody diarrhea, and neurological symptoms that resulted in extreme delirium and death. While pellagra was newly affecting the US, it had been raging in Northern Italy for decades. Luckily, by 1943 both countries eliminated the epidemic.[1] How? Very differently.

Before the discovery of the root cause of pellagra, the Italian government knew they had to make a move. People were suffering, and no one knew what to do, but one thing they knew for sure is that it was a disease of poverty. No rich Italians were walking around with scaly patches, cutting off their own penises in fits of delirium (yep, that happened). Thinking maybe it had something to do with food, the government passed laws that encouraged the poor to bake bread in community ovens, eat rabbits, and to drink more wine. All in all, a very Italian response to a public health crisis, but one that, shockingly, worked.[2] Not that anyone knew why. Or really cared. They were just happy to be rid of this horrible disease. And there was more wine for everyone! A real win-win for public health.

The American response, on the other hand, was also utterly on brand: we moved away from Mother Nature and got busy in the laboratory. By 1940, researchers and doctors had discovered pellagra was caused by a deficiency in niacin, at the time a newly discovered vitamin. Poor people in the American South suffered from the disease because their diet consisted "almost exclusively [of] what was called the three M's: low-quality meat, molasses and meal (industrially refined cornmeal)."[3]

So, what did the US government do? Instead of giving everyone bread and rabbits (we'll get to why that worked soon), they decided it was the food itself that needed to be modified, not people's diets. As a result, the government asked the food industry to begin enriching white flour with vitamins like niacin, thiamin, and riboflavin. Later, other foods like white rice and cornmeal would be enriched as well. It was a screaming success, and within a year, cases of pellagra became rare to nonexistent.[4]

By then, Italy too had seen success with its bread, bunnies, and vino. Although it took longer to eliminate pellagra, by World War II, it was no longer an epidemic. The reason it worked? Yeast. Niacin is found in yeast, so by supplying more bread and wine (which in its unfiltered state contains yeast), the poor were able to ingest enough niacin to avoid pellagra.[5] America's approach was to hammer the disease with food science and find success overnight. Italy's approach was to encourage people to expand their diet with what was already available, even if it took a little longer.

If we just stopped there, this story would be nothing more than a pretty interesting vignette of cultural diversity. But thanks to our friend Mark Schatzker, food journalist and author of *The Dorito Effect*, we see it as something much more profound. In his most recent book, *The End of Craving,* Mark points to this seemingly innocuous fork in the road between the two countries as an actual watershed moment: the US, with good intentions, started to pave a path to nutritional hell. Despite succeeding equally in the battle against pellagra, the US has since been the sole loser in the battle against metabolic diseases like diabetes, heart disease, and obesity. If you compare the US and Italy, the disparity in obesity rates alone is shocking—37 percent in Mississippi and just 8 percent in Northern Italy.[6]

Right now, you're probably thinking that the difference is on account of Southern BBQ and sweet tea, but Mark points out that the Northern Italians (in the past and present) actually eat incredibly rich diets.[7] They load on the butter and pork fat and pile up the meat. Not to mention the copious amounts of wine they drink. They also are known for their sweet treats like tiramisu and gelato. These are not the Italians of Sardinia feasting on the well-known Mediterranean diet. So, what the hell is going on here? How are Northern Italians able to eat like kings and still enjoy relatively good health?

If you're starting to think that you just need to get your hands on an Italian passport to win the well-being lottery, we don't blame you. But before we satisfy your curiosity, we're going to be a little annoying and withhold the punchline, because while this story has something important to tell us about food, it has something even more important to tell us about why food is so nettlesome. It's not because we don't love to eat it; it's because it can feel so damn confusing to eat "the right way." Why do Northern Italians, who generally eat high-fat, high-carb, high-sugar diets stay healthy, while Americans experiment with extreme diets every January with little success? How is it possible that drinking more wine improved health outcomes? Isn't bread bad for you? How could adding a simple vitamin to your flour protect you from an epidemic while potentially making you sicker at the same time? Why would the exact place that was hit by the US pellagra outbreak eighty years ago be the same region that has the highest rates of obesity and metabolic disease in the country? The story of pellagra and food in contemporary America is a story of good intentions and unintended consequences, confusion and paradox, interfering with nature and ultimately, needing to get back to it.

What you need to know about food and nutrition before we go any further is this:

It's a shit show.

Go to the local library and find the section where the nutrition and diet books live, and you will see the madness on full display. There may only be a cool two hundred in your local library, but over 5 million diet books were sold in the US in 2016 alone, and the diet industry at large is a $60 billion industry.[8] There is a lot of money to be gained by trumpeting a "new" and fresh perspective on what everyone should eat. The result is a deafening scream of contradictory guidelines—low carb, no carb, all carb! No fat, low fat, all fat! No meat, fake meat, all meat! If you're living in the US, you know exactly what we're talking about. It's impossible to tune it out completely. But the resulting cacophony of opinions and conflicting science is exactly what turns people off about thinking about the food they put in their bodies. If nothing is for sure, if nothing is set in stone, then who the hell cares—let's all go eat cupcakes and guzzle Bloody Marys! We have all felt the need to deploy the screw-it attitude about food on occasion because we are exhausted by the uncertainty of it all—the obsession and the calorie-counting and the hassle and the money spent on juice cleanses. Who needs it? No one.

But we do need to eat, and wouldn't it be nice if it wasn't something that was going to make us sick or tired or give us cancer? In this chapter, we'll do the work for you in terms of filtering out all the noise, bunk, biases, and agenda. The *mindbodygreen* podcast has hosted over four hundred guests who are nutrition experts in some respect, so we have truly heard it all. One week, a guest will share their strong feelings about kale and tell us all about why it's not as great as anyone thinks, and then a couple weeks later have another guest on talking about how kale is a superfood that will change your life. One expert demonizes beans; another thinks they are the key to longevity. Would you be surprised if we told you bananas are controversial? Probably not. It's the Wild West out here, folks. One of the reasons there is more information available about food and nutrition than ever is the same reason there is more misleading information than ever: social media algorithms. These algorithms create a feedback loop that incentivizes extremes, specifically anger. Scott Galloway, author of *Adrift*, recounts how researchers from Wharton Business School looked closely at articles from the *New York Times* that went viral and found that the most common factors were anxiety, awe, and anger. "For every standard deviation increase of anxiety elicited, the probability of an article making the most-emailed list went up by 21%. For awe, it went up 30%. But the most powerful emotion was anger, increasing virality by 34%."[9] Keeping this in mind, it's easy to see how many food influencers like doctors, nutritionists, and other self-styled experts are rewarded for polarizing points of view. How many famous influencers do you see out there scooping up billions of likes and clicks because they are talking about the Mediterranean diet? Not too many. Why? Because unlike other food trends (carnivore, vegan etc.), that diet is incredibly well balanced and uncontroversial. In other words, no one is sparking tribalism or vitriol and capitalizing off it. The world has seen this phenomenon play out disastrously in the political arena, where polarizing content is incentivized because it drives views, which translate to revenue.

We in the world of well-being have watched all of this unfold in real time. After all, it's our job to watch the trends and patterns of health. But more than just listening to it all, we have personally tried most of the food trends and diets out there: vegetarian, vegan, raw vegan, keto, paleo, and full carnivore; recipes based on Ayurveda and Traditional Chinese Medicine, and cleanses galore. And after more than a decade of experimenting and researching, we have come to two realizations that aren't sexy and might not drive clicks, but they are foundational to a healthy, joyful-not-painful mindset about food.

1. The science is too young to stake your life on most new food trends. From registered dietitians to preventive cardiologists, everyone knows that the state of food science and nutrition science is not ideal. There is so much we don't know, so many flawed and contradictory studies, so much more research to be done. Where there is research, it can be difficult for a layperson to figure out which studies to trust. Driven by their own biases, scientists and experts can find "evidence" to support a lot of claims, further undermining public trust. Modern food science began in 1926, when the first vitamin was discovered, which means the field is still in its infancy compared to many other fields.[10]

2. There is no one right way to eat for everyone. Despite the raft of diet books that come out every year flogging keto or paleo or whatever, we have yet to find one single diet that works for both of us—and we are just two people! To further make the point, we have two friends who are both healthy and thriving later in life—one is paleo (Mark Sisson, sixty-nine years old) and the other is vegan (Rich Roll, fifty-six years old). Who's to say that one is right and the other wrong in terms of their nutritional philosophy? What do they have in common? Not much other than that they both avoid processed foods and are extraordinarily active. We get that it would be simpler if you could just follow a list of requirements in a book, what to eat and when, but we have learned over the years that it doesn't work. Why? A couple of reasons. First, depending on genetics and lifestyle factors, one person could ramp up their consumption of meat and their lipid panel numbers would catapult them in a higher risk category, while another person could see their numbers improve. We're all unique, listening to your body is the name of the game. Second, because food is more than fuel—it is about joy, ritual, and comfort, and what eating approach brings everyone these gifts is wildly different. What is sustainable is what makes you happy, and it's unrealistic to think any specific diet could ever make everyone happy.

So, should we all just throw up our hands and go to the Sizzler buffet for dinner and Dairy Queen for dessert? Sorry, no—as much as our 1990s inner children would love that. While there is no one diet that works for everyone and the science is young, there are universal building blocks you can use to find an eating philosophy that works for you. These fundamental guidelines are common sense and have held up against repeated rigorous scientific review. They are also what the experts we consult with constantly all agree actually work, and what we use as our own personal North Star. Our perspective on this chapter is that you should listen to what all the experts are saying, then tune out the points of disagreement and the trendy new advice. That includes videos from content creators who lack letters after their name but make really compelling videos. We all know that people have opinions. And everyone has a new diet that has worked for them, so they are talking about it at the neighborhood block party (which is now social media) and getting you all excited that it could work for you too. We are optimistic beings, after all. But what we've found over the years is that the gold is in the overlap. If you listen closely enough, there *are* some places where the experts agree unequivocally, and those are the gold nuggets that we are going to highlight in this chapter. That is the low-hanging fruit of better nutrition, and we have found they can help get you 80 percent of the way to maximum well-being. Interestingly enough, the guidelines we'll share are also pretty radical for how balanced they are. These days not being controversial is about the most radical position you can take.

So, after having acknowledged that we are all deeply tired of the cultural obsession with what to eat, why exactly should you spend the time to read yet another word about nutrition, never mind take the time to build a new philosophy for yourself?

Because it's not as hard as you think, and because it's important.

If you've picked up this book, chances are that you've heard it all before, or you have experienced firsthand the impact of nutrition on your well-being. Jason certainly has. If you look at him now at six foot seven inches and two hundred pounds, you might not see it, but he is no stranger to what experts call weight cycling, aka, losing weight and then gaining it (for him, between twenty-five and fifty pounds) many times over years or decades. It started his sophomore year in high school when he tried to put on muscle for basketball, but since he had no idea how to do this skillfully (think lots of breaded chicken parmesan, white pasta, and gross protein powders), he'd add some muscle but would gain even more weight around his midsection. When basketball started up, he was bullied by his high school coach, who had a treasure trove of fat jokes to hurl at Jason during practice, destroying his confidence. Eventually, he'd lose the excess weight over the course of the season, then when summer came, he'd put it all on again, eating tons of processed foods and making regular trips to 7-Eleven for Gatorade. To get back in shape he'd go on the Atkins diet and take other extreme measures to lose it. This cycle happened again and again throughout his teens and twenties, when he played college ball (where he folded beer and late-night pizza into the mix). Jason's yo-yoing weight journey was harmful to his physical, emotional, and mental health. While the weight swings became less severe in his thirties, they didn't totally stop until his early forties, when he finally figured out which food and lifestyle choices supported his metabolic health. For some people, like Jason, the impact of diet is obvious, but for others it is reflected not in weight gain, but in inflammation and metabolic disease.

For the purposes of getting to the why-it's-doable part, that's all we're going to say about why it's so important to eat right. But we *will* say this: what you eat and how you eat is incredibly consequential. You don't wake up one day and flip a magic switch, rendering you diabetic, inflamed, or tired. After all, you make dozens of food choices every day. Any one of those is not such a big deal, but over time, harm or health accumulates. It happens over time. Which is good news, because you have ample time to use food as medicine. And that's exactly what it is.

EAT REAL FOOD (EMPHASIS ON *REAL*)

Whole foods. Plant-based food. Organic food. Processed food. All-natural food. Local food. There are endless qualifiers for "food" in the nutrition world; some are straightforward, and others are just the marketing equivalent of jazz hands. Regardless, it can all get pretty confusing pretty fast, so we'll try to keep it simple.

- Eat real food.
- Eat real food.
- Eat real food!

What does that mean? Real food is food that is in its original form or is as close to that as humanly possible. These are foods that are not processed, are rich in nutrients, and are free of additives. Think blackberries, avocados, arugula, broccoli, walnuts, garlic, sweet potatoes, grass-fed beef, wild salmon, or pasture-raised eggs from your neighbor's chickens (eat those chickens too, if on offer). Whole fruits and veggies are the first things that spring to mind when we talk about real food, because they are most recognizably in their natural form. Things get a little trickier when you move on down the line to grains, meat, and dairy, all of which can show up on the grocery store shelf either minimally processed or highly processed. But for those of us who are able to eat a diet of primarily real food, the benefits abound. For starters, you'll benefit from lower rates of type 2 diabetes, heart disease, and cancer.[11] You will be eating a diet rich in antioxidants and micronutrients like vitamins and minerals. You'll be feeding your gut microbiome the fiber it needs to digest properly, maintain immune health, and keep your blood sugar in check. You will starve the plaque-causing bacteria that live in your mouth and explode your budget with dental bills. And once you get on the real-food train, you'll benefit from fewer cravings for sugar and highly processed food.[12]

For years now, we have all heard the news that processed foods are bad for us. Things like high-fructose corn syrup and trans fats are two highly publicized examples. When we think of highly processed foods, we think of McDonald's, KFC, or food you might buy at the gas station. But do most people think about yogurt, pasta, or even oatmeal as being processed?

Nope.

But as real-food visionary and endocrinologist Robert Lustig, MD, says, "It's not what's *in the food*—it's what's *been done to the food* that counts."[13] In other words, people get a little too hung up on the whether it's sugar or fat or salt that we should be avoiding in our food, and forget to look at the other dimensions of what's on our plate. For instance, depending on which brand you happen to snag at the store, your yogurt might not be just cow's milk fermented with some good-for-your-gut microbes—it could also include fat replacers and "natural flavors" that are just chemicals designed to smell like the real fruit they have neglected to actually include in that "blueberry" yogurt. Artificial sweeteners are everywhere, and some like aspartame are associated with a greater risk of cancer.[14] So we have starches, gums, thickeners, and sugars going in, and fiber, fat, and micronutrients are coming out, and often we have no idea what the wizard is doing behind the curtain to make it all happen.

Trying to decode a food label at the grocery store has never been a more mystifying endeavor. Many of these highly processed foods can even be labeled organic because you don't need pesticides to develop compounds in a lab. Likewise, many of these chemical additives are derived from plants, which gives the food industry legal cover to call them "natural." Even more alarming, as the term *plant-based* has gained popularity, brands are scrambling to put that qualifier on everything from crackers to fake meat.

Time out: Allow us to hop on our soap box for a minute about this. Just because something is plant-based doesn't mean it's good for you. Oreos, Coke, and Doritos are mostly plants! But they are ultra-super-duper-highly processed plants—so processed, in fact, that they more closely resemble a high school lab experiment than what pops out of a garden or field. Fake meat is the latest innovation in deception. At its core, this product is about emulating a whole food that is notoriously difficult to replicate in terms of taste and texture; this is achieved by utilizing a bunch of new ingredients, like soy leghemoglobin (heme), that have not been tested for long-term toxicity and are genetically modified to boot. This lab meat might taste more like real meat than ever before, but at its core it's still lab meat. Its proponents claim that it is a more sustainable option than real beef, which is certainly true if you eat burgers every day, but the argument is on less solid ground if you eat organic grass-fed local beef once a month.

As savvy as we are about nutrition after all these years, even *we* have gotten caught in marketing booby traps laid for us by the food executives. For instance, fake fats are notoriously hard to spot. There is an array of fake fats added to foods that are patented under names like Simplesse but stealthily hidden on your food label as "milk protein."[15] When you read "milk protein," it sounds pretty wholesome, a lot like real food, right? It's not, but that's the whole point of the wordplay. In the end, all the linguistic trickery explains how Greek yogurt could contain no fat, no added sugar, and no real fruit and not taste like total garbage.[16]

But in the end, processed food *is* too good to be true.

In the mid-twentieth century, when we began to process our food supply in earnest, we started down a dangerous path. We began a long, expensive, disastrous experiment with our food that included tinkering, adding, subtracting, and shuffling around key components of whole foods. Whether it's genetically modifying food or enriching it, we have fundamentally changed the food supply, and as a result, the food supply has changed us. As US corporations were experimenting with how to make food more profitable and palatable and easier to produce, they were also playing with our long-term health by testing the impacts of their new inventions only on our short-term health. If they tested a new modified starch on a bunch of rats and they didn't immediately die (or die within six weeks), that was considered good enough. But no one studied the long-term metabolic effects of all this tinkering with the food supply.[17] The belief was (and still is in some places) that if the additives that you put in are safe, then changing the chemical composition of the food as a whole must be safe too. The argument goes that our bodies don't care if we have yogurt with artificial sweetener that is technically nontoxic. In fact, it's good for us from a calories-in, calories-out perspective—what our body doesn't know won't hurt it, right? Unfortunately, that couldn't be more wrong. It matters where our calories come from. The fundamental miscalculation that the US made in the 1940s when it decided to start enriching food is the same one we make today when we continue to eat those highly processed foods. We underestimate the profound complexity and intelligence of the human body. Your metabolism is nobody's fool, but if you treat it like one, you will see a range of unintended downstream health consequences.

There is so much we don't know about the impact of all the additives we are putting in our food. The food industrial complex is not interested in funding that kind of research, and the amount of research scientists can do is far outstripped by the breakneck speed of food technology. But what we do know is more than enough to have you shopping the perimeter of the grocery store forever. There are lots of ways that processed food is bad for us; added sugar, salt, and fat and hidden pesticides like Roundup immediately come to mind. But we want to highlight two lesser-known reasons for sticking to foods without a label (have you ever seen a label on an orange?) or with as few ingredients as possible.

Your Body Is Nobody's Fool

When you sit down to crush an entire pint of low-calorie, keto-friendly Halo Top ice cream, never forget that your taste buds, nervous system, and hormones are smarter than you are.

Processed foods that add flavorings, additives, and other compounds are designed to trick your brain into thinking it's eating something with more fat, sugar, or salt in it than it really has. This was a major miscalculation on the part of food science. One of the reasons we have the ability to taste at all is because our brain likes to predict things.[18] In order to properly metabolize different kinds of foods, we have to expend different amounts of energy. To help us do that more efficiently, our brain needs to know what to get ready for—protein or sugar, fat or carbs? What those foods taste like is the information our brain requires to warm up our metabolism appropriately. But the real genius happens after we taste and eat our food—it's called post-ingestive learning, and this is how we learn to like, want, and even crave food.[19] For instance, if a food gave us an awesome amount of brain-building fat, we're going to remember what that tastes like, so we can properly identify it in the future and come back for more.

Until we started playing mad scientist with our food supply, our brains could rely on foods that taste sweet to have a commensurate number of calories, or a piece of meat that tastes rich and fatty to have a predictable level of fat and protein. But now, if you eat a yogurt with Simplesse in it, your body is not getting the same number of calories that it would expect to get from such a sweet, fatty dairy product. This creates what scientists call a "nutritive mismatch"—and the biggest problem with this is that your body starts to make up for all that uncertainty, all that prediction error, by sending your body the message that it had better go get more calories, pronto.[20] For instance, a disappointing caloric scenario: You eat Simplesse-laden yogurt, your tongue picks up on creamy texture and tells your brain you've got lots of fat coming in, but then your stomach just gets "tiny protein balls" instead of rich fat.[21] Can you really blame your metabolism for feeling totally ripped off? It's hard to be upset with our brains and bodies for wanting to make up the caloric difference in light of our trickery. So much better to feed them the real-deal, full-fat, absolutely delicious real treat, as opposed to the impersonator du jour. You'll be full faster and honor your body's wisdom at the same time.

Elaborating on the example he gave in the book, Schatzker told us in an interview, "There are so many ways we've changed food to constantly deliver a message that is out of sync with the actual nutrition; this is why I think we're seeing an outsized desire to eat."[22] Right now, 58 percent of calories in the American adult diet are coming from ultra-processed foods; that number is 67 percent among children and adolescents.[23] When you look at that statistic and then look at the spiraling metabolic health of the nation in the last thirty years, what ails us starts to come into sharp focus.

The Case of the Disappearing Fiber

We mentioned earlier that it's not just what's in processed food that is problematic; it's what is taken out. One of the healthiest, most critical part of real foods is the fiber they contain. To get back to basics: fiber is a complex carbohydrate that can't be digested or broken down into sugar, so it sails on through our gut and out the other end. But along the way, it has an extremely important job to do: it keeps our blood sugar in check, helps us feel sated, and feeds the healthy bacteria in our intestines.[24]

Despite all of that, the food industry seems hell-bent on discarding fiber from food. Robert Lustig cites a simple example: orange juice. It seems like orange juice should be equally as healthy and nutritious as a whole orange, but metabolically, you might as well be drinking sugar water with some vitamin C added to it. When you drink that OJ, what has been discarded is the fiber, which is exactly what slows down the sugar punch of an orange, because fiber slows the digestion of carbohydrates and the absorption of sugar. The fiber matrix of the orange, as opposed to the juice, allows your body to digest and absorb in a way that is healthier for your liver and won't spike your blood sugar.[25]

A side note about metabolic health: Why should we care about blood sugar? Why should we care about metabolizing our food optimally? Metabolic health—the state of having your blood sugar, blood pressure, and cholesterol in normal ranges—is make it or break it for us humans. If we are not metabolically healthy, we are at greater risk for diabetes, heart disease, and stroke. While all public health eyes are on the obesity epidemic, more and more research is coming to light that shows we all should be paying more attention to our metabolic health, which is largely what causes obesity in the first place. Because while weight gain is the most visible sign of metabolic dysfunction, far more of us are unhealthy than are fat. In fact, according to one study only 12 percent of us, or one in eight Americans have "optimal metabolic health," which means that if we want to be healthy, it's not only the numbers on the scale we should be paying attention to.[26]

Which leads us back to fiber.

Right about now you might be thinking about our old friend Metamucil, or psyllium husks, or whatever brand of soluble fiber you might add to your smoothies or cereal. Isn't adding that in enough to make up for our low-fiber diets? Not exactly. It certainly helps. But there are two types of fiber—soluble and insoluble—and both are equally important. You can add a bunch of soluble fiber to your diet, but if you aren't eating whole foods, you are missing half of the fiber equation. The combination of both types of fibers is what suppresses your insulin response and confers huge metabolic benefits.[27]

The importance of fiber to a healthy diet and overall well-being can't be overstated. Renowned gastroenterologist Will Bulsiewicz, MD, really opened our eyes to how fiber deficient we are collectively and how deeply important it is to everyone's health. One of the wilder statistics that we've come across—which is saying something—is that 95 percent of Americans are fiber deficient.[28] This is really alarming when you realize that by adding more fiber to your diet—not a lot, and not even the recommended daily amount—you reduce your exposure to six of the top ten causes of death in the US (heart disease, stroke, diabetes, kidney disease, cancer, and Alzheimer's).[29] To get specific, during our interview Bulsiewicz told us about a new study that looked at the interplay between increased fiber consumption and the success of cancer immunotherapy. Will told us, "They discovered that you were substantially more likely to have a good response to the immunotherapy, to live longer, and to survive your cancer, to the point that for every five grams of dietary fiber intake, these people had increased their likelihood of survival by 30 percent."[30] It's important to note that the threshold for fiber intake for this study was 20 grams of fiber, not even the recommended amount of 38 grams for men and 25 grams a day for women ages 19 to 50.

Even though fiber is the eight-hundred-pound gorilla when it comes to what is taken out of highly processed foods, there is a lot more that ends up in the trash. According to Lustig, things like "vitamins, polyphenols, polyamines, flavonoids, and other antioxidants" are also discarded, important micronutrients and phytonutrients that we desperately need to keep all of our body's systems humming along.[31]

Big Takeaway: When you eat a bunch of fake food, the experience does not bring your body a lot of joy. It will just make you want to eat more and more and more, until you get sick.

Eat real food and you will feel full and happy—and be healthier as a result.

INTEGRATION TIPS:

This is where going back to basics really pays off. Despite the complexity of all the science behind what is metabolically optimal and what is actually in our food, doing the right thing for our bodies is dead simple: Eat real food. If it's got ingredients you can't pronounce, and it comes in a box or a can or a pouch, it's something you should really look at more closely. Some cans just have beans, some have beans and a bunch of processed seed oil and salt. Spending the time to check out the label is worth it! After all, now that you know all the dirty little tricks of the food industry, you can be on high alert for all their clever label phrasing. We're also including some tips for navigating the grocery store and eating in a way that is flexible for any budget.

■ Don't bite off more than you can chew (pun intended); you want to make small tweaks to your diet that put you on a trajectory toward more and more real food in your diet. Our friend and rock star nutritionist Maya Feller, RD, has helped hundreds of people change their health, and she says that every time someone tries to completely overhaul their food life, she knows it won't be sustainable. Starting small is how you make this a life change, not by starting another temporary diet.

▪ Start by looking at the meals that are your favorites, the ones that work for your family's food culture right now. How could you make tweaks in the right direction? If spaghetti and meatballs is your favorite, try making the pasta sauce at home instead of buying it. If you'd like to cut down on refined grains, substitute a lentil bean pasta for your usual white-flour pasta for some added protein and fiber. Throw a few vegetables into the sauce, and you've already substantially improved the nutritional profile of your meal.

▪ If money or food accessibility is a barrier (and even if it's not), lean heavily on canned and frozen foods. Plenty of food that is packaged isn't highly processed; you just have to read the label to figure out which is which. You can get frozen spinach, frozen broccoli, canned wild fish, and beans and eat just as healthfully as the person who has the resources to go to an expensive health food store. The simplicity of real food also lends itself to affordability, despite what a lot of people think. We're not professional meal planners or cooks, so we rely on organic whole foods like black beans, extra-virgin olive oil, and wild sardines. Because of their simplicity, even though we choose exclusively organic foods for our family when we can, we find we are still able to put together meals based on real-food building blocks that are affordable and delicious. For more info on our weekly grocery list and favorite brands, head to thejoyofwellbeing.com/groceries.

▪ So many struggles with integration of real food are about time. The allure of processed food is how expedient it is in the moment—just grab a package and go. But the benefits of that time saved do not outweigh the costs to your health and happiness. In order to make cooking real food more manageable from a time perspective, think about doing some meal prep for the week ahead if things are hectic in your day-to-day. Cooking up some rice and beans, cutting up some veggies, and packing lunches ahead of time will help you integrate real food more seamlessly. If prepping for the whole week feels overwhelming, just prep for two days. Two days of eating well is a great place to start!

- Create some go-to meals for weeknights. Make them as easy and fast as possible. Don't worry about eating the same thing over and over again. It's not boring—it's a survival tactic! With two kids and a busy life, we have a menu for the week, which makes grocery shopping and meal prep as efficient as possible. We have found our regular Monday night meal of red-lentil pasta with broccoli to be both delicious and relaxing.

- This is one that you may have heard before, but is worth repeating: your plate should be mostly vegetables. When you're planning meals, consider how you can bump up the servings of veggies. When you are at a restaurant, order the meat as your side dish and vegetables as your main—not the other way around.

CIRCADIAN FASTING

In the last chapter we talked about the power of our internal clock, or circadian rhythm, and how it acts on every part of our physiology. Well, we're popping back in here to tell you that we weren't kidding, and there's more where that came from.

For a few years now, one area of interest related to eating is not what to eat, but *when* to eat it. As the mindbodygreen research team knows, it seems like we don't go a day without seeing an article on intermittent fasting (IF) and its potential health benefits—improved cognitive function, weight loss, and extended life span, to name a few.[32] So what is it? In the medical world, intermittent fasting is called time-restricted eating—meaning that you are restricting the period of time you eat to a set number of hours each day. Time-restricted eating typically consists of confining all your eating to a window of a certain number of hours, ranging from four to twelve, and fasting the remainder of the day. But with so many popular iterations of IF out there, each with potential perks and pitfalls, it's hard to know which option—if any—is right for you, or if it's even safe. The truth is, this area of science is still young, and there's a lot that needs to be verified with further research. But that said, many reputable experts we've spoken to *do* see a benefit to various forms of intermittent fasting for most people—when done responsibly and in a way that's in tune with your goals and current health status. The most responsible, low-barrier, and seamless way to get the benefits of time-restricted eating without having to think about it too much or work with your doctor to see what is safe for you to do is simply to do a twelve-hour circadian fast most days.[33]

How this differs from intermittent fasting is simply that you are timing your meals with the rise and fall of the sun and the corresponding surges and dips in cortisol. It also means that eating your biggest meal either at breakfast or in the middle of the day instead of at nighttime is the priority. If you decide to do a shorter eating window that requires skipping a meal, some studies show that there is greater benefit to skipping dinner as opposed to breakfast (which is more common but not as well supported by the science).[34] The timing is important too, because cortisol has a significant effect on your thyroid hormones, which affect metabolism of the food you eat. When cortisol rises in the earlier hours, your metabolism is also up and running, and you more effectively use the food you eat as energy. When cortisol dips later in the day, your metabolism simultaneously slows down, which makes it more likely that your body will store the food you eat as fat. Amy Shah, MD, a double-board-certified physician and expert on intermittent fasting for women, explained it to mindbodygreen like this: "All of our cells and organs have clocks that determine when our genes should be turned on and turned off... You can't do all actions in the body at once. So, when the sun goes down, usually the actions of digestion are turned off and the actions of repair and restoration are turned on. If you eat late at night, you may get slower digestion, inappropriate acid production, and more insulin resistance. This leads to fat gain, GI symptoms, and even diabetes."[35]

Circadian rhythm fasting also considers the role of insulin. When you eat, especially if you eat a meal that has a lot of carbohydrates, your body releases insulin in response to the rise in blood sugar. According to researchers from a study that was published in *Cell* in May 2019, if insulin rises at odd times—like when you eat a meal late at night—it can actually disrupt your circadian rhythm and increase your risk for long-term health problems, like type 2 diabetes and heart disease.[36] Insulin also promotes the storage of body fat, especially if you eat too many carbohydrates or calories.

Timing your meals with your natural circadian rhythm has also been shown to help improve inflammatory diseases, like rheumatoid arthritis and inflammatory bowel disease; infections; metabolic disorders; certain cancers; and central nervous system disorders, like multiple sclerosis and Parkinson's disease.[37] It's even been touted as a powerful way to combat internal and external signs of aging.[38]

While the overall timing of your meals is important, it's not the only thing to consider when following circadian rhythm fasting. Felice Gersh, MD, a board-certified obstetrician with expertise in hormonal management, recommends eating no later than seven p.m. and says it's also important that your circadian rhythm is actually functioning as it should. The circadian rhythm diet relies on a predictable rise and fall of cortisol and other hormones. Artificial lights, extended screen time, and unpredictable sleep schedules can all negatively affect your natural circadian rhythm and throw your hormones out of whack. Eating with your natural sleep/wake cycles can help start to balance your hormones, but if you're scrolling through Instagram on your phone until two a.m., it can negate all your efforts.

To reap the full benefits, Amy Shah recommends getting your sleep schedule in harmony with your eating schedule by going to bed between nine p.m. and eleven p.m. and waking up between five thirty and eight a.m. each morning. And don't forget to grab a few minutes of sunlight first thing in the morning to reset the hypothalamus and help with better hormone regulation. Aim to restrict eating to a twelve-hour period (the majority of the other twelve hours will be spent sleeping) in line with your circadian rhythm.

INTEGRATION TIPS:

- If twelve hours of fasting feels like a stretch, start slow and focus on nighttime. If you usually go to bed at nine thirty, try to close the kitchen by seven p.m. after a light meal.
- In the morning, if you wake up early and hungry, make the wait more comfortable by having a couple of glasses of water. Front-loading hydration is a good idea anyway.
- You can drink black coffee or tea and still be in a fasting state—just leave out the creamer.
- While it's not a good idea to have a heavy meal in the evening— it can impact your sleep among other things—make sure you include some healthy fats and protein at dinner to keep you full and sleeping well throughout the night.

HYDRATION

Whether you are constipated, hungry, tired, headachy, sick, hurt, hypothermic, or even a smidge brain-foggy, the first thing any doctor will tell you to do is drink water. It's the health equivalent of the IT guy asking you, "Have you tried turning the computer off and on?" Likewise, "Have you had enough water?" is the first and last question whenever something is wrong with our bodies, but it should really be the question we're constantly asking ourselves throughout the day no matter how we're feeling in the moment.

Kristen Willeumier, PhD, is a neuroscientist and researcher who designs and studies therapeutic approaches to rehabilitating brain function in athletes with mild traumatic brain injury. Through her work studying the brains of hundreds of NFL football players, she observed how important brain health is and helped design protocols to heal the brain through nutrition and lifestyle changes. She says, "One of the first things that I do when I teach people about taking care of their brain health is to make sure they are drinking enough water. I have taught thousands of people about how to get brain fit… The number one thing people don't do is drink enough water."[39]

So, what does all that boring old water do for our brain and body exactly? It flushes out toxins, keeps your blood pressure normalized and your skin clear, keeps you metabolically active, and can even improve your memory.[40] In a study of adults aged 51–70 years, there were remarkably zero chronic disease deaths in people who met the hydration criteria and did not already have a chronic condition.[41] Willeumier points out that hydration is critical to help your brain age well. When building her database of healthy brain scans (to use as points of comparison in her NFL study), she saw a lack of perfusion (healthy blood flow) in the brains of folks who were otherwise healthy. What this showed her was that if they didn't correct those perfusion problems and protect their neurons, they would be at a higher risk for cognitive issues as they aged. The first place to start with increasing blood flow to the brain? You guessed it: water.

INTEGRATION TIPS:

- A good rule of thumb is to drink half your body weight in ounces. So, if you weigh one hundred and fifty pounds, you should drink about seventy-five ounces of water a day. How to fit it all in? If you don't want to lug around a giant Yeti bottle (like Colleen does) with you all day, you could stash a jug of water in the fridge (at work or home) and keep refilling your cup all day. At night you could put an empty water glass next to your coffee machine or tea as a reminder to start your day with water.
- Remember, you can get up to 20 percent of your daily water intake from hydrating fruits, veggies, and green juices. Use those as your cushion for the days when you fall a little short on water intake.

WEIGHING IN ON THE HOT TOPICS: SUGAR, ALCOHOL, REFINED GRAINS AND FATS, MEAT, AND DAIRY

As much as we have no interest in being super prescriptive, we do know that inquiring minds want to know more about certain food groups—especially those where the information about their role in a healthy diet is confusing or controversial. There are plenty of people who have very strong opinions about each of these categories of food—many extreme. From where we stand, villainizing whole food groups (remember the war on fat?) is what has gotten us all into a heap of nutritional trouble. When you go on a quest to eliminate dairy from your life, or sugar, you end up right back where you started—eating a bunch of fat replacers and additives that have no business in your body and then eating more and more and more. Even worse, you miss out on stellar sources of nutrients (micronutrients, phytonutrients), like calcium, vitamin D, B vitamins, and even macronutrients like protein. On the other side of the equation, there are people who have allergies and sensitivities that make certain exclusions necessary for feeling their best. The only realistic choice when it comes to what foods to eat is to stay true to who you are, what your body needs and wants, and what you need and want to be happy and healthy. Everyone's metabolic situation is different and should be honored. Everyone's family, lifestyle, and goals are different and should be taken into consideration. You won't get blanket statements from us about what should be on your plate or in your glass, but we won't totally hold out on you. Here are some more nuanced recommendations for living your life and enjoying food while keeping some bumper lanes up for your health.

Sugar

Sugar is probably villainized more than any other food right now. And while most experts agree you should limit your intake of sugar to no more than 25 grams of added sugar a day, you should also remember the 80/20 rule and take into consideration the dictum to eat real food. If you're going to have a chocolate chip cookie, have the best damn chocolate chip cookie you can get your hands on. That means a full-fat, gluten-tastic (if you can tolerate gluten), loaded-with-butter cookie from the bakery down the street. For the love of Mother Nature, don't waste your life on Chips Ahoy! And don't forget to enjoy the hell out of that bakery cookie—in our house we call it a "treat," not a "cheat," in order to come from a place of abundance and joy as opposed to scarcity and guilt.

Alcohol

The advice about alcohol is always changing and often contradictory. Depending on what study you read, a glass of wine a day is good for you or it causes cancer. But if Giuseppe from Sardinia and the other Blue Zone centenarians are any indication, many of you can consume alcohol moderately and in a way that doesn't damage your health. If you are someone who can handle drinking moderately—a few drinks a week—go ahead and enjoy it (preferably with friends and not alone). For instance, we have family dinner on Sundays, and Jason takes that opportunity to enjoy a lager with a grass-fed burger. While you shouldn't give free rein to your inner day-drinking college student, drinking earlier in the day is actually better in terms of how alcohol impacts your sleep, heart rate, and recovery. Also, it comes down to the individual: you've got to know what your limit is and understand that certain drinks may impact you differently depending on lots of factors. For instance, Colleen can tolerate only one margarita or one glass of prosecco without it impacting her sleep, and she tries to have it as early in the day as possible. Context and setting are also important. Are you having a couple of glasses of wine with friends and family, or are you drinking by yourself? Are you having to lie to your doctor about your drinking habits? (Don't worry, we've all been there, but it is a red flag!) Final note: If you don't drink, don't start.

Refined Grains and Fats

The key word here is *refined*. As we saw in the discussion of real foods, the more processed or refined something is, the less healthy it is. In the case of refined grains, the less you eat them the better. Why? Unfortunately, when grains are processed, they are stripped of dietary fiber and most of their nutrients. In the case of white flour, wheat has been stripped of its bran and germ. That's why many experts recommend staying away from refined grains completely. We simply look at it as another treat that we look forward to. For instance, we love fresh sourdough bread—it's one of life's true high points. And when we were vacationing in Italy we ate like Italians—plenty of pasta and bread. But in the majority of our day-to-day life, we've found our bodies are happier with fewer refined grains in our bellies.

Refined fats like seed oils are a hot topic in the nutrition space. New research is emerging that highly refined oils like corn, canola (rapeseed), cottonseed, soy, sunflower, safflower, grapeseed, and rice bran can cause inflammation. According to family physician and *New York Times* bestselling author Cate Shanahan, MD, these oils are deemed unhealthy for two reasons: They're highly refined (farther away from the original plant goodness), and they're high in a particular type of polyunsaturated fatty acids (PUFA) known as omega-6 fatty acids. When they're exposed to chemicals in the refining process, they're essentially stripped of their antioxidants, vitamins, and minerals. Since omega-6 PUFAs lead to pro-inflammatory downstream pathways in the cells of our body (and cells make up tissues and organs), consuming too many of these fats over time can lead to inflammation. Americans are currently consuming excessive amounts of omega-6 fats from cheap oils. Meanwhile, we're dismally underconsuming another type of stellar PUFA, omega-3s (EPA and DHA especially), which are anti-inflammatory. It's a delicate fat-balancing act, which we're currently failing as a nation.

"For all foods, we have to consider the nature of the fats," Shanahan says. Traditional fats, like butter, are closer to whole foods than refined oils are. "You don't need high heat, you don't need complicated equipment, you don't need refining machinery," Shanahan says about butter. "You just let the cream rise to the top, skim it off, and then you start churning it around, and that's butter."[42]

The same can be said of olive oil, coconut oil, and avocado oil when they're cold-pressed and unrefined. Traditionally, these oils are squeezed straight from the fruit, or the seed of the fruit, and are not stripped of their antioxidants and minerals.[43] Since olive oil is the most used on this list of good fats, we want to mention that all olive oil is not created equal. If you're looking to get the health benefits of this superfood, you should always be shopping for extra-virgin olive oil. Look for oil made from Greek Koroneiki, Italian Moraiolo, or Spanish Picual olives. It also matters when you buy your olive oil. According to our podcast with chef Ryan Hardy, "The level of those polyphenols is at its highest when it's harvested, and then it quickly drops down." You also lose flavor as your oil ages, so look at the label carefully next time you're stocking up.[44]

Meat, Fish, and Eggs

Most functional medicine doctors will tell you to eat wild fish, occasional pasture-raised chicken and eggs, and grass-fed meat. Wild fish is better than farmed fish, if you can get it, and we recommend sticking to SMASH (salmon, mackerel, anchovies, sardines, herring) fish for less mercury exposure and high nutrient density. SMASH fish are rich in the all-important marine omega-3 fatty acids EPA and DHA, and they're also a great source of protein. Eggs are high in protein as well, and try for pasture-raised and organic if you can. Grass-fed organ meat is back in vogue and backed by science; incorporate that into your diet if you can stomach the texture (sadly, we can't). If you're looking for permission to go vegetarian, pescatarian, or vegan—permission granted. When done thoughtfully and with the support of the health professionals in your life, going meatless is a fine option, though you'll likely have to supplement to make sure you're getting the diversity of nutrients you need. Some people are true carnivores and don't feel like they can live without it, and that's fine too—just be careful to keep an eye on your lipid profile and other biomarkers of health and adjust accordingly.

Dairy

There's no reason to hold back on full-fat, organic, grass-fed dairy unless it makes you feel bad. An hour or two after you eat dairy, do you feel bloated and gassy? That's probably a strong sign that your body is having a harder time digesting it. If you eat it and you feel fine, you're probably okay. Know your body and use moderation. If you are having trouble listening to your body, ask your healthcare providers about blood tests that can help you understand how your body interacts with dairy. Some people land on a spectrum of lactose intolerance, while others might have a dairy allergy to contend with.

The bottom line on balancing what you eat, as Michael Pollan famously said, is "Eat food. Not too much. Mostly plants."[45]

We leave it up to you to figure out what works best for your unique needs to fill in the blanks:

- 80 percent = Whole, unprocessed foods. Lean heavily on vegetables. Think of the perimeter of the grocery store, and choose foods that don't require labels when you can.
- 20 percent = Everything else. The inner aisles of the grocery store.

INTEGRATION TIPS:

- Think about what your nonnegotiables are and keep those as a part of your life. Keeping the 80/20 rule in mind, how can you move some of the not-so-healthy foods that you eat into the 20 percent category? Maybe that means saving wine for the weekends, and pizza is something you do to celebrate family wins. As you do an inventory of what you eat and what you value and what healthier choices would be, think about what you can't live without day to day. For instance, if you absolutely love the taste of a tablespoon of maple syrup in your coffee every morning, that's a nonnegotiable—do it and love it and don't look back.

▪ Ultimately, family meals are meant to be joyful. What are your favorite family traditions? Think about meals or dishes that can be made slightly healthier to ease yourself and your family into more healthy routines through thoughtful substitutions.

FINAL THOUGHTS

This chapter threw a lot at you in terms of the science of eating, but ultimately the real message is the importance of keeping your relationship to food simple and joyous. At the end of the day, that is what all the science points to. If you do want to make changes to your diet, make sure that it jibes with the way you already live your life, your budget, and what makes you happy. Make a ritual around your family dinners by setting the table, lighting a candle, singing a song—whatever brings you joy. We hope you're convinced by now that it's not impossible or overwhelming to make small changes that make a big impact. In fact, if you go slow and low, much like cooking a nice organic, grass-fed, and humanely raised rib roast—we promise you'll discover a delicious transformation.

THAT EXTRA 20 PERCENT

SEEK DIVERSITY

One way to go the extra mile and really get into the joy of cooking and eating real foods is to think beyond the standard "health food" fare of broccoli and blueberries. There are plenty of ways to branch out beyond your own culture and enjoy the diversity of foods that are delicious and healthy. For instance, have you tried bok choy, kimchi, jicama, Chinese long beans, prickly pears, sour cherries, or papayas? Finding these may be a challenge if you don't shop beyond your local grocery store, but that's where the extra 20 percent comes in—embrace the challenge!

USING FOOD AS MEDICINE

Most people over the age of thirty or so get blood work done every year. Some people know their numbers, others just hear "normal" from their doc and forget about it. If you want to go the extra 20 percent and use food as a precision tool for your health, it helps to pay attention to the numbers and ask for more tests than your doctor normally orders. There are so many tests out there, but these are the ones that will help you identify any hiccups with your health, because usually if these are out of whack, there is something larger going on. This is even more important if you have a family history of heart disease or metabolic disorder. If you want some general guidance on what the recommended numbers are, there is always the internet. But if you want some curated guidance on which ranges are not just the norm but actually optimal (something your doctor doesn't always mention), we have more information for you on our resource page at thejoyofwellbeing.com/labs.

Fasting glucose and fasting insulin

These two are hugely important for identifying any early-onset metabolic issues that might be sneaking up on you. Just a heads up—some doctors are very resistant to ordering fasting insulin, but it's always worth it to ask.

Lp(a)

This isn't on a standard lipid panel, but it should be. If this number is high, you have almost triple the risk of having a heart attack at a young age.[46] Especially if you have any history of early death due to heart failure in your family—get it done! More than 20 percent of the population has high Lp(a) and would benefit from medical intervention.[47] Genetics play a significant role, and lifestyle doesn't have much effect on this number, so if you're low, you probably don't have to take this test again.

Homocysteine

This amino acid is broken down by key vitamins like B12, B6, and B9 (folate). If you have high levels of this, it means your B levels are perilously low, which ups the risk of blood clots and stroke. When homocysteine builds up unchecked, it can also contribute to dementia and heart disease.[48] For Jason, this one is personal. A few years ago, he felt physically fine, yet after a routine blood workup, discovered he had a homocysteine level of 63.3 umol/L. (For reference, high homocysteine is defined as anything higher than 15 umol/L, so his was especially shocking. At first his doctor thought the labs were a mistake!) There are no side effects of high homocysteine levels; it's just something that is undermining your health quietly in the background. Luckily, because Jason was aware of a family history of cardiovascular disease, he tested and caught the problem early. He was able to treat it successfully with a specific array of bioactive B vitamins and get his homocysteine down to normal levels.

Estrogen, Testosterone, and Thyroid Status

Estrogen and testosterone are two essential sex hormones to have in balance in your body; make sure you are within normal ranges. Another critical set of hormones to keep an eye on are thyroid hormones (aka T3 and T4). While women are disproportionately impacted by thyroid health issues (hypothyroidism and hyperthyroidism), everyone would benefit from working with a hormone-focused practitioner to assess thyroid status via a comprehensive thyroid panel (not just TSH, but also T3, T4, reverse T3, and thyroid antibodies). Sex and thyroid hormones have whole-body effects, so they are important to prioritize and optimize.

Hemoglobin A1C

This is one you've likely heard before in the context of diagnosing and treating diabetes. Some doctors will only order this if your blood glucose levels are in the prediabetic range, but because blood sugar is so critical to understanding your baseline overall health, getting a six-week snapshot of your average blood sugar level (which is what the A1C provides) is a great idea.

Uric Acid

One marker that may be less familiar is uric acid, which is a waste product found in the blood, created when the body breaks down chemicals called purines. High levels of uric acid are commonly associated with gout, a form of arthritis, but that's not the only thing they may indicate. Endocrinologist Robert Lustig says, "Uric acid is basically a proxy for sugar consumption, because of the way uric acid is made in the liver. If your uric acid is high, that means your mitochondria aren't working well, and you've got a problem."

ApoB

This test is a must if you are concerned about heart disease. There is increased consensus among experts that points to "apo B lipoproteins as the fundamental initiating causal factor in atherosclerosis."[49] In other words, your ApoB number gives your doctor a much better understanding of the level of buildup of cholesterol on your artery walls. This test is not one typically ordered by your doctor, but you can request it as part of an advanced testing panel, like with Lp(a).

Vitamin D and Omega-3 Status

While there are many nutritional status tests, two of the most important to know are vitamin D and omega-3. Why? Our nation has epidemics of vitamin D and omega-3 underconsumption and deficiency. For vitamin D, the test is serum total 25-hydroxyvitamin D, aka 25(OH)D for short. Vitamin D insufficiency is a 25(OH)D level less than 30 ng/mL. That's a number to avoid. Your actual goal level is around 50 ng/mL according to vitamin D and endocrinology experts. To assess your consumption of EPA and DHA omega-3 fatty acids, there is a wonderful omega-3 status test known as the omega-3 index, which was developed by nutrition and lipid researcher William S. Harris, PhD. An omega-3 index of 8 percent or higher is the goal, for overall health but also specifically to benefit your cardiovascular wellness.

Chapter Five

Just ~~Do~~ Move It

So, what does your workout look like?"

This is a question we get a lot when we first meet people and they find out that we run a health and wellness company. Considering what a pillar of health physical activity is, this question is second only to "What diet do you eat? Keto? Vegan?" Wherever small talk abounds—parties, conferences, school drop-off—we get these questions, and we brace ourselves for the disappointed looks we get when we answer. In the case of diet, there is no label for the way we eat; it's far too personalized to put in a box. And in the case of exercise, we also don't strongly identify with a plan or a tribe, like CrossFitters or Peloton users. Instead, this is what we say: "We walk a lot, do a small amount of cardio, and do resistance training two to three times a week. We also have an unwritten rule that we take the stairs if it's under five flights."

Cue the confused looks and slight twitch of disappointment as their smiles start to droop. Pretty quickly after that we see the raised eyebrows of skepticism, followed by "Wait...that's it?" When we confirm, "Yep, that's it," the conversation is usually over and on to the next topic. As much as we wish people would be more curious about why we do what we do, they usually don't get past the skepticism. While we don't claim to know what others are thinking, our best guess is that they either wonder if maybe we're not as healthy as we look or suspect that maybe we're not giving them the whole story. And maybe they're a little bit right about that last one; it's possible we hold back getting into the details because we don't think it's that interesting. But in the course of writing this book, we've paid more attention to what we love about those walks, how restorative and full of intention they are, and how utterly critical they are to maintaining our health and happiness. We've also gained not only strength but a lot of peace of mind from our resistance training. In the course of writing this book, two out of three of our living parents have ended up in the hospital for extended stays. We think a lot about the protective layer that our resistance training routine gives us now, and how it will also help keep us out of hospitals in our later years. So, here's what our "workout" really looks like.

Mornings in our house are a chaotic whirl to get out of the door on time for our daughters' school drop-off. Colleen usually throws on yoga pants to accommodate her ongoing aspiration to be able to move when there's a break in her schedule and maybe get in a gentle ten minutes of sun salutations in her office before the first call of the day (yoga pants are 100 percent appropriate in our office, by the way). Once we return from drop-off, we take a fifteen-minute walk to our office. If we have extra time, we'll extend the walk and make it a moving meeting, talking through our agenda for the day, whether it's work or child related. We always opt for the stairs whenever we can. Once we're behind our computers, we make it a rule never to sit for longer than thirty minutes without getting up to pace around a bit, and about two or three times a week we'll manage to get some resistance training in (free weights, kettlebells, machines, or some body-weight exercises). And that, friends, is it. If you don't count our walking time, we literally "work out" for twenty to thirty minutes three or four times a week.

We want to be crystal clear: this is not a prescription.

It's a *description* of what it looks like for one set of humans to thread exercise and movement into their days without having to think about it too much, pack an extra set of clothes for the gym, worry about showering, or cram in a certain number of minutes on an expensive exercise bike. And the wild thing about all of it? We know that it's all we need to do right now. This routine alone is getting us over 80 percent of the way to optimal health. Do we spend a lot of time or money on it? Nope. Do we subscribe to rigid rules around minutes or calories burned or heart rate zones achieved? No way. Do we do it in our apartment while our kids are playing with Legos? Sometimes. (We believe it's important for our girls to see us working out and to inspire healthy habits at a young age.) Did we intentionally build it into our lives so that we would barely notice we were doing it? Hell yes, we did.

The big flashing-light message of this chapter is dead simple: move your body in a way that brings you joy (so you'll keep moving it) and do a little strength training.

Moving your body, exercising, working out, gently stressing your body so it can build back stronger—whatever you want to call it—is critical to your health. Unless you have been living under a rock for the last seventy years, you know this. Like the advantages of eating whole foods, the importance of exercise is a giant point of overlap in the stacks of research about how to improve health span and life span. We did not evolve to sit on our butts all day, that much is clear. Exercise in various increments, from three seconds to thirty minutes, has been shown to be protective against a panoply of diseases of the body and mind that wreak havoc on our well-being. The Mayo Clinic reports that exercise can prevent, manage, and lower the risk of death from stroke, metabolic syndrome, high blood pressure, type 2 diabetes, depression, anxiety, cancer, arthritis, and falls.[1] According to Jennifer Heisz, PhD, author of *Move the Body, Heal the Mind*, in one study that looked at two thousand middle-aged men who were tracked over twenty-two years and grouped according to their fitness level, the dementia risk was "nearly twice as high for the less fit than the more fit."[2] This is as far as we will get into the big-picture benefits of exercise (since that could be another entire book), but we will drill down more into the wild benefits of exercising *less* than you think you need to, and the advantages of moving your body in ways that might not leave you carving out sweat angels on the gym floor but will be more than enough to get you to 80 percent.

Now, for the paradox. If we all know movement is so important for our health, and we are barraged day and night with ads for new exercise equipment, programs, and plans, why aren't we doing it? The Cleveland Clinic published an article in 2018 reporting that 80 percent of Americans don't get enough exercise.[3] This is the constant refrain from the medical establishment: get more exercise. The entire world is yelling and screaming about how important it is, and yet none of it seems to move the needle in terms of getting people to actually do the damn thing.

Let's be straight about something: *It. Is. Hard.* Many of us work at least eight hours a day at jobs that require us to be sitting behind a computer screen. Standing desks are great, but they only get you so far—especially when you go home and collapse on the couch, order takeout because you're too tired to cook, and then binge-watch Netflix (hey, we've all been there). That is a lot of time to be sitting still when you compare it to the near-constant movement of our hunter-gatherer ancestors. So, what do we do about it? How do we get around a world built in complete opposition to our evolutionary design? How do we get ourselves to *move*? We think this is a two-part problem. First up: motivation.

MOTIVATION IS A BEAST

In the health and wellness world, motivation is the beast to slay. Entire books have been written about how to hack motivation. Why?

Because depending on your life stage and circumstances, motivation is highly variable, which means exercise can feel either impossible or easy to do. We certainly remember a time before children, when finding the time and motivation to work out didn't feel that hard. Many people in that life stage right now turn—as we did—to fitness classes not only for exercise but also for social connection and community building. A report authored by two Harvard Divinity Students, Angie Thurston and Casper ter Kuile, revealed that millennials were finding in fitness what people in the past have found in religion: ritual, social connection, and purpose.[4] Based on this and our own personal experience, we say if you have time for a class, go for it! You certainly won't be alone. Zumba classes alone grew exponentially in 2022—potentially symbolic of people seeking joyful dance in community as a reaction against the loneliness of the pandemic. In an email exchange with Zumba CEO Alberto Perlman, he told us, "People are coming back to Zumba classes in droves to get their cardio, their dance fix, their joy, but most importantly, their community back."

But if you are struggling with motivation to move, it's not your fault. You're not lazy; your brain is. What we mean by this is that it's not a character flaw; it's an evolutionary mechanism that was once there to help us conserve energy but is now sabotaging us. A million years ago, our brain created default settings for our biological functions that had to do with energy expenditure based on a very active life. The result is a mismatch with our current circumstances—that is, we don't need to worry about not finding a woolly mammoth for dinner, but our bodies still think we do. According to Jennifer Heisz, "The brain views all exercise as an extravagant expense and only wants you to move if your life depends on it ... Your lazy brain would rather you save your energy for later, when you *really* need it."[5] Our brains are masters of efficiency because they needed to be in order to live long enough to pass down genes to the next generation, but now most Americans live in a world of relative abundance, so we don't need to conserve high levels of energy. The result is a lack of desire to move at a time when we need to move more than ever. So how do we get around this?

Throughout the chapter, we'll talk about ways to integrate movement into your life and sideline the motivation problem, but here's where we start: a change in mindset. Instead of looking at what you're not doing in the present and panicking, instead of trying to hit a number or a recommendation or mimic what worked for someone else and beating yourself up when you're just not excited about doing it, try focusing on how you want to feel now and in the future. Not what you want to look like. Not what numbers you want to put up on the leaderboard. Not what your doctor tells you that you should do. Do you want to feel stronger and less stressed? Do you want to sleep better and have the energy to play tag with your kids in the backyard or say yes to a hike on the weekend? If you don't know, figure it out. This is the unequivocal number one must-do if you want to build new habits around exercise.

Why? Because by visualizing these tangible returns on investment, the joy of being someone who moves their body and reaps the rewards, you are actually much more likely to follow through on making exercise a sustainable part of your life.[6] Before you read any further, we recommend that you answer those questions for yourself. And if you feel great right now and are moving your body regularly, consider this permission to ditch the sneaking suspicion that you should be "doing more." If you're moving in a way that works for your life and you feel strong and rested, don't let anyone tell you that you need to get into kettlebells or Pilates or parkour (unless you want to, of course).

The second part of motivation mindset disruption is to think about what you want your body for in the future. Note that we didn't say "what you want for your body" (to lose ten pounds, to have less wrinkles, etc.), but what you want to use your body *for* in terms of living your best life. There is no denying that even the most healthy and happy among us are going to get older. When that happens, strength and energy wane unless you are (and have been) taking steps to keep yourself as vigorous as possible. No one is saying you've got to be Jack LaLanne—you can park yourself in front of the TV at the rest home if you want to! But most people *want* to be active, strong, and clear for as many years as possible. We know that at seventy-five years old, the body stumbles over a steep cliff in terms of deterioration. Yet, many of us want and intend to live well past seventy-five. Think about what those years might look like. Do you want to be able to walk to pick up coffee? Get down on the ground and play with grandchildren?

This is worth a visualization exercise.

Sit and close your eyes for a minute. Think about what you want to *be doing* when you are seventy-five—what do you see? Are you paddleboarding on the Gulf Coast in Florida? Are you climbing the stairs of your five-story walk-up in the East Village without getting winded? Are you doing tai chi in the park? Are you teaching your grandkids how to play tennis? Now think about what you want to be doing in your eighties and beyond, what does that look like? What do you need your body to be able to do? For us, it's all about the grandkids (should we be so lucky)—we want to be able to pick up babies and chase toddlers and be capable of watching them all weekend without breaking a sweat. For you it might be as simple as wanting to be able to carry your own groceries. Or maybe you want to be cognitively clear enough to keep writing poetry well into your golden years. Maybe you want to be able to keep riding horses or swimming in the ocean, or simply driving your car. To do all of those things, you have to move and keep moving for decades before that. Most people don't, which is why degeneration, disease, and a terrible quality of life is the fate of far too many older Americans. But if you use how you want to feel as a North Star when it comes to making day-to-day choices about taking a walk, taking the stairs, and lifting those weights, you're less likely to get caught in the motivational quicksand.

MOVEMENT OBSTACLE COURSE

The second reason why people find it so difficult to integrate movement into their lives is the lack of time and money. A lack of time and money is a serious, real-life constraint. There's no arguing with that. But you can argue with the misperception that moving your body requires lots of time and money in the first place. This perception—that you have to work out at the gym every day for at least thirty minutes and spend money on a membership/trainer/bike/tread—was born of the fitness industrial complex and the distorted reality of the internet. Part of the reason why we get such puzzled looks when we talk about our not-a-workout is cognitive dissonance. After all, here we are, representatives of the wellness world, and yet what we do doesn't line up with people's understanding of what it means to be healthy. This is because their understanding comes largely from what healthy looks like on social media: an elaborate home gym with a Peloton, matching activewear sets, and, of course, rock-hard abs. All of the fitness gurus that we follow on Instagram and the celebrities who do indeed have their own battalion of trainers would have us believe that to look as good as them and to be as healthy as they are, we have to do what they do—which sometimes involves throwing down huge sums and spending hours on their bodies. We know that's not reasonable for a normal person, so we might tell ourselves, *Well, if they're spending two hours, we have to spend at least thirty minutes. And if they have a personal trainer, we at least have to get a Peloton.* In other words, they have skewed the algorithm in our brain.

In reality, physical fitness and health doesn't require as much as we think. Remember Giuseppe from Sardinia? What would he think of a treadmill? Walking up and down the same hill every day for years, moving throughout his daily life, that was all more than enough to keep him healthy. And according to the latest science, even Giuseppe was probably doing way more than he needed to. Just by doing his daily chores he was partaking in the world's best wonder drug for dementia: walking. A study of 78,430 adults living in the UK found that clocking around 10,000 steps per day (9,826, if you want to be exact) was correlated with a 51% risk reduction in dementia. What's more, just 3,800 steps per day was associated with a 25% reduction in dementia risk, and those who walked at a higher intensity (cadence) were associated with an even lower risk.[7] Every other day it seems there is a headline in the *New York Times* Well section that could pass for an *Onion* headline: "Stronger Muscles in 3 Seconds a Day," "Can 4 Seconds of Exercise Make a Difference?" or "A 2-Minute Walk May Counter the Harms of Sitting." As crazy as it sounds, these real headlines reflect a sea change in the scientific literature in the last ten years that all points to shorter bursts of aerobic activity—done consistently—as being just as effective in promoting health as mindless cardio done for long periods of time. This is good news for anyone who lives in a time-crunched world of ever-encroaching lunch meetings and family, friend, and work obligations. The same goes for resistance training. In fact, a meta-analysis of weekly weightlifting for strength showed that doing one session of weightlifting per week gave people nearly the same gains as working out multiple times.[8] Obviously, if you are lifting weights once a week, you're not going to be entering into any bodybuilding competitions anytime soon—but if you focus on the quality of that session, what you will do is build enough muscle mass to keep your body healthy and happy and be well on your way to lifting your own groceries at eighty-five. The biggest evolution over our thirteen years at mindbodygreen has been a shift from mindful movement being the fitness routine to a bigger focus on strength and resistance training to build muscle for healthy aging protection. For those just starting out, it's important to remember that something is better than nothing—hence our three-seconds-a-day example—but more is still better when it comes to improving health span.

One final word on why shorter, easier, and less financially fraught movement choices are a better way to go: habit building. Behavioral researchers and habit experts alike agree that the number one thing you can do to sabotage a new habit is to make it too hard.[9] If you make it time-consuming, expensive, cumbersome, inconvenient, or just plain painful, it (of course) disincentivizes you from doing it again. In the moment it might seem like a good idea to push through a vigorous workout even though it hurts and you are tired, but it's actually sabotaging your ability to do *any* workout in the future. You are chewing through all your motivation in one go instead of using little bites of motivation to help you lace up your shoes and take a pleasurable walk that you will look forward to doing again. For this reason alone, we're begging you to cancel the phrase *no pain, no gain*.

MOVEMENT MACRO TIPS

So much of the popular conception of exercise frames it as a painful, joyless slog. These ways of exercising are giving movement a bad name and creating an unsustainable, unattainable ideal of what we have to do in order to be in shape and feel good. Here's where we throw it all out the window and start over. Instead of having a rigid idea of what exercise looks like, focus on how you want to move in your life. Stop thinking about what you should do—what do you *want* to do? It could be as simple as walking to work and taking the stairs, because that's all the time you have in this stressful moment of your life. It could be joining adult gymnastics, it could be surfing in the summer and snowshoeing in the winter, it could be taking a walk in the woods while birding, it could even be hopping on your Peloton. Whatever you like to do and have time to do, *do it*. That is really all you have to remember: move that butt, in any way you can.

In order to guide you a little into this new Wild West of exercise you like that will make you happy (what a concept!), we have tips for how to make whatever movement you choose to do more successful and sustainable. Here are some guiding principles.

It should bring you joy (or at least not pain).

Move in any way that brings you joy or fulfillment, or at least doesn't hurt. Play tag with your kid. Go dancing. Find something that you want to do again and again, or experiment with new kinds of movement every week. Make it play. Here's a thought: what if we could get back to how we used to move our bodies as kids, without any higher purpose other than to have fun?

Listen to your body.

What used to feel good or what used to be your fallback position for exercise you liked might not work for your body or your energy levels anymore. Colleen used to love to run fast and for long stretches. For a while that was what her body wanted, but now the intensity of those workouts combined with her energy levels as a mom of young kids? No way. That would just deplete her further, so instead she focuses on more restorative, gentle movement like walking and yoga, combined with resistance training, which she has significantly increased now in her forties.

Choose something that doesn't bring more stress to your life.

Sometimes you have to balance what your body wants and what your schedule wants. Jason used to ride the subway all over New York City going to five different yoga classes a week. Then we had kids and the business ramped up, and slowly the number of classes a week he was able to attend whittled down to zero. Instead of getting frustrated or down on himself about it, he looked at the reality of his life and found other ways to fit yoga into his schedule in smaller increments. He started lifting weights to supplement and found that this balance just worked better for his life now.

———

By now you're sensing a theme, right? Find a form of exercise that makes you happy and works for your life. We can't really say this enough, because it's so important, and one of the biggest mistakes we see people make on their health journeys is trying to fit a square peg in a round hole. In the case of exercise and movement, more than any other category, the secret to healthy is to be happy with whatever you're doing so you will keep doing it. But because some of us don't like too many choices, we wanted to offer up some low-hanging exercise fruit—two things that you can fall back on whenever you run out of ideas or if you just want to be 100 percent sure you're getting in your 80 percent. Two things we know for sure: you need to move, and you need to maintain muscle mass in order to maintain health and well-being throughout your life. In the next two sections we'll talk about two ways you can accomplish that without having to spend much time or money. In fact, they are two of the most accessible activities around. You can incorporate them into your day and do them in short bursts of time, making it entirely possible to do what every doctor in America wants you to do: move it.

So, let's dig into why walking isn't just for old people, and lifting weights isn't just for bodybuilders at the gym.

WHY WALKING IS FITNESS'S
BEST-KEPT SECRET

For Annabel Streets, walking is more than the number of steps on her smartwatch or a way to get to the store. Before she even knew she was writing a book about walking (*52 Ways to Walk: The*

Surprising Science of Walking for Wellness and Joy, One Week at a Time), she was learning how to love something that so many of us take for granted: putting one foot in front of the other. Although it would turn into an emotional, spiritual, and social journey, Streets started her adventures in walking from a place of pure physicality. After years of driving everywhere and sitting for long stretches at her desk, she began to notice the toll it was taking on her life in the form of what she called "curious changes to my body (rounder, softer, achier, stiffer, stooped) and to my mind (anxious, unsettled, discontented)."[10] As an antidote to all these unwelcome changes, she embarked on an experiment that had two rules: one, walk everywhere, and two, change sedentary activities to active ones. She began walking everywhere—even in the rain and cold, when she was tired, when she was alone, when it was muddy, and at night. All the excuses we make not to move, not to walk, jumped into her awareness—it's boring, it's too far, it's not the right time of day, it's too hilly, and so on. Streets called bullshit on all of it and refused to be deterred. She bought herself good shoes, warm clothes, and plenty of rain gear and decided to suck it up and *walk*. This decision changed her life, her body, her mind, and her spirit. Her daily walks became a means for "unraveling towns and cities, of connecting with nature, of bonding with our dogs, of fostering friendships, of finding faith and freedom, of giving the finger to air-polluting traffic, of nurturing our sense of smell, of satisfying our cravings for starlight and darkness, of helping us appreciate the exquisitely complicated and beautiful world we inhabit."[11]

The pace of our lives and the distorted mindset that we have cultivated about walking not being "real" exercise have made this option largely invisible when it comes to what we think about as "working out." While plenty of people walk for their health, a large subset of people think it isn't good enough, it's the bare minimum, or it's something that you will do when you get old and can't do anything else.

We rarely pat ourselves on the back for a nice twelve-minute walk despite research that shows even a short jaunt is capable of altering over five hundred metabolites, which are molecules that bolster our heart, lungs, and brain.[12] We either forget, or never knew in the first place that a ten-minute walk is enough to boost creativity and improve memory.[13] Many people believe that if they're not sweating and breathless, it's not worth it. And while high-intensity interval training (HIIT) *is* a wonderful way to improve your health, it's not for everyone, and more importantly, it's not necessary for everyone. In fact, for some people HIIT workouts can be too intense, tipping over into the type of physical stressor that weakens and damages the body.[14]

In order for the movement that you do to get you 80 percent of the way to optimal health, you need to improve blood flow, stress your body in a balanced way so it can build resiliency, and make sure it's pleasurable enough to sustain over time. Walking hits all these marks and more. Because it's a flexible practice, it's something you can make work for you if you haven't gotten off the couch in years or if you are already a triathlete. You can walk slow or fast, on a flat road or up a steep hill, on uneven terrain or on the sidewalk, and for as long or short a distance as you please. Walking is free and easy to access no matter where you live. If you live in a more rural place, congratulations, you have the opportunity to commune with nature! If you live in the city, congratulations, every grocery store run, appointment, and social meet-up is now a chance to take a walk.

Annabel Streets reminds us that one of the reasons why such a simple thing is such a boon to our mental and physical health is that we were built to walk. Not to yank on a rowing machine in the basement, or cycle in a dark room with loud music, or sit in front of a computer. Every part of our body, from our neck to our feet, from our bones to our muscles, is designed to walk.[15] Think for a second about the iconic image "The March to Progress." You know the one:

it starts with an ape on all fours and ends with a hunter-gatherer *Homo sapiens* with a spear resting on his shoulder. This is an illustration of 25 million years of evolution represented by a sequence of species from early apes to early humans. Here we see one of the most important aspects of that change illustrated *as a walk*, highlighting bipedalism as the pinnacle of our evolution.

Because walking has been a constant for millions of years, our body systems and our biochemistry have adapted to it elegantly, folding in all sorts of added bonuses for us when we engage in this evolutionary pastime. Here are just a few of the ways we can get back to our biological roots and take advantage of built-in health optimizers.

Walk by the water.

While researching her book, Annabel Streets found strong evidence that walking by water confers the most benefits of walking in any landscape. Whether it's the sound of water rushing, the teeming wildlife, or the shimmering surface catching our eyes, one thing is for sure, we humans like water. For over twenty-five years researchers have been churning out data that shows how being near water changes our biomarkers (think heart rate, cortisol, etc.), kicking off a total vibe shift. We are more contented and even altruistic when we are near this primal landscape.[16] Studies also show that people who live by the sea are happier and healthier than those who live farther inland.[17] There are many theories as to why, but for Streets it's just common sense: for millennia we were nomads, and the importance of water to survival and the need for it was quickly encoded into our genes. Even now, when we find ourselves walking beside water, it puts us at ease, cortisol levels drop, and our brains can relax. On a personal note, Jason has noticed a huge shift in his heart rate variability (HRV) metric since we moved to Miami. Now that we live in an apartment with a view of the water, his HRV quickly started averaging 100ms (the higher the better for HRV). When we lived in

New York City it was 84ms. Coincidence? Maybe, but Jason believes it has everything to do with the soothing water we're so lucky to have nearby.

Walk in the woods.

Another landscape that has wonderful effects on immunity, blood pressure, and mental health is just as primal—the woods. The place where we used to go to forage the plants and animals we needed to keep our ancient bellies full continues to be a place that sustains our good health. According to researchers at the University of East Anglia, spending time in nature has pretty wild health benefits. They reviewed the data from 140 reports spanning twenty countries and including 290 million people and found that nature time "reduced risk of type 2 diabetes, cardiovascular disease, premature death, high blood pressure, and stress."[18] Other studies have shown similarly remarkable benefits: the woods improved the grades of students who did their lessons near trees, people who had more foliage in their neighborhoods were mentally sharper, and children who grow up in the forest have more diverse microbiomes.[19] Many researchers believe we have compounds known as terpenes to thank for all these benefits. Trees give off a multitude of terpenes, which are powerful phytoncides that have been shown in experiments to do everything from mitigate cancer to reduce lung inflammation. One study showed that a terpene known as delta-limonene was even more effective than antidepressants in treating those with clinical depression.[20] Terpenes are also nature's sleeping pills. Emerging studies have shown that two different terpenes abundant in pine tree forests are linked to better and longer sleep, and one study in Japan (land of the forest bathers) found that walking in the afternoon made the biggest positive impact on sleep.[21] Kind of makes you want to hug a tree as the sun goes down, doesn't it?

Walk in the city.

As city dwellers who might not get to the woods as often as we'd like, we were cheered to hear from Streets that the city is full of untapped walking benefits. You might not be passively absorbing terpenes, but you are giving your brain a much-needed workout if you can do one thing—get lost. This is a great way to get to know your city better, activate new neurons, and help yourself to an extra dose of dopamine.[22] "The brain loves novelty. Confronted with something new or different, our brains immediately build new neural pathways, improving our memory and our capacity for learning in the process," says Streets.[23] Considering you're not in danger of running into a bear or truly getting lost, a weekend wander seems to us like a great way to build our brains and move our bodies—especially when there is a coffee shop on every corner. You can't say that about the forest!

INTEGRATION TIPS:

How you integrate more walking into your life is going to largely depend on your schedule and where you live, but the first obstacle is going to be all the excuses that inevitably bubble to the surface. We'll tackle a few below, but the biggest thing to remember is the freedom that walking gives you. If you can build it into your life, you can say goodbye to any guilt or nagging worry that you're not getting enough exercise to keep you healthy. The reason walking and just generally moving (taking the stairs, choosing the hill, etc.) is better for you than you may know is that you are more likely to do it. It is a sustainable practice that brings immediate benefits and (unless you're injured) doesn't hurt. Has anyone ever come back from a walk through the park and said, "Wow, I really feel worse?" Nope. And here's the straight talk: in order to stay healthy, you have to move your body in any way you can. No excuses.

- Integrate your better-sleep practice with your movement practice and pop out for an early-morning walk in your neighborhood to soak up the sun. Double down on the goodness!

- Most experts agree you shouldn't sit still for too long, so for those of us chained to our desks during the day, we have to get creative. We need to move and we need water. At least every hour, get up, refill your water bottle, and do some quick stretching and pacing around. Even if you're just walking in circles around your office, remember that you're helping pump blood into that big ole brain of yours, so technically it counts as work, right?

- One thing that we have learned walking through rain, snow, and sleet is that having the right gear is the difference between bitterly cursing the weather as you grump-hustle down the street and walking at a normal pace, marveling at the beauty of the falling snow or the way the rain smells. Layers are key, and remember, when in doubt, it's always better to overdress than underdress. And on the inevitable day that you underdress for a winter walk, just remember that being exposed to the cold (while safely protecting your fingers and toes) helps you generate uber-healthy brown fat (more on that later), so it's all for a good cause.

- Always take the stairs. Make it a hard-and-fast rule, no excuses. Jason walks up all twenty-two flights of stairs at a fast pace once a week in our building for his workout. His golden rule is that if it's five flights or less, he takes the stairs. For anyone worried about being late, it's literally seconds or a few minutes difference at most when compared with taking the elevator if we're talking less than five flights. Everyone has that time. And if it's difficult, start with one flight and go from there!

WHAT ABOUT CARDIO?

We know the cardio question is on everyone's mind when they think of movement. How breathless and sweaty do you need to get to keep your heart strong and your artery walls smooth? How long do you need to stay in that zone? We stand by what we said in terms of needing to do less than you think. Plenty of people have made it well past one hundred simply by lifting heavy farm equipment and walking up hills. Many people who have physical jobs are probably in better shape than they think they are. For instance, in one illuminating study of London transportation workers, researchers found that people who had more physically demanding jobs (conductors) had a lower incidence of coronary artery disease than workers who had less physically demanding jobs (drivers).[24] These conductors were likely walking up and down the platform and heaving bags, day in and day out. No elliptical or heart rate monitor required.

That being said, most of us are pretty sedentary, which means we have to be intentional about challenging our cardiovascular system so it can stay in good working order. Experts agree, more is always better.[25] We don't think about cardiovascular workouts, or any kind of workout, in terms of blocks of exercise per se, but we think we should try to move as much as possible and within the movement try to get slightly out of breath for a few minutes each time (biohackers call this zone 2). Again, take the stairs as much as possible. Walk at a fast pace as much as possible. If you like running, go for a jog. But always try to be moving and try to push yourself when you can.

In short: get that heart rate up. Not a lot, not all the time, maybe not even enough to sweat through your T-shirt, but occasionally you should hoof it up a hill or two. In the Blue Zones research, the third biggest predictor of living to one hundred in Sardinia was how steep your village was. The more elevation, the more opportunities to challenge your heart and build resilience. In the case of the centenarians of Sardinia, it was the result of the environment—they simply had to walk up a lot of hills to live their lives—but for the rest of us, we need to set the intention to make our own damn hills.[26]

USE IT OR LOSE IT, BABY

About a year ago, it was a very ordinary day spring day in Brooklyn when it occurred to a tall man looking in a mirror that, somehow, some way, he had gone and lost his ass.

For weeks leading up to this discovery, Jason, the assless man in question, had begun noticing that he was a little light on the scale. Because, as you know by now, he's a tracking nut. Jason does weigh himself occasionally. After clocking in at 205 pounds for years, suddenly he found himself ten pounds lighter. At six foot seven inches tall, ten pounds is not that much, but data hound that he is, it bugged him that he didn't know the reason. He wasn't eating less, and he wasn't moving more. What the hell was going on? Then, he looked in the mirror one day and saw that he had...old-man butt. Things were just a little flatter, a little less there, if you know what we mean. His legs were also noticeably thinner, once he thought about it. This led pretty quickly to the realization that while nothing about his routine had changed, something about his routine had been missing something for a long time. The truth was, he hadn't done squats or lunges, or any type of lower-body resistance training since his basketball days ended in 1998. So, despite the fact that he was walking everywhere and using stairs, middle age was upon him. The old workout wasn't cutting it anymore in terms of muscle mass. His upper body strength was good, thanks to consistent upper body resistance training, so the difference between his upper body and lower body was noticeable. Someone not too concerned with how ripped they are might think it was one of those things that just kind of happened. Most people would probably just shrug and move on. But once again, because we do what we do, Jason saw this new development as a red flag. Not because he really cared what his butt looked like (as long as Colleen thinks it's cute, who cares?), but because at forty-seven years old, he knew that if there's one thing you don't mess around with, it's sarcopenia.

The clinical definition of sarcopenia is "a syndrome characterized by progressive and generalized loss of skeletal muscle mass and strength."[27] In real-people terms it just means if you don't use your muscles, you lose your muscles—and that's very, very bad. While a drastic reduction in muscle mass and strength is always a health risk (think disability, decreased bone density, diminished quality of life, and death), the older you get, the faster you lose it. This starts happening as early as thirty years old. You heard that right—thirty. And every decade thereafter people lose between 3 percent and 5 percent of their muscle mass.[28] In the abstract, that might not sound like much, but muscle loss is just as scary a health risk as diabetes or cancer or heart disease. Muscle loss is serious business.

Despite what some people might think, sarcopenia is not a "normal" part of getting older; it's a condition that you can prevent and reverse simply by building muscle. If you don't, and your muscles degenerate, it impacts your metabolism, your immune function, and your ability to recover from illness and injury.[29] When you've got sarcopenia, you're not only more likely to fall and break something in the first place, but there's a solid chance you're not going to make it out of the hospital in the last place. As our friend and fitness guru Mark Sisson says, "Muscle also provides a metabolic reservoir for support and recovery from physical trauma—injuries, wounds, damage to our tissues."[30] Even more alarming is the reminder that **the heart is a muscle**, which means it too is affected by a lack of strength, which of course impacts cardiovascular health.[31] Sadly, sarcopenia is more common than you might think, with up to 13 percent of people in their sixties suffering from it and up to half of people in their eighties living with it.[32]

So now you can understand why Jason's missing butt was a concern in the first place. He was reminded how quickly you can lose muscle mass and strength when you are not actively using it. And this brings us back to the most important thing to remember about this chapter (and honestly, this book): the point is not to just live longer; it's to live better. When you are seventy-five, if you have spent the last several decades only walking, you may still not have the strength that you need to do the things that you want, the activities that make you happy, like picking up your grandbabies or playing in your local pickleball league.

So, the second component to moving your body in a way that builds health span (not just life span) is to do some sort of resistance training. While we wish our daily walks after school drop-off were enough, we have learned the importance of resistance training (meaning weights or body weight) for maintaining muscle. For women, there's another big reason that this type of training is critical—bone density. Like muscle loss, we lose bone density as we age—up to 1 percent a year after the age of forty. If unaddressed, this can lead to osteoporosis in both men and women (though more women suffer from it). In this scenario, the muscle loss and bone loss work together to increase your risk of injury and permanent disability. If you're over sixty-five, there's a one in four chance that you'll fall, and if you do fall, studies show that your chances of falling again double, and if you fall and break your hip, then there is a 30 to 40 percent chance that you will die within a year.[33] And even if the worst doesn't happen, your independence and mobility can be significantly hindered.[34] Muscle strength and bone density are intimately connected, and despite the downsides of losing both, this connection is actually good news, because when you build muscle, you build bone. Study after study has shown that a short amount of strength and/or resistance training can help increase not only your muscle mass but your bone density as well. Both feats can be accomplished at home doing equipment-free body-weight training or resistance training with free weights or machines.

PROTEIN POWER TIP

While protein has been long associated with body building, more and more studies are showing that sufficient protein intake for everyone is important to supporting muscle mass and strength (and therefore bone density) as we age, and thus critical for longevity. Activity level, age, muscle mass, and overall health all impact the amount of protein we each need to stay healthy. Like everything health and wellness, some providers will suggest more and others will suggest less, but many scientists believe the current recommended dietary allowance (RDA) for protein is overly conservative. Right now, the RDA says that you should consume approximately 0.36 grams per pound of body weight per day. What many people don't know is that this is considered the minimum requirement to survive (not thrive). So, what do we need to eat in order to lay down sufficiently strong muscle throughout life, especially given the risk of muscle decline in older adults? Probably double the RDA (.70-.75 grams of protein per pound of body weight per day) if you're looking to build and maintain muscle, particularly in the setting of an active lifestyle that regularly incorporates resistance training (which we highly recommend!). We use the word "probably" here on purpose—the science here is still emerging. For some of us, this intake comes naturally; for others, this might be very difficult, and we may need to more intentionally incorporate it into our diet by way of protein powders. One of our guests on the podcast, Gabrielle Lyon, DO, who calls her practice Muscle-Centric Medicine, reminds us that amino acids are critical to making the best use of your body's muscle-generating abilities. Without going down a rabbit hole on amino acids, you want to make sure that you are getting approximately 2.5 grams of leucine (a particularly pivotal branched-chain amino acid) for every 30 grams of protein that you're consuming in a meal in order to promote muscle protein synthesis. For the plant-centric people, that might even mean strategically considering incorporating some animal protein sources or supplements (e.g., grass-fed whey), for the sake of your muscles and whole-body health. (For more on our favorite sources of protein, go to thejoyofwellbeing .com/protein.) We've come to realize that many people who "eat healthy" and get their five to seven helpings of fruits and vegetables are missing optimal levels of protein (Colleen is raising her hand here). If you're an omnivore or a flexitarian, some of the best protein superstars are beef, eggs, dairy, fish, and chicken. If you lean plant-based, getting adequate protein to build and maintain muscle is more challenging, but there are many forms of healthy plant proteins that we can turn to: lentils, beans, nuts, tofu, quinoa, and oats. You can also use protein powder as a supplement if building or maintaining muscle is a priority. As you're paying more attention to building muscle, remember that nutritionally you can power up your muscle gain with protein. While we're not fans of counting anything when it comes to food, this is an exception. It's worthwhile to check in with how much protein you're getting and make sure you're at levels that will support your muscle and bone health. Many of the experts we talk to say that unless you are already being intentional about adding protein, it's safe to assume you're not getting enough. When you're deciding what to put on your plate, take a minute to think about how you might add even a little more protein to what you're eating—even a few nuts here and a little chicken there will help. Again, it might be challenging to meet protein recommendations, but it's necessary if you're serious about maximizing health span and longevity. Science is emerging here, so check back at thejoyofwellbeing.com/protein.

Like moving your body, *using* your body to lift things is necessary when it comes to health and happiness. When you hit fifty years old, that's when experts say muscle loss really starts to ramp up, but they also stress that getting started on muscle strength in the decades before middle age is critical. Likewise, experts say it's important to build your "bone bank" early on to help protect your bones later. If you are starting from a good baseline of strength, when the inevitable decline happens, you will be in a much better situation.[35] So, basically, that means it's use it or lose it after thirty. Time to flex!

So how can we "use it" in a sustainable way?

For someone like Giuseppe, who was lifting bags of grain and shoveling heavy loads of sheep dung well into his seventies, resistance training was built into his life. But if your job doesn't require much physical activity or heavy lifting, you'll have to find another way. The good news is that it doesn't take much time to maintain a healthy level of muscle mass and strength, and you don't need to go to the gym and hang out by the barbells to do it. Body-weight resistance training (think push-ups, planks, and air squats) will help you build muscle just as well as free weights, which are also a great choice—it all falls under the heading of resistance training, which is what you need to do to fend off sarcopenia and bone loss.

Peter Attia, MD, a well-regarded longevity expert, talks a lot about sarcopenia on his podcast *The Drive*, and points out that you don't need to turn into an Olympic weightlifter to stay healthy from a muscle perspective. He says, "If you have low muscle mass, provided you have adequate strength, you're okay. And this is good news because people come in all shapes and sizes. Having big muscles is great for sure, but it turns out that it's what those muscles can do that probably matters more."[36] This is important to know from a sustainability and time perspective. If you want to have big muscle (mass) and be able to lift a Smart car, you are going to need to spend a lot of time at the gym and have access to increasingly heavy weights. But if your goal is just to maintain adequate strength throughout your lifetime, you're in luck. If time is your biggest obstacle to weight training, a new study published in the *Scandinavian Journal of Medicine and Science in Sports* and conducted by a university in Japan checks that excuse off the list. The *New York Times* reported that the study followed the progress of thirty-nine healthy college students (and ten as a control group) as they spent three seconds a day working on their biceps strength. Five days a week, for those three seconds, they either pulled or pushed as hard as they could on a lever that acted as resistance. At the end of this month-long, sixty-second-total experiment, researchers discovered that the students in one sub-group (the ones lowering the lever like in a biceps curl) had improved their muscle strength by 12 percent. Despite the fact that the students didn't gain muscle mass, the study's authors still point out that "every contraction counts" when it comes to resistance training.[37] This small effort shows us that it doesn't take much to get our muscles working, so even if you can literally only find three seconds a day, it's way better than no seconds a day. Of course, we recommend that you do more than sixty seconds a month—but the point is that even if you do twenty to twenty-five minutes two to three times a week (which is what we do), you are putting mega money in the muscle bank. More is usually better, so if you want to resistance train more frequently, please do. In the words of Peter Attia, "If you have the aspiration of kicking ass when you're 85, you can't afford to be average when you're 50."

INTEGRATION TIPS

- We keep weights by the couch in our home, and for those of you who have busy lives, this just might be what you need to do to get your weight training in. If you have access to free weights, great! If not, the next time you get up for your two-minute movement break, do some air squats or push-ups, or even hold a plank. Now you know that even three seconds helps, so why not go for more? And while you're doing more, do it right— really nail your form and make sure you're not putting yourself at risk for injury. Go to joyofwellbeing.come/strength for more guidance on resistance training.

- Intensity matters. If you're only going to do a limited amount of weight training (let's say ten minutes a couple times a week), then you really should be maxing out your repetitions, which means that you should be straining your muscles as much as possible without hurting yourself. To achieve this balance, keep doing repetitions until you can no longer hold the proper form. If you find yourself doing endless reps before your muscles start to shake, you probably need a heavier weight, champ.

- If you don't have free weights and you have no intention of getting any, no problem. Get down on the floor and use your body weight as resistance—push-ups, air squats, sit-ups, or pull-ups anyone? Check thejoyofwellbeing.com/strength for a few of our favorite body-weight strength exercises.

- To make the experience more enjoyable, listen to your favorite music or even a podcast when you work out. Some people like to watch TV while they lift. We have a friend whose guilty pleasure was watching *The Kardashians,* so she made a rule that she could watch as much as she wanted as long as she was lifting weights. Jennifer Heisz, professor of kinesiology, reminds us that it's all about building a "dopamine bridge."[38] If you're new to lifting weights and working out, you may have to build up your enjoyment of exercise. Listening to music or watching your favorite show will increase dopamine, which makes you feel good and start to build that connection between movement and enjoyment.

- Whether it's Jazzercize or Zumba, the most important cardio exercise is the one that you actually do, so find something that you love to break a sweat to.

- A fun way to get your heart rate up is to make like a kid and jump rope. (Jason jumped rope nonstop during his basketball days.) Most jump ropes are inexpensive, and you can even try a weighted rope, which can help with strength and is inexpensive. Skipping rope can be great for resistance training, cardio, and coordination, and it can help with cardiovascular health. Start with just a few minutes a day.

FINAL THOUGHTS

What we loved most about writing this chapter was that when we looked closely at the research, what our experts said, and what we have experienced, we discovered that the two things you must do broke down perfectly into two categories: what you have to do to feel good now and what you have to do to feel good later. There's a beautiful symmetry to it that is all about intention, for now and for the future. Prioritizing movement right now, whether that is walking, HIIT workouts, or jogging will give you immediate benefits. After every single workout you do, the brain is infused with neurochemicals like dopamine that make you feel fabulous. It gets the blood flowing, increasing clarity and creativity. It gives you a boost in mood and a reduction of anxiety. And you don't have to wait for muscles to grow. It's like an ATM in the sense that you can always pull money out when you need it; all you have to do is move your body.

Right now in the US, we're in a mental health crisis, in large part because there is a lot lacking when it comes to treatment. The first line of defense is usually antidepressants or anti-anxiety medication. Unfortunately, one in three people don't respond to antidepressant drugs. That's a lot of people who are suffering with no good option for feeling better. Many people don't know that exercise is on par with antidepressant drugs in terms of effectiveness at alleviating symptoms of depression.[39] In fact, according to Jennifer Heisz, "In studies, when individuals who haven't responded to anti-depressants start exercising, they usually see significant reductions in their symptoms."[40] Exercise is known to help people reduce anxiety and build resilience to everyday stressors. It's quite simply the most important thing we can do for our mental health aside from getting a good night's sleep. We need to move our bodies now more than ever.

And we also need to plan for the future. People are living longer than ever, but there are alarming signs that point to a reduction in quality of life. In short: they aren't *living* better. From 2007 to 2013, the CDC reported that death rates of older adults from falls increased by 30 percent.[41] It is a significant jump that some experts speculate is due to "longer survival after onset of common diseases like heart disease, stroke and cancer."[42] This means that advances in medical technology might be extending our lives, but we aren't strong enough to enjoy living those longer lives. We haven't planned for our long life, and we haven't been using our bodies in middle age with the intention of being badasses in our old age. Admittedly, this statistic about falls paints a pretty grim picture of today's older Americans, but it doesn't have to be that way. Advances in medicine have also shown us how to take a different path, one that leads to many vigorous decades and plenty of babysitting the grandbabies. We just have to choose it.

THAT EXTRA 20 PERCENT

POSTURE AND BREATHING

To prevent injuries and maximize your movement, whether you're walking or lifting weights, you've got to pay attention to posture and breathing. From chapter 2, you already know why it's so important to breathe out of your nose, but we acknowledge this gets more difficult with exertion. That's why it's extra credit! As far as posture, chest lifted and open, neck lengthened, and arms swinging will help you get the most out of your walks. While you're lifting weights, it's important to keep your core engaged no matter what exercise you're doing—this will protect your back and work multiple muscle groups at the same time.

INTERVAL WALKING

You've heard of HIIT, but have you heard of HIIW? There's a way to make just about any exercise into an interval exercise where you work hard for a minute or two, and then go back to a regular pace for five minutes—rinse and repeat. Walking is no different. You can mark your intervals by city blocks or telephone poles, or even just timing it on your watch or phone.

RESISTANCE TRAINING WITH EQUIPMENT

While you can certainly build strength without equipment, you may be able to build your muscles more quickly with the regular gym fare. Because the internet is the internet, there are literally tens of thousands of videos to help you build a routine that works for you and show you how to get the most out of weights if you choose to use them. For more information about workouts, including some exercises that helped Jason bring his butt back to its original form and gain back five pounds of muscle in his lower body including his posterior, check thejoyofwellbeing.com /strength.

Chapter Six

Stress

One of Jason's most haunting memories is of a cold shower.
It was circa December 31, 1994, at Sacramento State University, and Jason and his fellow Columbia teammates were wrapping up a three-game Northern California road trip. After the game the team shuffled into the locker room, sweaty and disappointed by their loss to Sacramento State. Worse still, they knew they had to immediately get on a red-eye and fly back to the East Coast. That alone would have been enough to elicit some groans from the team, but when they entered the basement and felt the chill of the unheated concrete locker rooms, everyone yelped. And that was before they learned that the only water coming out of the two dozen showers was *cold*. Jason had a choice. Sit in his own stink for the long flight home, or brave the icy cold blast of the arena's punishing shower situation. Half the team gave it a hearty hell no, but Jason decided to suck it up and go for it. In a lucky life with few regrets, this choice stands out as an incredibly bad one. It was effing freezing. He lasted about fifteen screaming seconds before he ran for his towel. Ever since that fateful frigid day in California, of all places, he has stayed as far away from cold water as possible.

Colleen, too, is not a fan of being cold. She has a condition called Reynaud's, which is overconstriction of the small blood vessels in the fingers, toes, ears, and nose in response to cold exposure. When she stays out too long in the winter, Colleen's fingers turn white and she loses feeling in her toes. As someone who grew up in California, she didn't realize what a problem this was until she moved to the Northeast and learned the true value of mittens. She has absolutely no desire to take cold showers and swears her ears go numb just listening to the Sacramento State story.

Now, why on earth would two people such as ourselves, based on what you just read, even entertain writing an entire chapter on cold therapy?

Because as much as *we* hate it, the science that is developing around the physiological benefits of cold immersion is strong and exciting. And it's a practice that is incredibly accessible and easily integrated into your life, should you so desire. Showers are basically free, you have to take one most days of the week anyway, and emerging evidence tells us that you may get a significant benefit from only one to two minutes of cold per session. If you're at all open to it, we think it's well worth a try considering the striking benefits-to-barrier ratio. This book is all about highlighting the health practices that are underpinned by strong science and easily integrated into your life. We're not personally fans of it, but it fits our metric for sharing and for some people it just might be life-changing.

FOLLOW THE RESEARCH, NOT YOUR PREFERENCES

One of the many problems with the wellness world is that so-called experts refuse to talk about the benefits of things they don't like—for instance, have you ever heard a vegan talk about the health benefits of wild salmon? We sure haven't, despite the fact that research shows that for some people, omega-3-rich fish is indeed part of a healthy diet. So many people have practices, worldviews, and philosophies around health that they are passionate about but that limit the conversation about what might work wonderfully for someone else. We see this all the time in the podcasting world; many hosts only bring on guests that reinforce their existing beliefs, making authentic conversation among the curious a rare thing. The whole reason we started mindbodygreen, and why we're writing this book, is to open up the conversation and make space for individualized health. We recognize that there's a good chance at least half the people who read this chapter don't share our hang-up about the cold, or are at least open to trying it. If you're one of those people, this chapter is for you. And, if you're like us, we still recommend you read on in case there is any wiggle room inside you for a new adventure.

WHAT'S SO GREAT ABOUT FREEZING YOUR ASS OFF?

In two words: hormetic stress.

As with most things in life, stress in neither all good nor all bad. While we think about stress as the ultimate villain when it comes to our health and well-being, it's actually a little misunderstood. Of course, too much stress on the body—whether it be extreme temperatures, hunger, physical danger—is bad. But researchers and scientists also agree that *not enough* stress on the body can be just as bad. Our bodies evolved in a stressful world (running from lions, famine, and, you know, the Ice Age), so a little bit of stress on our systems actually helps keep things in balance. While chronic stress—long-term sustained stress—is notoriously harmful, short-term, low-dose exposure to stress releases a deluge of hormones that activate a whole range of physiological processes that can help boost metabolic and immune health.[1]

This "good" kind of stress is called hormetic stress, and it represents the Goldilocks zone of stress exposure. In an article in *Ageing Research Review*, author Elissa Epel says, "hormetic stressors, acute intermittent stressors of moderate intensity, can produce stress resilience, the ability for quick recovery and possibly rejuvenation of cells and tissues."[2] Exposing ourselves to hormetic stressors can help us live longer and better, manage autoimmune disorders, prevent heart disease, and improve memory—and the science behind this is growing. The stress can be dietary (which is what we are gunning for when we do circadian fasting), physical exercise, mental exercises like word games, and extreme temperatures (hot or cold).[3] By engaging in breathwork that pushes your limits of CO_2 tolerance, you're also triggering hormetic stress. Now you see that when we say everything is connected when it comes to health and well-being, we really mean it. Exposing yourself to hormetic stress in the form of these different practices pays huge dividends when it comes to ongoing health and happiness (not to mention longevity), because it elicits a beneficial evolutionary response that is ultimately restorative.

The beauty of hormetic stress is that it is, by definition, short-lived. That's good news when it comes to cold exposure, because not everyone wants to be like the extreme athlete and living legend of cold-water immersion Wim Hof. If you haven't heard of this wild man from the Netherlands, let us enlighten you. Wim Hof is known for such feats as running a half marathon barefoot above the Arctic Circle, swimming underneath ice for sixty-six meters (seventy-twoish yards), and holding the Guinness World Record for longest ice bath (1 hour, 52 minutes, and 42 seconds). No one needs to be Wim Hof to get the benefits of cold immersion, but he is a helpful reminder that the human body is capable of much more than we think it is. And by challenging our physical selves, we can get a little closer to the "good" stressors that have contributed to human health for eons.[4]

Now it's time to drill down a little on the benefits of the polar plunge. Although the science is still emerging on how this brand of hormetic stress helps us, what we already know is fascinating. What's even cooler is how it lines up with the lived experience of so many people who have been singing the praises of cold-water swimming for thousands of years. Thanks to the bravery of research subjects and journalists who are willing to expose themselves to extreme discomfort, we know more than ever about why humans are total wimps when it comes to dealing with the cold, and why, despite that, our bodies love it.

DOPAMINE HIT

For those who love cold-water swimming, there is nothing like the rush. Jack Dorsey, founder of Twitter and known biohacker, says a cold plunge is "better than caffeine."[5] Katherine May, bestselling author of the book *Wintering: The Power of Rest and Retreat in Difficult Times*, devotes an entire chapter to her love of winter swimming. Describing how it feels to get out of the water after a swim, she says, "Gazing back at the water, I felt the urge to do it all over again, to go back and exist in those crystalline seconds of intense cold. My blood sparkled in my veins."[6] To us, accounts of the high and the addictive allure of cold water sounds eerily similar to the way people describe the ecstasy of certain controlled substances. And for that reason, it wasn't a shock to discover that the primary reason some people feel their blood sparkling is because in a way, it is actually sparkling—with dopamine.

The second you jump into cold water—below sixty degrees—your body loses heat, fast. Water leaches warmth from your body more than twenty-five to thirty times faster than if you expose your skin to air of the same temperature. As a result, your body tries to rein in the dangerous heat loss by quickly releasing fight-or-flight hormones like dopamine and norepinephrine. One study showed that a cold plunge at fifty-seven degrees increased levels of dopamine by 250 percent and norepinephrine by 530 percent, while also ratcheting up the subjects' metabolic rate by 350 percent.[7]

Why is this important? Because increased levels of these brain chemicals, in an effort to marshal all our resources to keep warm, significantly impact and regulate mood and mental clarity. Dopamine in particular is central to our reward system, the part of our brain responsible for managing feelings of pleasure and motivation. Alcohol and drugs also stimulate these dopaminergic pathways, which is why those substances are so addictive.[8] When dopamine is secreted, and the reward system activated in a healthy way, it operates as it was intended—to help us perk up when we need to and find the motivation for things like building shelters, finding food, and getting the hell out of that cold water. For us modern folk, a healthy hit of dopamine might not be necessary for our survival, but it can shake us out of our daily torpor of desk sitting and doomscrolling. This might save our life in an altogether different way: by helping us find the motivation, energy, and mood stability that is critical to our well-being.

Maintaining mental health, whether it's fending off anxiety and depression or just finding more pleasure in life, has never been more important. We think this might just be one of the best reasons to consider cold-water therapy. Unlike some of the other benefits that we'll get to, the dopamine surge happens each time you get in the water. So even if you try it only once, you'll still benefit from the dopamine rush of the bracing cold for up to two and a half hours after exposure.[9] In an article in the *Washington Post*, NYU neuroscientist and cold-water lover Wendy Suzuki, PhD, said, "I can tell the difference when I forget to do it. It's just generally activating. I feel so alive."[10]

BROWN FAT IS WHERE IT'S AT

Scientists have known for a while that animals like bears and mice and human babies have a special kind of fat that acts as a kind of built-in heater. Because bears, mice, and babies can't shiver to get warm, they rely on what's known as brown fat to help them manage the cold. Until recently, scientists didn't believe human adults had brown fat, but a flurry of research in 2009 showed that we do in fact have "the capacity for nonshivering thermogenesis."[11] In other words, they discovered that some adults maintain cozy little deposits of brown fat on their necks, collarbones, kidneys, and spinal columns. The amount every person has is different, but in each of us brown fat operates the same way—as an energy powerhouse. Unlike white fat, brown fat is packed not with lipids that just sit there, but with mitochondria, which store more energy and won't lead to a higher risk of heart disease and metabolic dysfunction. In fact, brown fat is a metabolic boon, because once activated it takes sugar and white fat and turns them both into energy. Cold exposure "activates" this brown fat, and repeated exposure increases its volume.[12]

While white fat is what we're all trying to stay away from, we would be wise to stockpile as much brown fat as possible. Looking at over 130,000 PET scans of cancer patients at the Memorial Sloan Kettering cancer center, Tobias Becher, MD, of Rockefeller University in New York found brown fat deposits in about 10 percent of the scans.[13] (This is assumed to be an undercount because some of the protocols patients must abide by before receiving a PET scan actively inhibit brown fat activation, making it harder to discern on the scans.) Once they identified the patients with brown fat, Becher's research team was then able to crunch the numbers and look for an absence or presence of common cardiometabolic conditions compared with the patients who did not have discernible brown fat. What they found was eye-opening. People with brown fat had a lower incidence of type 2 diabetes (4.6 percent vs. 9.5 percent), a lower incidence of abnormal cholesterol, and a lower risk of coronary artery disease, hypertension, and congestive heart failure. Even more surprising, the people who were obese in the study had the most significant protection from brown fat when it came to cardiometabolic conditions—effectively neutralizing the risk posed by their excess white fat.[14]

NEXT-LEVEL BURN

One of the biggest areas of interest from researchers is how cold affects metabolism. Specifically, they want to know what spurs that higher caloric burn during and after cold exposure. While the mystery behind the mechanism is not entirely unraveled, so far experts think there are two ways that you burn extra calories. One of those is by activating brown fat. Within minutes of immersing your body in cold water, the body loses heat quickly, and brown fat activates, burning energy like a demon to try to warm you up. The second hypothesis is that for those who don't have as much brown fat, shivering is what induces the increased metabolism. Simply put, you've got a heck of a lot of skeletal muscle, and if it is all contracting and spasming, that takes a lot of energy. There's a reason why it's critical to give people with mild hypothermia lots and lots of calories—otherwise, they will run out of energy needed for shivering, and that's when life-threatening hypothermia sets in.

Interestingly, if you have more brown fat, it takes longer for you to get cold and for your body to begin to shiver. You become more and more adapted to the cold, which is great because brown fat gives you greater metabolic gains. People with brown fat who are exposed to cold will burn almost twice the calories of those who are exposed to cold but have less brown fat to help them out.[15] But don't forget, they both burn more calories than a person who doesn't brave the cold in the first place (pointing fingers at ourselves here).

INSULIN SENSITIVITY

Burning calories is great, but have you tried increasing your insulin sensitivity? That's where the real health advantage is. Because caloric burn is easier to quantify than other metabolic gains, less research has been done on humans about how cold exposure impacts things like glucose control and insulin sensitivity. However, a handful of studies show the promise of cold-water exposure for people with metabolic dysfunction, specifically those who are prediabetic or diabetic. When researchers from the University of Texas studied two small groups of men, they found that when exposed to the same cold conditions (a room at sixty-six degrees Fahrenheit, wearing suits that were filled with circulating cold water), the group with brown fat demonstrated improved stability in blood glucose levels and insulin sensitivity. In order to prevent diabetes and other metabolic conditions, having stable blood sugar over time and maintaining insulin sensitivity are vital. What this study, published in the journal *Diabetes*, shows us is that cold exposure may be a valuable nonpharmaceutical avenue of disease management for the over 25.8 million people living with diabetes.[16] There's still much more research can tell us about insulin sensitivity and cold therapy. If you have diabetes or any kind of metabolic disease, always talk to your doctor about whether or not cold therapy is a good idea for you.

IMMUNE RESET

When the body goes into fight-or-flight mode, it's prepared for a fight, and likewise, it's prepared to get hurt. It's been shown that mild stress can mobilize a constellation of immune cells—monocytes, neutrophils, and lymphocytes—that begin circulating in the blood, ready to help shore up any damage to come.[17] Since cold water triggers this sympathetic nervous system response, it makes sense that hormetic stress could help strengthen our immune systems. A recent study in the Netherlands of over three thousand people backs this up, showing the power of cold showers to trigger a protective immune response. Compared to the control group that took warm showers, the three cohorts that were asked to blast themselves with cold water over the course of a month had a 29 percent reduction in sick days taken. The three cold-shower groups were asked to turn on the cold water for thirty, sixty, and ninety seconds, but the benefit of reduced sick days didn't significantly change between cohorts. For those of us who aren't fans of freezing our butts off, it's good to know that thirty seconds may be enough time to garner protection against sickness.[18]

Another immune-related, possibly long-term benefit of cold exposure has to do with inflammation. We all know that cold exposure reduces short-term inflammation—there's a reason NFL players are compelled to sit in ice baths after games—but many experts believe it could also be beneficial to attenuating long-term or chronic inflammation.[19] This kind of inflammation is an overreaction of the immune system that we see in autoimmune disorders like rheumatoid arthritis, lupus, inflammatory bowel syndrome, and multiple sclerosis.

HOW TO REAP THOSE COLD REWARDS

There are plenty of ways to intentionally build cold exposure into your life. Most of the existing research on cold exposure and its many health benefits is on full-body, up-to-the-neck immersion in an ice bath, pool, or other cold body of water. The reason for this is purely practical—it's simply easier to control all the experimental variables that way. In an immersion tank, you can more precisely measure the effects of cold because you can control the temperature and how much skin is exposed to water versus air, regardless of differences in body weight, height, and surface area, whereas in a shower, you can't really control for any of those things. Since the science is just beginning, researchers haven't yet gotten there. But that doesn't mean that you can't still get the benefits of cold exposure other ways; it just means that there are no evidence-based protocols—yet.

Most of the researchers and experts we talked to agree the important part about cold exposure—no matter how you do it—is to get uncomfortable. Andrew Huberman, a neuroscientist from Stanford

Medical School and the popular host of the podcast *The Huberman Lab*, says, "You want to get uncomfortably cold, but not dangerously cold."[20] In other words, you want to get to the place where your mind is screaming to get out, but your body can still stay in the cold safely, without tipping over into hypothermia or tissue damage. That might sound vague, but this is one of those practices that is really about listening to your body and adjusting as needed. Here are some general guidelines to think about whether you are taking an ice bath, jumping in the ocean, or partaking in a cold shower:

- **Safety first.** If you have any heart problems or a family history of heart problems, talk to your doctor before trying cold immersion or exposure. The benefits of this practice come from the extremes that it pushes your body to in terms of hormetic stress, but one person's hormetic (safe) stress is another person's cardiac stress. In rare cases, cold-water immersion has been linked to dangerous cardiac events like heart arrhythmias.[21] One way to reduce this risk may be to start at higher temperatures, and as your body becomes increasingly adapted to the cold, you can handle lower and lower temperatures more safely. Also, if you have a circulation disorder, like Raynaud's, this practice probably isn't for you—Colleen urges you to keep those fingers and toes safe. Again, when in doubt, it's always a good idea to talk to your doctor. Be smart about anything you try.
- **How cold is cold enough?** There is no definitive number, but among experts the consensus seems to be that brown fat activation happens when you get below fifty-nine degrees Fahrenheit (fifteen degrees Celsius).[22] That being said, what counts as "uncomfortable" for a person without much brown fat might be above this temperature range, so you have to experiment a little with your comfort/discomfort zone. Shivering also is a good indicator that you're cold enough.

- **How long is long enough?** We'll dive into specific recommendations in a minute, but a general principle—whether or not you're going for a walk in the wintertime without a jacket or taking a cold shower—is that the lower the temperature you're exposed to, the shorter the amount of time you need to be exposed to it. Keep this in mind when adjusting to how the temperatures might change throughout the year. For instance, in the wintertime, the cold water you can get in your shower could be ten to twenty degrees colder than what you'd get in summertime.

- **How much of my body needs to be in the water?** As much as possible! If you're fully immersed, going in up to your neck is plenty. If you're in a cold shower, some people prefer to duck their heads in and out, thus avoiding a terrible ice cream headache.

- **How long before I see the benefits?** If we're talking about mood, the answer is immediately. Every instance of cold-water exposure will boost your dopamine and norepinephrine and may offer benefits like mental clarity and improved mood.[23] The effects of brown fat take a little longer to see because brown fat itself takes longer to accumulate. No one knows for sure how long; Susanna Søberg, PhD, author of an important study on winter swimming and metabolism, believes that after just one season of swimming twice a week, you may see a benefit.[24] Consistent cold-water exposure over time will help you build up your brown fat stores and see the greatest overall metabolic benefits.

- **What time of day should I do this?** A cold-water plunge or an icy shower are certain to wake you up, so common sense tells us that the best time of day for this would be in the morning. The science behind this is rooted in the fact that after the body's reaction to that initial cold, it will start to heat up and elevate your core temperature as well as dump adrenaline and dopamine into your bloodstream. This is an added bonus of focus if you have an important morning meeting. But because your body wakes up and becomes more alert as your core temperature rises, don't try a cold shower right before bed.[25]

DON'T BE SHY—JUMP IN

In the fall of 2021, a study published in *Cell Reports Medicine* had the cold-water-loving corner of the internet abuzz. Susanna Søberg devised a protocol to study the effects of cold on the bodies of seasoned winter swimmers with brown fat. These were healthy men already trained in winter swimming, so what the results really show is the power of brown fat to improve our health and just how little time in the water is needed to reap those rewards. The protocol for the cold-water exposure piece of the study is pretty simple: two or three cold-water swims a week, totaling eleven minutes each week. That might sound like more than three minutes in the cold water for each dip, but actually the participants were going back and forth between cold-water swimming and the sauna (more thoughts on saunas later). If you were only doing the swimming part, you could simply try to build up to three minutes for each session, or get in and get out a few times. For your bravery, the rewards you can look forward to are higher brown fat activation, increased metabolism, being warmer (thanks to thermogenesis), increased resilience to cold, better glucose balance, lower insulin production, and a more well-adapted immune system.[26] One important principle shared by Søburg is to always end cold. To increase metabolism, minimize hot showers and saunas after the last cold exposure (it's okay to go back and forth between exposures until then). This forces the body to rewarm itself, keeping that brown fat stimulated and helping stoke your metabolism.[27]

If you live by a cold water lake, river, or ocean, this protocol might just be for you. Aside from being scientifically proven to be good for you, it's also a chance to connect with nature and community. Throughout the world there is a network of cold-water swimming clubs that thousands of folks belong to. Some swim every day; others swim just once a week—we've even heard of one that only goes out when there's a full moon! Mark Harper, MD, PhD, a cold-water swimming researcher and enthusiast, has been winter swimming with the Brighton Swimming Club in the United Kingdom for thirteen years. Besides the buzz he gets after his daily swims, he talks about the sense of community that his participation brings as his favorite part of the endeavor.[28] Every day at seven a.m. he can go down to the water and find a clutch of people ready to run madly into the water with him. The people who do this kind of cold-water swimming rarely do it alone—there's something inspiring and motivating about having someone else around while you're freezing off your bits (as the British say). No matter how many times you do it, the lead-up to the plunge never gets easier—the primal dread of being cold remains, which is why having an accountability partner is so important, not to mention safer. On the other side of things, when you emerge from the water, your skin numb and adrenaline coursing through your bloodstream, it's also so sweet to share that moment of victory. As we'll see in chapter 9, social connection and community building is just as essential to our overall health and happiness. So, if you have the access to a body of water, why not make it a twofer? Cold water and community go well together (or so we've heard!).

THE BEST WAYS TO INTEGRATE COLD INTO YOUR LIFE

One of our favorite cold-therapy enthusiasts is the *New York Times*–bestselling author of *Beyond Training: Mastering Endurance, Health, and Life* and fitness expert Ben Greenfield. When we had him on the podcast, Jason joked that it seemed like Ben was always in the cold—either outside working out in the cold with minimal clothing, showering in the cold, or doing extreme cold plunges in the barrel he has in his backyard. Ben responded that it wasn't always easy for him, and in fact he used to despise the cold. And while he still doesn't unequivocally love it, he said, "If you have the right mindset it grows on you. And you pair that with knowing all the benefits and how good it is, eventually it turns from a hate-hate relationship into more of a love-hate relationship."[29]

That's the real talk. You might never love cold-water exposure, but you can learn to hate it a little less and focus on the intention you are setting to do right by your body and get closer to that 80 percent of maximum well-being. If this is one path of your personal health journey that you'd like to take, we recommend setting yourself up for success by making it as easy as possible to stick with it. If jumping in the ocean in February is the way you want to approach it, and you think that is sustainable for your life—fabulous, we say grab a buddy and go for it. But we also recognize that for most people, the recommendations below are going to be a lot easier to fold into their lives. Depending on your level of personal dread when it comes to the cold, you can try these in any order, and work up to the ones that seem harder. It's all about finding the practice that feels doable. Let's check it out:

Take a shower.

For those without access (or time) to partake in the full cold-water swimming experience, showers are the easiest and fastest way to expose your body to that good low-dose, short-duration stress that it craves. While cold showers haven't been as rigorously studied as full immersion, many experts agree that there's no reason to think you can't get the same benefits from a cold shower. In fact, it may be the perfect way to get started with cold exposure because you can more slowly build up your cold tolerance. Søberg recommends shooting for thirty to ninety seconds per shower.[30] If you want to try and mimic her protocol, you could try cold for thirty to ninety seconds, then turn on the hot water for thirty to ninety seconds, then go back and forth a few times. Just remember to end on cold, and don't go stand in front of the heater when you get out. Dry off if you want to, but it's even better to stand there for a few minutes and let your body air dry and warm itself naturally. That will enhance the metabolic gains.

How long and how often you partake should also change depending on how cold your shower water gets and how long you typically stay in. While there is no definite consensus on how many times a week you should do this, the most overlap seems to cluster around three or four times a week. Bottom line: there is no reason to think that you can't do cold therapy every day if you want to—our friend Ben Greenfield sure does.

Practical Tip: Take your time working up to the thirty-second mark, and don't get down on yourself if it takes a few weeks. It doesn't matter how short a duration you start with; if you keep with it, your body will reward you with progress. That progress is key to maintaining motivation, so keep a timer in or near the shower so you can reliably clock how long you're in there.

Take off your jacket.

This is another easy, low-tech way to expose yourself to cold. If you live in a place that actually gets cold (sorry, Floridians), this one is as simple as peeling off your layers. When you take your daily walk, leave the coat at home. If it's really cold, protect your hands with gloves, but keep your neck exposed and try to stick it out as long as possible.

Turn the heat down.

If you work from home, this is easier than if you go to the office, but it's still worth a try no matter how much you are at home. If you turn the thermostat down, not only will this save on energy costs, but you can help your body build brown fat stores by exposing it to continuous cold temperatures. Even if you can't stand it during the day, definitely keep it around or under sixty-five degrees when you sleep. Lower temperatures in the bedroom are also part of good health hygiene, helping you achieve better, more restorative sleep. Double win.

SAUNAS AND ACCESSIBILITY

Some of you may be scratching your heads about why we chose cold therapy and not hot therapy. If you reasoned that hot temperatures, like cold temperatures, can trigger hormetic stress in the body, you're right. There is emerging science around the cardiovascular benefits of consistent sauna use—something that Scandinavians have been engaging in for ages. So why didn't we recommend it in this chapter? If you remember from the introduction to the book, we made a pledge not to recommend or go too deeply into a practice that is inaccessible to most people. It may be science-backed, and it may help your well-being, but if most of us can't access a sauna, what's the point? It becomes just another one-percenter recommendation like all the others churned out by the wellness industrial complex. So, here's what we say: If you have access to a sauna, awesome, use it. If you don't have access to a sauna, you could try a hot bath instead, *if* it brings you joy. Andrew Huberman, PhD, recommends a hot Epsom salt bath before bed as a way to help the body modulate temperature in a way that helps trigger melatonin production.

ANCIENT PRACTICES AND
EMERGING SCIENCE

We would be remiss if we didn't mention that of all the chapters, this one is an outlier. The science is there, but it is young and not yet bulletproof. Like many ancient practices, cold-water immersion is something that is understudied. Plenty of researchers are ready and willing to conduct the research, but they are short on funding. Why? Call us cynical, but there's not a lot of money to be made from telling people to take a cold shower or jump in the ocean. It's just a fact that pharmaceutical companies are the ones with the big research dollars to spend, so any area of interest or potential solution that doesn't involve a pill is likely under researched. We see this when it comes to research on breathwork and nutrition especially, which are also places where we'd like to see a lot more science. All that being said, the science that does exist for cold-water immersion is quite promising; combined with the fact that cold-water therapy has been around for a long time, can be done safely and easily, and *may* give you a huge return on investment, that was enough for us to want to share it with you.

FINAL THOUGHTS

Well-being is the result of the cumulative effect of a set of daily decisions over time. In this sense, knowledge is power, and so is the practice of discernment. In other words, now that you know what you know—what will you do?

When we first learned about the powerful benefits of cold exposure, we were surprised and intrigued. The more we learned, the more we had to recognize that it made sense with what we already knew about the importance of hormetic stress. We experimented a little (very little) with it personally, we listened to others who had different perspectives, and ultimately we each had to reflect on whether or not this one was for us. Cold-exposure therapy is a health practice that is a nice-to-have, but it's not a must-have, which makes it a great opportunity to practice listening to yourself, reflecting on your health journey, and taking a holistic view of the question of whether or not to do it. Now you have the facts about what cold exposure can do for your body: it is healthy for you. But will it bring you joy? Will it fit into your life in a way that is seamless, and will it foster at least a love-hate relationship (as opposed to the hate-hate)? Those questions apply to many potential healthy habits, which is why refining your process of reflection, discernment, and deliberation is just as critical to your long-term journey as any cold shower will ever be.

THAT EXTRA 20 PERCENT

If you have access to a sauna and a cold shower, you can fully partake in the evidence-based protocol out of Denmark. Lots of gyms and YMCAs have saunas and showers, so this is within reach for those who really want to take it the extra mile. It's pretty simple: you want to shoot for a back and forth between sauna and cold that equates to a total of eleven minutes of cold and fifty-seven minutes of hot per week, and you must end cold. That's it. Here's what it could look like if you went to the gym twice a week:

- **Day 1:** Ten-minute sauna, two-minute cold shower, ten-minute sauna, two-minute cold shower, ten-minute sauna, two-minute cold shower.
- **Day 2:** Ten-minute sauna, two-minute cold shower, ten-minute sauna, two-minute cold shower, ten-minute sauna, two-minute cold shower.
- **Total cold time:** Twelve minutes
- **Total sauna time:** Sixty minutes

Chapter Seven

Regenerate

We all know that the best way to communicate and connect about important subjects is through storytelling, which is why when we started writing this chapter, we looked for a story of ordinary people affected by the climate crisis, like the devastation of polluted water supplies, the destruction of entire towns due to extreme weather, or simply someone who was going about their business until a personal tragedy woke them up to the reality that human health and the health of the environment are inextricably, beautifully, and profoundly connected. It took us a long time to write this chapter, and not because we couldn't find a story to start it off; instead, we found too many.

Here's just one: Fred Stone, a third-generation dairy farmer in Arundel, Maine, had to euthanize 150 dairy cows after the soil on his farm and the milk from his cows was found to contain extraordinarily dangerous levels of perfluorooctanoic acid (PFOA) and perfluorooctane sulfonic acid (PFOS), known as PFAS (PFAS also include PFHxS and PFNA).[1] These chemicals are found in the coating of Teflon pans, stain-resistant couches, firefighting foams, and waterproof clothing, and in industrial and municipal waste products.[2] Research on the harmful effects of PFAs is ramping up, because what we do know about them is alarming. According to one article about the PFAs crisis from the University of Maine, "They have been linked to harmful health effects in humans, including immune system disorders, thyroid hormone disruption and cancer. They also don't break down readily and can biomagnify—or increase in concentration as they move through food webs. PFAS used decades ago are still circulating in the environment, in animals and plants, waterways and even in peoples' bodies, which is why they're often called 'forever chemicals.' "[3]

This is why Fred Stone's farm was just one tip of a thousand icebergs, not just for farmers in Maine, but for hunters and anglers as well. In late November 2021, just as the deer hunting season was winding down, the Maine Department of Inland Fisheries and Wildlife issued a rare "do not eat" advisory to hunters in six communities in the central part of the state. Unsafe levels of PFAs had been found in local deer meat, which is a huge food source for many rural families. By then, over thirty-eight thousand deer had been harvested, which, by one hunter's account, meant the meat could have been shared and eaten by over one hundred thousand people.[4] As officials in Maine and from the Department of Environmental Protection scrambled to investigate the breadth of the contamination, Maine residents, many of whom are legacy hunters and anglers, were left wondering what exactly is in the meat they are eating and the water they are drinking. Personally, we don't eat elk or hunt deer (we love Bambi), but this story illustrates the larger issue at hand: we are poisoning our planet and our wildlife in unprecedented ways.

So, where did such high levels of PFAs come from in the first place? In the 1970s and '80s, across the US, spreading sludge from wastewater treatment facilities and paper mills was billed as a good way to improve the quality of the soil for agriculture. According to the people who wanted to offload the sludge, it was a free fertilizer that would be a boon to crop yields.[5] In Maine specifically, the first indication that PFAs were a problem came from the groundwater around military bases that had been contaminated by firefighting foam used for training purposes.[6] If you can take a step back from the horror of them, the forever nature of these chemicals is fascinating. If anything, they are evidence of the vastly interconnected nature of our ecosystems and ourselves. PFAs start in a Teflon pan or your new couch, show up in our bodies and then our waste, which ends up on our farmland, which ends up in the hay that the cows eat and the water they drink and is passed to the milk that they produce, which we then consume until it makes its way into our bloodstream, which eventually leaves our bodies via the toilet, and then out in the world it goes to start the whole cycle all over again. Or maybe the PFAs come from the water-resistant coating on the bottom of the cardboard pizza box leaching into the crust, or from the burn-resistant coating on the inside of your microwave popcorn bag, or from the wrapper on your burger that miraculously keeps grease from staining your pants as you maneuver through the evening commute.[7] The more you read about PFAs, the more you realize they are everywhere—all over the world, in every part of our lives, even inside of us—and they are here to stay. According to an article in *Wired*, PFOA (one of the four PFAs) specifically has "a half-life of 92 years in the environment and two to eight years in the human body."[8] Fred Stone stopped spreading the sludge on his farm in 2004, but that didn't stop the forever chemicals from poisoning the cows and ruining his livelihood almost fifteen years later.

After reading dozens of stories like Fred's about the destruction wrought by forever chemicals, floods, hurricanes, lead in the water supply, animal extinction, deforestation, drought, and rising seas, and the devastation felt by climate refugees and victims of pollution, we felt wrung out. Not joyful. We talked about which terrible, horrible, very bad things that we should cover in this chapter so that you would know what's going on in the world. (Spoiler alert: we're not going to do much of that, because chances are, you know what's going on.) For a little while we got lost in the sadness and overwhelmed by the enormity and breadth of the problems we are facing as a world seemingly just waking up to a nightmare. Our experience of writing this chapter is not unique. It's a microcosm of what everyone everywhere who stays informed about what is going on around them experiences. If you are reading this book, we know you are not someone who denies that the climate crisis exists or that humans are the cause of it, so we'll skip that. It is crushing to read the news some days, but even more crushing to be a person or a community *in* the news. And soon, we all will be.

Why? Because it's all about connection.

Before we started mindbodygreen in 2009, phrases like *mind-body-spirit* and *mind-body-soul* were pretty common. We chose *mind* and *body* for the first two parts of our three-pronged philosophy because it's pretty obvious that the mind and body are not separate—they're one. So, let's say that we've nailed the *mindbody* part: we have a spiritual practice, we have strong emotional connections to friends and family, we're breathing through our noses, we're moving our bodies, we're eating real food...Does this mean we're healthy? Well, maybe...or maybe not. There's another piece of the well-being puzzle: the *green* part. If we are (unwittingly or not) using harsh chemicals and toxins in our cleaning products and eating foods bathed in pesticides, that easily negates all the spinach we're eating. If we are displaced because of wildfires in our communities and find ourselves living in a shelter, there will be little time to worry about the best form of exercise for our metabolic health. We are not separate from the earth and the environments that we inhabit, or the animals we eat and coexist with. To live and act as though we are a species apart is not only dangerous for the earth; it's dangerous for us as well. Which is why we chose the name mindbodygreen. Not three words, one word—because it's all connected. That's not to say we have it all figured out, but we do think it's a solid daily reminder that these three pillars of health and happiness are tightly linked.

THE GLOBAL IMPACT

The degradation of our environment and the loss of biodiversity in the world affects us all. Just as every part of our body is connected— our digestion, our breathing, the nutrients that we feed ourselves— there are a million different environmental ripple effects that act on each cell and system, reverberating throughout us. We are not a closed system; we are open to the world, and we bring it inside when we eat and when we drink and when we breathe. When you understand that on an intellectual, emotional, and spiritual level, you understand that things need to change.

We can begin by looking at the two broad levels of impact of the climate crisis and other ecological disasters: personal and global. For instance, it's a personal catastrophe when you find out that your drinking supply is contaminated by lead, and it's a global catastrophe that wildfires are so widespread they don't even make the news anymore, with some populations more personally impacted than others. One level of environmental suffering is not more important than another, and taking responsibility for both is critical to human health and happiness.

For too many years we have been complacent in the delusion that the environment is someone else's problem: The health impacts from air pollution are for the people affected by them in China to deal with, just as the people whose homes and lands are devastated by tsunamis in Southeast Asia have to deal with their problem; even closer to home, hurricanes and floods wipe out American cities, but that's for those cities and communities to deal with. In the last few years, wildfires, pandemics, drought, and extreme weather events have brought the realities of our changing world home to all of us. As the planet warms and the years pass, no one will be untouched. This is a problem for both our bodies and our minds, and—if you're the spiritual sort—our souls. Extreme weather events and ecological devastation threaten our most basic physiological needs. Food, water, warmth, rest, security, and safety all sit at the bottom of Abraham Maslow's famous hierarchy of needs—they are foundational. This is the most obvious, red-flashing-light problem that we face, because not much matters when these basic requirements get disrupted or threatened. But even if we live in a place where we have, so far, been shielded from the worst physiological impacts of the climate crisis, the next level of Maslow's hierarchy of needs is still in peril: psychological and self-fulfillment. Living in the grip of eco-anxiety and feeling chronically stressed by the horrifying news headlines makes it impossible to be truly emotionally *well*. On a deep, spiritual level, the earth is part of us—every plant, every animal, every living thing—and when it is hurting, so are we, even if we are in denial about it. We live in community and connection with other living organisms. Once upon a time that statement would have been viewed as just some cheesy, New Age BS. But we know better now.

We know that trees literally talk to each other. Through complex, underground fungal networks, trees send out distress signals, feed young saplings that are struggling, and form close relationships with each other that allow them all to flourish.[9]

We know that three-quarters of our food crops rely on pollinators like honeybees, bumblebees, and butterflies.[10] Unfortunately, almost 40 percent of insect species worldwide are in decline, and almost a third of all species are facing extinction.[11] Invasive species, pesticides, and global warming are upending complex ecosystems at a dizzying rate.

We know that the widespread use and abuse of antibiotics in agriculture has unleashed dangerous antibiotic-resistant bacteria. Antibiotics transformed human healthcare in the twentieth century, saving millions of lives. Unfortunately, that progress is under a direct and rising threat of antibiotic resistance.[12] By aggressively using antibiotics on healthy animal populations, the agricultural industry has put us all in danger.

For decades we've exploited and extracted resources, driven thousands of species to extinction, and polluted our world. The repercussions of those actions are coming home to roost.

THE PERSONAL IMPACT

There is no shortage of big, obvious ways that climate change is affecting us, but we should be just as concerned about the invisible and insidious damage to our bodies as the result of the way we have treated the earth. The climate crisis is not just extreme weather; it is also the negative effects on human health caused by environmental toxins from industrial farming, plastics, and pollution. These impacts are the most obvious expression of the connection we have to our environment, because what we do to the earth is what we do to ourselves. We are what we eat, drink, breathe, microwave, carry food in, and wear on our bodies.

About six years ago, while Colleen was pregnant with our firstborn, we did a "plastics sweep" of our house and started to phase plastic out of our lives as much as possible. For years we had been hearing about the dangers of endocrine disruptors like BPA, and with a vulnerable bun in the oven, we knew it was time to act. We started with the low-hanging fruit and threw out all our reusable plastic items like plastic storage containers, drinking cups, bowls, plates—everything. It didn't take long, and it wasn't that expensive for us to replace the items we tossed with glass or stainless steel or ceramics. But once we became more highly attuned to the presence of plastic, we realized that our home was just the start.

Plastic is everywhere.

Every package you order from the internet is encased in mind-boggling layers of it. The takeout food you get is wrapped in it or its packaging is coated in it. The food you buy in the grocery store is held by it—we can usually only find one or two brands of any given food that comes in something other than a plastic container. The toys that many preschool kids play with are primarily made of plastic. Water bottles, to-go coffee cups, fishing nets, dental floss, insulin pumps, the lining of metal cans, you name it—plastic. The famous 1967 film *The Graduate* has probably the most prescient movie scene in history. Dustin Hoffman's character is getting career advice from his father's friend, Mr. McGuire, who says, "I just want to say one word to you. Just one word…Plastics." He then goes on about the great future that there is in plastics and tells Hoffman's character to think about getting into the business. It's hard to believe, but in 1967, most consumer goods were still mostly made with wood, glass, metal, and aluminum. Now, just like Mr. McGuire said, it all boils down to one word: *plastics.*

We have flooded our environment with plastics to the extent that microplastics—tiny pieces of plastic that come from broken-down consumer goods—can now be found in the farthest corners of the world. From the sea surrounding the Antarctic peninsula to the depths of the Mariana Trench, scientists have found microplastics. But you don't have to go that far to find them; you can simply go to the bathroom or prick your finger, because they have been found in human stool and, more recently, our blood. A small but breakthrough study in *Environment International* found plastic in the blood of humans for the first time. According to an article about the study in *Smithsonian Magazine*, "The participants could have been exposed to microplastics through air, water and food, but also through personal care products, like toothpaste or lip gloss, that might have been accidentally ingested, dental polymers, parts of implants or tattoo ink residues."[13]

Why is all this so bad? Well, there are the obvious ways plastic hurts the earth—the fact that only about 10 percent of all the plastic manufactured in our lifetimes has been recycled, that marine organisms are killed by the millions because of plastic polluting our oceans, and that plastics manufacturing is a major driver of climate change. But plastics also act on the human body in invisible and insidious ways.[14] Plastic is, of course, made of and with chemicals, many of which are harmful to human health. They leach into our food from plastic containers, especially when heated, and can also get into the body when babies chew on plastic toys or drink from plastic straws. All of these exposures are, according to one journal article, "linked with severe adverse health outcomes such as cancers, birth defects, impaired immunity, endocrine disruption, developmental and reproductive effects."[15]

While there is a whole alphabet soup of chemicals that are harmful to human health, research has shown phthalates and BPA/BPF/BPS to be particularly dangerous. The former makes plastic soft, like the flimsy water bottle you get at the gas station, and the latter makes plastic hard, like a sturdy reusable water bottle that can go in the dishwasher. Both of these chemicals interfere with human hormones like estrogen, progesterone, and testosterone, which is why they are commonly referred to as endocrine disruptors. Many scientists and environmental experts have linked the rise of these endocrine disruptors in our environment to disturbances in reproductive function such as declines in fertility, higher rates of miscarriage, and changes to the number and quality of eggs in ovaries.[16] From 1973 to 2011, the total sperm count of Western men dropped by 59 percent, which makes sense when you know that exposure to endocrine-disrupting chemicals can reduce levels of testosterone in males.[17] Shanna Swan, PhD, a leading environmental and reproductive epidemiologist from Mount Sinai Medical Center, found that pregnant women who were exposed to endocrine disruptors were giving birth to male children with measurably smaller penises and anal-genital distance. In other words, the chemicals that the pregnant women were exposed to lowered the testosterone levels in their male fetuses enough to have physically measurable impacts. Scientists have been observing this exposure effect in male frogs, for instance, for decades, but to see it shown in humans is alarming, to say the least.

In her book *Countdown: How Our Modern World Is Threatening Sperm Counts, Altering Male and Female Reproductive Development, and Imperiling the Future of the Human Race*, Swan reminds us that these chemicals are disruptive to far more than our reproductive health and have been connected to problems with our immune, neurological, metabolic, and cardiovascular systems: "To make matters worse, an individual's genetic susceptibility to certain health conditions, coupled with exposures to other chemicals and lifestyle habits, can increase the effects produced by a particular EDC [endocrine-disrupting chemical]."[18] Research in this area is new and emergent, and while scientists are moving as fast as they can, the complex health effects of chemicals on our bodies is a frightening unknown.

Even more disturbing is the fact that these endocrine-disrupting chemicals are found not only in plastic but in thousands of household and personal care products. We already talked about how PFAs (also endocrine disruptors) are found in everything from your frying pan to your new sofa. Well, phthalates can be found not only in plastic water bottles, but also in soaps, makeup, fragrances, body lotion— all things you put directly on your body's largest organ.

All of this can feel incredibly overwhelming. Plastic—everywhere. Chemicals—everywhere. Which are terrible? Which are okay? Which do we just not know anything about? It's enough to make you want to move to a deserted island and fashion your clothes out of coconuts and reeds. This, on top of the global problems of climate change, can feel like too much to handle. Many of us get stuck here, overwhelmed and paralyzed by fear. Others say, "Screw it, it's too much. I'm just going to stick my head in the sand and keep doing what I'm doing." These are both reasonable emotional responses. But staying stuck in those gears for too long will not lead to a happier, healthier life.

The best way to combat our own eco-anxiety and to help the planet that sustains us is to *do something*. It is empowering to act. And even if those actions don't feel like enough when you begin, if you keep doing what you can, you'll be moving the needle on your own flourishing—and everyone else's too.

So where do we even begin? How do we choose what to do?

There is paralyzing eco-anxiety about what is coming for us that we can't control. And then there is paralyzing choice overload about what we can control. Should we never drink from a plastic water bottle again? Should we start using those beeswax coverings instead of cellophane? Should we go vegetarian? Do we need a water filter? What about getting an electric vehicle? Is the cost of installing solar panels really worth it? Is microwaving plastic *really* that bad for you? My moisturizer says "no parabens"—is that good enough? Should I plant a tree in my backyard or make a bee-friendly garden instead?

What has the most impact? What does the most good in the world? Like eating, exercise, and everything else in life, there's no silver bullet, no one-size-fits-all solution to living green. And you are only one person, with only so much time and money—so what actions get you the biggest bang for your buck? From where we stand, that is the critical question to ask when you are thinking about making changes for environmental good. It's all about return on investment. Because we're business owners, that concept is always skipping through our heads. And in the next sections, we will share the actions you can take on climate that will yield the biggest return on investment. These changes we lay out are all important, accessible ways we can safeguard our health, help keep our communities safe, and move toward a regenerative future for every living thing. And like everything else in this book, the key is to choose among the options and find the best ways for *you* to act on this issue. What are the actions you may take out of despair but can do with joy?

WHAT DO WE DO?

Most of the changes that will make a real impact on both environmental toxins and the rising temperature of the earth—cutting carbon emissions on a global level and policy changes—are above our pay grade. As individuals, most of us don't have access to the kind of power that shifts environmental policy on the industrial or global stage. But we can't get bogged down or sidelined by what we *can't* control, or else we abdicate the responsibility that we have to do what we can. On the macro level, we have the power of the ballot box, and we can protest with our dollars. Do that, and feel good about it. And then turn the focus back on what you can do in the realm of lifestyle change. For us, that has been the most grounding way to deal with what feels like daily setbacks and horrible news.

Imagine two circles. One is filled with the most impactful changes humankind can make to help end the climate crisis and live in harmony with Mother Earth. In the other circle is a list of what we personally control in our small, beautiful lives. If you imagine these circles as a Venn diagram, there is an overlap area. And there is a *lot* in the middle. Actually, there is way too much in the middle, because you are just one person living one life, and most of you can't fully devote yourself to climate justice or tracking down every chemical that goes into every product in your house.

The good news is that there are so many things you can do!

The challenging news is that there are so many things you can do.

One of the reasons we're in this crisis in the first place is the complexity of the issue. For one example, is it more important to eat local food or organic food in terms of carbon footprint and overall health and well-being? We could literally spend the entire chapter talking about that, and there are many good-faith disagreements between scientists and activists about this very topic. Organic farming operations require more land and so in some cases may have a larger carbon footprint than conventional farms. On the other hand, non-organic farming contributes to pesticides in our water and soil, which we know is harmful. In the end, the answer seems to be "it depends"—it depends on where you live, what you have access to, and what foods you are eating.[19] Trying to hold all this information in your head and make the best choice is a frustrating task, and yet we all want to do better. In our interactions with experts and in our own lives, we have found that the best way to contribute to the health and well-being of the world and its people is to choose a few things that are simple, unequivocally good for you and good for the world, and easy to integrate into your life. We rely on the climate experts in our circle to help us understand exactly where we can make the most impact, and how to make it happen. The following areas of action are unequivocally good for the earth, good for your personal health, and easily integrated into your life. Of course, there are big-ticket items you can and should do if you have the resources—buy an electric vehicle, put solar panels on your roof—but what we've chosen to focus on are changes that everyone can make, regardless of income level, geography, or available time.

Eat a Plant-Rich Diet

Paul Hawken, world-renowned environmental activist and author of *Drawdown: The Most Comprehensive Plan Ever Proposed to Reverse Global Warming*, is someone whose advice we take very seriously. *Drawdown* was published in 2017, and in the years since Paul's conclusions have stood the test of time. So when he tells us that the top three things we can do to help regenerate the earth on a personal level revolve around food—what we eat, where we get it from, and how much of it we waste—we listen. First up: eat a plant-rich diet. In chapter 3 we talked about the importance of eating a plant-rich, whole-foods diet for your health and longevity. Well, it turns out this is a double-your-money kind of lifestyle change, because it's one of the most impactful green actions you can take to help mitigate global warming, *and* it's good for your well-being. Because there is some confusion about what is meant by a plant-based or plant-rich diet, we want to be super clear about what we mean.

Unfortunately, plant-based can be highly processed.

These days foods can be "made of plants"—remember Doritos, Oreos, and Impossible burgers—and still be problematic. Think of all the carbon emissions unleashed into the environment through industrial food manufacturing—not good. As in chapter 3, we are talking about plants that are whole and as close to their natural form as possible. Focus on shopping the perimeter of the grocery store and you'll be in good shape.

Plant-rich means being thoughtful about the meat you eat.

Notice that we're not suggesting that it's necessary to go full vegetarian or vegan (unless you want to!), but rather to have a diet that is *mostly* plants. Most experts agree that plants have a lower impact on carbon emissions than meat and dairy, so even simply cutting your meat (particularly beef) intake in half will have an impact.[20] But Hawken reminds us that it's more effective from a land regeneration standpoint to use herding animals wisely (i.e., not how the meat industry is currently using them, which is utterly appalling) than it is to abandon all animal husbandry.[21] When animals are raised responsibly—that is, not stuffed with corn and soybeans on a feedlot—and eaten judiciously, they can be a great source of nutrition and enjoyment. This is a good reminder that abandoning your bimonthly grass-fed burger for a fake-meat burger is not necessarily the greener choice. Fake meat is a less nutritious option (less nutrient dense, full of canola oil, and genetically modified), and according to Marco Springmann, PhD, a food researcher from Oxford University, it's not necessarily that much better in terms of emissions. Cellular-based meat produces five times the emissions as chicken and comes in just under conventional beef. Plant-based meat releases roughly the same amount of emissions that chicken does, but about five times the emissions of legumes and vegetables.[22] Not to mention the emissions from the manufacturing, processing, and shipping of all the ingredients that go into fake meat, which are difficult to calculate. Making an Impossible Burger involves the production of about twenty-one different ingredients, including genetically modified soy. There is no question that factory-farmed beef is problematic, but the carbon footprint of fake meat is still highly debated. The point is that eliminating animals altogether is not a silver bullet solution, and it's one of the reasons why we are so excited about the potential of regenerative agriculture.

Support Regenerative Farming

The second food-related action item from Paul Hawken is about where we get our food and what systems it is supporting or undermining. There is a burgeoning movement in agriculture to return to farming practices that are regenerative as opposed to extractive. Before the advent of manufactured pesticides and genetically modified, "Roundup Ready" monocrops like soybeans and corn, farmers were able to farm the same land for centuries with no loss of fertility and greater carbon sequestration.[23] Unfortunately, current Big Agriculture practices are terrible for maintaining healthy soil ecosystems, which is bad news from a land use perspective. But it's also alarming because scientists are starting to understand that soil health contributes greatly to the nutrient profile of the plants we eat. It turns out vegetables are not monolithic: a potato grown in the wild is not the same as a potato grown by a commercial farm. In fact, our vegetables are what *they* eat—in other words, what's in their soil. An article in *Civil Eats* reported that "recent studies have found that crops grown with regenerative practices contain higher levels of vitamins, minerals, and phytochemicals."[24] What this means for us is that by transitioning from industrial agriculture back to more resilient farming practices, we are not only helping safeguard food supplies for future generations, but we're also safeguarding human health right now. When you buy organic or from a small local farm or grow your own food, you are forgoing chemicals in your food *and* bumping up their nutrients. But regenerative agriculture isn't only about better-quality, more nutritious food. According to the National Academy of Sciences, regenerative farming practices sequester huge amounts of carbon dioxide (250 million tons in the US annually), another big win for supporting the planet and it's a practice we are very excited about.[25]

Cut Down on Food Waste

Here are some wild numbers. One-third of all food grown in the world is wasted each year, which equals 1.3 billion tons.[26] About half of that is wasted on the farm, and about half is wasted in the home. Whether that food is wasted because of imperfections, spoilage, or simply because someone wasn't hungry for dinner, what it means is that food ends up in a landfill (mostly), rotting and releasing methane into the atmosphere. But that's just one way that it hurts the environment, because what about all the water, energy, and carbon emissions that went into creating that food in the first place? What a devastating waste. According to all of the experts on the environment and climate change that we talk to, reducing your food waste is at the top of the list of things you can do to be green. While you can't control the waste at the farm or the supermarket, you can control what rots in your refrigerator. The bonus of this action is that it will actually save you money. It's time to leave the guilt of the fuzzy white strawberries behind and plan for eliminating food waste in your home. Here are some ideas.

Meal planning for the win.

Some of you reading this will groan. We know meal planning gets a lot of airplay in the wellness world for other reasons, but this is a worthy cause. Take twenty minutes to survey the contents of your refrigerator and make a meal plan for the week, *then* go to the grocery store and buy only what you need. There are about a hundred meal planning apps and how-to websites out there if you need help.

Embrace the freezer.

You can dramatically increase the shelf life of fruits and vegetables if you shop smartly in the freezer section. Frozen whole foods are just as nutritious as fresh ones and can dramatically cut down on the food waste. The freezer is also a great place for fruit that is on the edge of too ripe (hello, bananas!) and leftovers that you just can't stomach another night of but would be totally down for in a couple of weeks.

Clothing Waste

When we think of major contributors to climate change, we don't always look to our closets. And yet, the fashion and textile industries are huge producers of carbon emissions because of the petrochemicals they use to manufacture their products and the sheer number of clothes that are churned out every year. According to Paul Hawken, "In the US we buy a new garment of clothing every six to seven days on average. About 8 to 10 percent of global emissions come from the clothing industry."[27] That's more than the total emissions from international flights and shipping.[28] Like plastic, a disturbingly small percentage of clothing gets recycled. According to a *Bloomberg News* article, roughly 87 percent of the materials used to make clothing ended up being incinerated or sent to a landfill."[29] Like reining in food waste, getting a handle on clothing waste gives us a huge return on investment, in large part because clothes are a big household expense. Here are some tips.

Buy less fast fashion.

Simply put, buy less clothing that is cheap, not particularly well made, and produced by companies that exploit labor in the developing world to drive down prices. More chemicals are used less responsibly for manufacturing, more workers are harmed, and more waste is created. Environmental experts agree that we all pay a high price for cheap clothes. While some people argue that fast fashion is important from an affordability standpoint, that argument doesn't really hold water. The fast fashion industry isn't driven by people with smaller budgets, but by people with more disposable income buying more than they need. We all like novelty and a deal, but when you zoom out, it's actually a raw deal.

Buy more high-quality clothing.

We call this the "Marie Kondo does fashion" approach. If it doesn't "spark joy," don't buy it. The goal is to buy clothes that make you happy and that you will wear. Spend your money on quality, not quantity. Make investments, if you can, in clothes that are made from natural fibers that last longer so you don't have to replace them as often.

Shop secondhand.

A cheaper and ultimately more environmentally sound option for us all is to shop at secondhand or thrift stores. By wearing something someone else owned once upon a time, you are not only saving that item from the landfill, but you're also helping make all the energy and resources used to produce it count double.

For some of our personal suggestions about where to shop green go to thejoyofwellbeing.com/clothing.

Make Your Home a Safe Haven

Earlier in the chapter we talked about all the ways environmental toxins are invisible threats to our health. In the pages of this chapter, we have learned the importance of keeping our physical distance from PFAs, high levels of lead in our water, phthalates, BPA, and other endocrine disruptors. There's no way we're going to eliminate all exposures, even if we become obsessive about it. So, what *should* we do? The best we reasonably can. Here's what that looks like.

Filter your water, or at least don't drink it from a plastic bottle.

If you have the resources to invest in a home water filter, do it. As we have learned from the ongoing disaster in Flint, Michigan, we can't always rely on municipalities to alert us to problems with our water supply in a timely fashion. Not to mention, industrial and agricultural chemicals and pharmaceuticals can pollute your water in ways that are not monitored by municipalities.[30] If you get your drinking water from a well, it's even more important to filter it, considering what we know about PFAs contaminating groundwater. In short, what we know about water pollution is enough of a reason to be careful with our drinking water—what we don't yet know about potential exposures should send us running to the Environmental Working Group website to check out their guide to buying a home filter.

Eliminate plastics, especially around food.

This isn't as hard as it sounds, because in the past few years there has been more consumer demand for nonplastic alternatives when it comes to water bottles and food containers. This makes it easy enough to find your child a stainless steel water bottle or lunchbox, if you're up for it. The experts say that your best bet for food storage is glass, metal, and ceramics. If replacing plastic in your home is an expense you can't take on all at once, that's okay. You can mitigate your risk by not heating up foods in plastic. It's as easy as transferring your leftovers to a ceramic plate before you heat them up in the microwave— a small but mighty change.

Read the labels.

You should already be in the habit of reading food labels to make sure what you buy is as lightly processed and free from additives as possible. The next step is treating your household cleaners and personal care products with the same scrutiny. When it comes to cleaning supplies, Shanna Swan recommends going through your sprays and cleaners and looking for words like "danger, warning, poison, or fatal"—swap out those harsh chemical agents with products that are made out of easily identifiable ingredients. The cosmetics and beauty aisle at your local pharmacy is one of the most confusing places around. Because these products are not regulated as tightly by the Food and Drug Administration, their labels can contain misleading language like "all natural!" or "Pure and clean!"—descriptors that from a regulatory standpoint mean diddly squat. This makes it a lot harder to make the right quick decision about which products to buy. For personal products, in order to steer clear of harmful chemicals and endocrine disruptors, here's what Swan suggests you look for:

- **Buy:** organic, fragrance free or safe fragrance, paraben free, phthalate-free
- **Avoid if possible:** products in a plastic jar or bottle, products that say "Antibacterial," and many kinds of air fresheners (they're often full of phthalates).

We recognize it can be pretty hard to avoid buying shampoo in plastic bottles, but you can always buy them and transfer them to glass or aluminum containers when you get home.

Spend Time in Nature

In chapter 4, we talked about the power of nature to soothe our nervous systems, sharpen our cognitive abilities, and promote emotional well-being. Fostering a stronger connection with your environment will also help ease eco-anxiety and sustain motivation to live a greener life. In order to truly care about something, you have to know it. Whether you live in the city or in the country, ask yourself how much you truly know about the patch of earth you call home. Do you know what trees are in your backyard or in the park down the street? Do you know what birds are migratory, and which ones stay year-round? Do you know what pollinators are native to the land? Do you know which ones are threatened? It's one thing to live somewhere; it's another thing to truly inhabit a place. The more you learn about the flora and fauna in your area, the more connected you will feel to the living things around you and the ecosystems that sustain us all. Here are some ideas to get started.

Ditch the gym.

If you can, do your workout outside. Morning sunshine to regulate your circadian rhythms is already a good idea, as is moving your body. And we already know that being outside in the cold is good for you, so don't let a little dip in the mercury dampen your enthusiasm. You might have noticed by now that exercising or simply moving outside is one of the best things you can do for your health and happiness. By the end of the book, we will have recommended it in five chapters for five different reasons.

Go outside without your phone.

Considering 96 percent of Gen Z Americans won't go to the bathroom without their phone, it stands to reason that we could all do with a little space from our devices.[31] Even if you love listening to podcasts or music on your daily walks, try a digital-free day. Notice the birdsong, look up at the trees budding new leaves, and take note of the fat squirrels leaping from branch to branch.

Download an app to help you identify plants and animals.

There are plenty of free apps that allow you to take a picture of a flower and then identify it for you. They don't work perfectly, but even if you're dubious about the algorithm, it's fun to do some detective work and find out whether or not that tree down the street is a sugar maple or a Norway maple.

Create a green space bucket list.

Even if you live in Manhattan, plenty of green space is accessible by walking or public transportation. Do a little research and find out what parks and conservation areas are within a reasonable distance and check them off the list one by one.

FINAL THOUGHTS

There are two definitions of the word *regenerate* in the Oxford dictionary. One is the verb form, which means to regrow or replace tissue in a living organism. The other is the adjective form, which means to be "reformed or reborn, especially in a spiritual or moral sense." When used in the context of what we need to do to heal the earth and ourselves, both forms of the word apply. We need to repair the damage that we've done to Mother Earth by growing new tissue—planting trees, rebuilding soils, and cleaning up the mess we've made so our ecosystems can have a chance to heal themselves. Our friend Paul Hawken likes to remind us that regeneration is innate to every living creature. Every day when we sleep and when we eat, we are regenerating the cells in our body. We help other living things regenerate when we take care of our loved ones, our pets, and even our houseplants. If we can turn that care toward the environment and stop doing what we are doing that destroys life, the earth and all the living things on it will arc toward healing. Hawken says that "regeneration means to put life at the center of every act and decision."[32] And we believe that when we do that, we activate the second definition of regeneration: rebirth, or at least care, of our spiritual, moral selves.

THAT EXTRA 20 PERCENT

RESEARCH YOUR PERSONAL CARE PRODUCTS.

While we have yet to find a perfect resource for this, the most user-friendly and accessible is the Environmental Working Group's Cosmetics Database. The EWG is a respected nonprofit environmental organization committed to protecting health and helping families navigate consumer goods so they can make healthy choices. They produce many different consumer guides with easy-to-understand ratings systems. You can input any given product to see how it fares, or you can search by product type if you want help before your next trip to the store.

SHOOT FOR 120 MINUTES OF OUTSIDE TIME EACH WEEK.

Whether you spend that time outside all at once or split it up among several outdoor explorations, two hours is the number to shoot for. A large study by the European Centre for Environment and Human Health at the University of Exeter showed that people who hit that threshold were "substantially more likely to report good health and psychological well-being than those who don't."[33]

BUILD A "CAPSULE" WARDROBE.

You may have already heard of this trend of curating a small rotation (usually under thirty items) of high-quality clothing in order to streamline decision-making in the morning, save money on clothes, and commit to a signature style. If you've already done it—great! If not, consider doing it for all the reasons above *and* that it's good for the environment. Consider it the fashion version of meal planning—up-front thoughtfulness that makes your life easier and helps save resources that might otherwise go into the landfill.

SUPPORT REGENERATIVE AGRICULTURE.

Regenerationinternational.org has a map that helps you find farms near you. If you have access to a farmer's market, talk to farmers or local growers about their practices. For more ways to support regenerative agriculture, go to thejoyofwellbeing.com /regeneration.

Chapter Eight

In It Together

If you've ever watched *The Godfather*, or other movies or shows like it, you might have noticed that popular culture has a definite take on Italian immigrants: barrel-chested men with gargantuan bellies; rotund grandmothers carrying overflowing pots of pasta; and chain-smoking, hard-drinking people for whom a party is not complete without thick slabs of meat and cheese. Not to mention all of the guns and exuberant hand gestures. We're sure that there are plenty of holes in the big-screen version of Italian American life in the mid-twentieth century, but it turns out that the movies get a few things right. If you can look past the violent plotlines and horribly dated stereotypes, you'll also notice the other images and depictions that crop up—big families who live with each other or near each other, and a tight-knit community where trust, religion, and loyalty are valued. People who love to eat rich food, laugh and yell, hug and threaten, and have a definition of "the family" that goes well beyond blood ties.

Overall, the images of Italian Americans on the silver screen aren't exactly ones that exude health in the traditional sense. No one is devoted to exercise or green juice, going to the doctor is the last thing anyone has time for, and mental health assistance is anathema to the macho culture. But since we're talking Hollywood, of course there's a plot twist: all those tough guys with the big bellies might just be healthier than you.

In the real-life town of Roseto, Pennsylvania, scientists and researchers discovered a key to long life hiding in plain sight among Italian Americans: social connection. In the early 1960s, a local physician noticed that all of his patients from Roseto exhibited an almost shocking level of good health. Despite the fact that most of the men worked long, hard days in the slate quarry and their families ate lots of pasta and Italian sausage, smoked cigarettes and drank copious amounts of wine, there was a surprising lack of heart attacks in this one community. When he mentioned the strange phenomenon to a friend who was also a medical researcher, he kicked off a host of studies examining the lifestyle and health outcomes of the Roseto community. One study showed that in Roseto, the rate of heart attacks in people over sixty-five was half that of the nation, and for men under fifty-five there were *no* cases of heart attack.[1]

Just when we think we've got this whole health and well-being puzzle figured out, here comes Don Corleone…the paragon of longevity?

Don't reach for the cigars and meatballs just yet—there's a bit more to unpack here.

At first, the researchers who were working on the Roseto studies were scratching their heads. After all, what could account for such astonishingly low incidences of heart disease? Before they could figure out the Rosetans' secret to good health, researchers had to knock a few obvious things off their list, so they set up the study to control for environmental factors like water supply, geography, and health-care access. All of these factors were shared by four nearby communities, which the study used as controls. But when they looked at the health data over seven years in those communities, Roseto was the only town with a population-level low rate of heart disease. And what they found when they went to Roseto to get to the bottom of it would completely change the way that we look at what we now know is a key indicator of health: our relationships. Researchers hypothesized, and later confirmed, that what set Roseto apart was that it "displayed a high level of ethnic and social homogeneity, close family ties, and cohesive community relationships."[2]

This community of 1,600 people was founded by Italian immigrants in the late nineteenth century. And until around the late 1960s, the people in Roseto still lived as if they were in Italy, especially in terms of their social relationships, religion, and multigenerational homes. In a 2015 *PBS* documentary series about Italian Americans, filmmakers went to Roseto and spoke with elders who had been around for the original study. In fact, they were there to document what community members call the Big Time, an annual event that gathers together people with ties to Roseto, almost like a giant family reunion. There are parades, parties, and potlucks with lots of—you guessed it—pasta. Beyond the pure enjoyment of food and wine, what is so clear in the documentary is the real secret to the good life—care and connection.

Today, Roseto resembles the rest of America—it's no longer a cultural island—and so do its rates of cardiovascular disease. Since the early sixties, when Roseto's social cohesion started to break down, the mortality rates from heart disease also rose in the younger generation of Rosetans. The landmark study of Roseto that spanned fifty years tracked both mortality rates and the changing social traditions, confirming all of the earlier findings of other studies: older generations of Rosetans who benefited from that close-knit community in midcentury were far more protected from heart disease than their children.

When we watch the documentary about the Big Time, what sticks out to us is that everyone just looks so relaxed. The sense of community closeness that put Roseto on the map is evident at the reunion, even just as an echo of the past. This might be a once-a-year event, but it provides a brief window into what life in 1960s Roseto might have been like. You may know the feeling: extended family and friends around, wine flowing, boisterous laughter. Imagine family dinner every night, church suppers, and community gatherings. Imagine the relief you would feel knowing that you would be taken care of, no matter what happened, by your family or your neighbors. Imagine the joy in shared experiences, shared values, a shared life. We think one of the elders on the documentary said it best when he said, "Spaghetti is not the best thing for you all the time, you know. But I'll tell ya, if I'm gonna go, I'm gonna go with a meatball in my mouth."[3] That kind of security and exuberance for life was shared in Roseto on a deep cultural level in the early twentieth century. And because of that, they enjoyed immense health and longevity benefits. This phenomenon of increased heart health in tight-knit communities is now referred to as the Roseto effect, and the studies' core findings about the importance of social connection have been affirmed again and again throughout the years.

Having read the story of Roseto, you might be scratching your head. After all, it may seem like we're contradicting everything we just said in the previous chapters about nutrition and exercise, but it's a little more complicated than that. If you were to drop all your current ideas about healthy eating and moving your body, ignore everything we said in the last seven chapters, and start pounding the carbonara, you would not lower your rate of heart disease. While we might wish that were the case, it's simply not. Why? Because chances are, you do not live in a close-knit community like Roseto in the fifties and sixties. And *that* is what made the difference in their health. When you look at life and health holistically, you have to consider everything, not just what you put in your mouth.

We see this demonstrated by later generations of Rosetans, who began to skew closer and closer to the national average as the decades marched on. The Roseto of the fifties was more like a time capsule, or a transplanted community from Italy, than it was reflective of contemporary American communities, which were swiftly becoming more atomized. After all, the fifties gave birth to the concept of the nuclear family. People stopped living in multigenerational homes, and families began to spread out, building their own oases in huge suburban neighborhoods. They were going to work in all different directions, coming home, and waking up and doing it all over again without the same level of community engagement. Life in post– World War II America was more focused on efficiency, productivity, and wealth building than ever before. Family beyond your 2.5 kids was less and less of a focus, and communities were less intertwined. Sadly, as the decades wore on, this more isolated, less community- oriented way of life has only deepened. The advent of the internet and social media promised greater connection but delivered less. So, it's not that nutrition and exercise don't matter. They do, greatly. Especially when you are living without the security and stress resil- ience that communities like Roseto benefit from. What allowed them to eat the way they did and still live long healthy lives was the buffer to their stress response system that community and family provided. Seventy years later, we know beyond a doubt that the experience of strong social connection and the impact it has on our nervous system is fundamental to health and happiness. Without it, our hearts are less relaxed and full, and as a result, our biological systems are more vulnerable to death and disease.

Roseto was the tip of the iceberg, beckoning us to look more closely at the health and happiness implications of our relationships with other humans. New studies and research in the fields of immu- nology, neurobiology, and psychology have shown us that we need to weigh social connection equally (if not more) with other health and wellness practices. Understanding, of course, that we're never going to replicate Roseto, we can only learn from it and begin to integrate in our own lives its profound lessons about what it means to live the good life.

THE IMPORTANCE OF SOCIAL CONNECTION
TO WELL-BEING

Looking back on 2020, it's safe to say that at times it felt like we were all living through an unhinged, unintentional, and tragic social experiment, one that taught us a lot about ourselves, our government, and, perhaps most striking of all, how much we need each other. In order to stay clear of COVID-19, many people were forced (and chose) to isolate and social distance. Words like *quarantine* became part of our everyday vocabulary. Much of this was necessary to keep people safe, but there is no arguing that it had some seriously negative downstream effects. For well over a year, we were at varying points locked down, maintaining physical distance, unable to travel to see family, and enduring deep feelings of loneliness. The effect of all of this was catastrophic to the health and happiness of millions of people. At the time of this writing, over a million people have died from COVID-19 and many thousands more died or were harmed by the radical shift in our world that accompanied the virus. While not everyone has trauma with a capital *T*, we've all got plenty of scar tissue from years of trauma with a lowercase *t*, and we don't yet know the full extent of the harm.

In 2021, the American Psychological Association reported that at the beginning of the pandemic, 13 percent of Americans turned to alcohol or drugs as a way of managing their feelings about the pandemic. Some started using, while others just upped their usage. William Stoops, a professor of behavioral sciences at the University of Kentucky, is quoted as saying, "There's sort of a perfect storm of factors that we know increase drug use. People are more stressed and isolated, so they make unhealthy decisions, including drinking more and taking drugs."[4] Across the US, substance abuse and overdoses skyrocketed during the pandemic.[5] While there are numerous intertwined reasons why people turn to drugs and alcohol, the role of loneliness in mental health is significant. Social isolation both causes and exacerbates stress, and with fewer support systems available to help people cope during the pandemic, it's no wonder that self-medicating spiraled out of control.

Even for people with no prior substance abuse issues and good resources, drinking became a popular escape from reality. We say this from experience. It wasn't too far into spring of 2020 when a pop-up margarita cart appeared in an empty storefront that happened to be on our walk home from work. Did we stop by every single day for a month to have one or two (or sometimes three) margaritas? Yes. Yes, we did. Would we have needed to do that if we knew we were going home to a house full of extended family or friends with whom we could share our sorrows and worries and abject fear? Probably not. Loneliness is powerful. In fact, a study by Julianne Holt-Lunstad, PhD, a professor of psychology and neuroscience at Brigham Young University, compared smoking and loneliness and in a meta-analysis found that the mortality risk for loneliness is the same as smoking fifteen cigarettes a day.[6] Yikes.

We think this hard-won pandemic knowledge of the importance of social connection is something we can use to improve our lives. (Call us silver-lining people.) And because of this newfound understanding, we naturally got curious about the ways in which social health can impact personal health. This of course led us down a rabbit hole that began with the Roseto study but quickly took us to the more contemporary research being done about how strong social ties can impact everything from immune response to your microbiome. Here's what we found.

How Positive Relationships Calm Your Stress Response

We've already talked in previous chapters about how our fast-paced modern world has many people in a chronic fight-or-flight state and how terrible the downstream effects are: cardiovascular disease, diabetes, poor sleep. Well, it turns out that one beautiful evolutionary antidote to those elevated cortisol levels brought on by stress is other people. We learned about this during an interview with Marta Zaraska, a science journalist and author of the book *Growing Young: How Friendship, Optimism, and Kindness Can Help You Live to a 100*. Among many gems she shared with us was the story of how social connections can impact our vagus nerve, which is the longest and most complex nerve in the human body, one that plays a key role in regulating our stress response. When we are in close proximity to people we feel safe with, who show us love and affection, there is what scientists call a buffering effect on our fight-or-flight response.[7] This in part is because when we have real-life social experiences of connection with others, we engage the vagus nerve, which regulates the parasympathetic nervous system.[8] In fight-or-flight mode (the sympathetic nervous system) our body is revved up and pumping the cortisol into our systems so we are ready to do what we can to survive. When we are in the opposite mode, what is known as rest and digest, our parasympathetic system engages, and hormones like oxytocin and serotonin can help us get to a place of calm that allows us to do things like digest our food properly, reproduce, and think about the future. Basically, it's the opposite of survival mode—it's the living life mode. Inside our bodies is a constant, natural tug-of-war between the sympathetic and the parasympathetic. This is all good, as long as these two systems are in balance. Unfortunately, for many people, the sympathetic nervous system acts more like the bully on the other end of the rope. Luckily, we're not helpless: there are many ways to engage our parasympathetic nervous system to help the tug-of-war stay balanced. Activating and toning the vagus nerve may just be the biggest tool we have in our stress-reducing toolbox; it has been shown to help improve our mood, digestion, and immune system.[9] And for people whose fight-or-flight response is overactivated, social connection and the buffering effect it provides may be able to mitigate some of worst downstream effects of chronic stress.[10]

How Positive Relationships Can Strengthen Your Immune System

Our stress response system is intimately connected to our immune system. Think about it—you're in a forest and you stumble on a mountain lion. Your body is not only preparing to fight or run, it's (wisely) preparing to get hurt. A series of cascading hormonal reactions occur, one of which sends signals to the immune system to ramp up the kind of inflammatory processes that will help heal wounds. Interestingly, our stress response also downshifts the production of immune cells that guard against viruses and bacteria. If you're facing off with a lion, what's smarter, sending out the troops that heal wounds or the battalion that fights influenza? Unfortunately, having an acute, temporary stress response works out well for us only when we are actually facing the equivalent of a lion. When we are living as if every shadow and twig breaking is a lion, that is a chronic stress response—which is not where our bodies like to hang out, because it is so physiologically taxing. When we are chronically activating that stress response, researchers have found that we are inviting chronic inflammation (those first-responder immune cells just don't stop), which is linked to higher rates of cardiovascular disease, cancer, and autoimmune disorders.[11] This is all evidence of an immune system gone awry. When your body is in a chronic state of stress, it becomes its own worst enemy, disrupting the normal immune processes and functioning that we depend on.

It's well known that loneliness and lack of social connection can impart a huge amount of stress, triggering the kind of immune dysfunction that results from an overactive stress response. In that sense, it's not surprising that social isolation can make you more prone to illness. In one study, researchers even found that people who were socially isolated were 45 percent more likely to get sick with a common cold.[12] It doesn't take a Nobel Prize to figure out that the opposite is probably true—meaningful connection with others can improve our immune systems. In an article in *Psychology Today*, Emma Seppälä, PhD, wrote, "Social connection strengthens our immune system (research by Steve Cole shows that genes impacted by social connection also code for immune function and inflammation), helps us recover from disease faster, and may even lengthen our life."[13] It's no surprise that love is powerful medicine.

How Positive Relationships Can Boost Your Longevity

The science of longevity has some important things to say about social connection as well. In our interview, Zaraska referenced studies that demonstrated exercise lowers your mortality risk by 20 to 40 percent, and having a good diet is more or less the same at about 30 percent.[14] But, remarkably, being in a good romantic relationship, having friends, and being connected to your community can lower your mortality risk by 45 percent (similar to the 50 percent lowered risk found in Holt-Lunstad's meta-analysis).[15] Even though diet and exercise are critical to health and life span, these numbers suggest we are really missing something when we exclude social connection from the menu of healthy living practices. The wellness world is so focused on nutrition and exercise that it's easy to lose sight of our mental, emotional, and spiritual well-being. Humans are social beings. We evolved together, and we are still facing threats together, sharing discoveries together, and finding meaning together. It makes perfect sense that our physical health remains dependent on the strength of our connections to our tribe, whoever they might be. Science is just beginning to understand how critical these relationships are to our gene expression, stress response, immune system, microbiome, and even sleep.

While we wait for all the data to roll in about the mechanisms of this social and physical health connection, we have a pretty strong basis for action already. So then the next question is, how do we strengthen our social ties?

First, let's start with some definitions. Researchers and scientists who study human relationships and their intersection with our health define social connection a number of ways. In the previously mentioned meta-analysis of social connection and mortality risk, Holt-Lunstad describes the aspects of social connection that are most studied: how deeply we are connected to community, how supportive our social interactions are, and how much we think that our relationships are *actually* supporting us.[16] While those measures are used in scientific studies, it's not all that helpful for those of us who want to know exactly what kind of social connection benefits health and happiness. So, this is what we'll say: On a personal level, most of us know what it feels like to be in a relationship, whether with a friend, family member, or romantic partner, where we feel seen, supported, and connected in a way that makes our lives better. A strong social tie is the friend you know you can always call when things get really bad, even though they live three thousand miles away. It's a romantic partner who knows exactly what it means when your voice goes up an octave during a hard conversation with your brother and knows how to make you feel better after he leaves. A cohesive community is a web of individuals who act as a net, holding you up when it feels like everything else is dragging you down. Positive relationships are ones that challenge you, help you learn more about yourself, support your values and goals, and help you reach them. They make you feel physically, emotionally, and spiritually safe and strong. Put simply, healthy relationships make you feel good. Not all of the time (relationships are not supposed to be a cakewalk), but most of the time.

The bottom line on social connection is that good relationships are an essential part of what will help you be happy and healthy, throughout your life.

Everyone needs *their* people.

BARRIERS TO HEALTHY SOCIAL CONNECTION

While we learned a lot from the Roseto study in the 1960s, it didn't drastically reorder society and help us move toward more connection in our lives. In fact, if anything, modern life is becoming even more atomized and lonely. There are fewer multigenerational homes and more nursing homes and assisted living facilities. There is less real-life connection and more virtual connection. Our society is increasingly secular, which means fewer people gathering at the local church, temple, or mosque. When it comes to social connection, we face structural and cultural challenges, but perhaps none as big as the challenge of our increasingly digital lives. The initial promise of the internet and all things digital was that it would actually bring us closer together. Imagine it: you can talk to someone across the world whenever you want! You can send your beloved a message at all hours of the day, as many times a day as you want! There's no denying that there is something magical and hopeful about the internet. We certainly appreciate being able to FaceTime with loved ones when we're far apart. But, the dark side, the unintended consequences of an increasingly digitally mediated social life, are alarming to say the least.

In the last ten years researchers in neuroscience and psychology have discovered that the proliferation of social media sites and the uptick in usage have greatly impacted the mental health of young people, especially adolescent girls. (We have to be honest: this one keeps us up at night. In fact, ever since Colleen found out she was pregnant with a girl, she has been worrying about having a *teenage* girl.) While adolescent boys are also increasingly online, they spend more time playing video games with each other, whereas girls tend to be on heavily visual platforms like Instagram, TikTok, and Snapchat, which invite a toxic form of social comparison. In a wonderful (and terrifying) article in *The Atlantic*, social scientist Jonathan Haidt points out that for girls, interactions with Instagram don't end when they close the app. The perfect images of someone else's life tend to be something they ruminate on, sparking shame and anxiety.[17] For the heaviest users of social media, population-level rates of depression, self-harm, and suicide have skyrocketed since 2010, around the same time that social media platforms began expanding.[18]

The complex and chaotic social world of adolescents has always been a challenge, but when you think about the loss of context—an expression, a hand gesture, a tone of voice—that is experienced when you interact online, you start to see how quickly things can go off the rails. Kate Fagan's wonderful book *What Made Maddy Run* described the problem with text messages as a mode of communication: "It's an animated, easy-to-digest version: an exaggeration or a simplification, but not a reflection. And that would be fine if it weren't the main way we communicate with one another. We believe we're communicating with the humans we love and adore, and we are. But we aren't absorbing their humanity."[19] When we primarily use text message or social media to connect, *meaningful* connection becomes more elusive, and feeling truly seen seems almost impossible. Early in her book Fagan references a study that showed that instant messaging with people you love (in this case, teenagers and their parents) does nothing to stimulate an increase in oxytocin levels (the love hormone) or a reduction of levels of cortisol (the stress hormone). Basically, there is no benefit to that digital connection. But, interestingly, when researchers measured the oxytocin and cortisol levels of teenagers who were talking to their parents in person or on the phone, they found a reduction in cortisol and an increase in oxytocin.[20] In short: not all connection is created equal, and texting is not a substitution for the loving voice or touch of a parent.

Before you start to think we are self-righteous luddites, remember: we run a web-based media company. Obviously, digital platforms are a hugely powerful force, for both good and for evil—like everything else. The key to health and happiness with the internet is the same as with everything else: intention. Think about your current use of digital platforms and where you want to be with it. Less? That's probably the right answer for most of us, but maybe not. Some people are naturally better at self-regulating their online use than others (adolescents in particular are notoriously bad at impulse control), so this often comes down to knowing yourself. No matter what, don't forgo real-life connection for digital connection. You should aim to maintain a healthy balance of both. The more people swing to the heavy user end of the spectrum, the less satisfied with their social connections they seem to be. Importantly, exactly zero experts we've talked to recommend digital engagement over real-life interactions. The best thing you can get anyone to say about online interactions is that they are better than no interactions at all. The bottom line: treat social media and digital connection a little bit like sugar—a little is great and can bring you joy, but too much can damage your health and happiness.

BREAKING THE BARRIERS

The suburbs, social media, rugged individualism—it's increasingly obvious that much of the world is not set up for us to easily and readily connect with each other in meaningful ways. That means, unfortunately, we have to do a lot of that work ourselves. Of course, there are plenty of families and communities who get this right, are close-knit and supportive, and have healthy social ties. But for many of us, at least some of the time, it can feel like we are islands in a vast sea.

So, what's the first step in building social health despite the barriers? How do you connect *meaningfully* in real life?

We have to set an intention to get off the island. Then we have to pick up a paddle and jump in the boat. We need to do a diagnostic of the health of our relationships.

We have to show up for people, cultivate and strengthen friendships, and build networks of support where, disappointingly, there aren't any. The Dalai Lama said it best: Be the change you want to see in the world. The good news is, it's not as hard as you think—and depending on who you are, a little social connection goes a long way. There are plenty of ways to find the feelings of safety and support that make social connection so good for you. Here are the key categories of social connection, why they're important, and what you should consider about each.

FRIENDSHIP

It's something you've known since kindergarten: everyone needs a friend. Some of us are excellent at finding friends, and others of us, not so much. At one point or another in our lives, we will all struggle with connecting to others. Maybe it's relocating to a new part of the world. Maybe it's moving into retirement while our friends are all still working. Maybe it's just the crippling social anxiety we were born with. Maybe it's simply being male and middle-aged. Over the last thirty years there's been a precipitous decline in the number of close friendships that everyone has, but for men it's particularly bad. According to the Survey Center on American Life, "Thirty years ago, a majority of men (55 percent) reported having at least six close friends. Today, that number has been cut in half. Slightly more than one in four (27 percent) men have six or more close friends today."[21] This is one that Jason deeply relates to. While he has dialed in what foods and exercise he needs for well-being, friendship remains a struggle, he's lost touch with many of his friends from college and high school. We're all works in progress, and Jason knows this is an intention he needs to spend more time on.

We know friendship can be hard, but we also know that it's essential.

So, how many friends do I need?

This is a question we have asked ourselves and heard asked of our experts. A great article in the *New York Times* clocked the magic number at three to five, which lines up with the research as well as many people's gut sense. For instance, the *Times* reported on a study that showed that women who had at least three friends "tended to have higher levels of overall life satisfaction."[22] You may also have heard of Dunbar's number, which is a theory about how many connections the human brain can handle and maintain at once (150— not bad!). The author of the theory, anthropologist and psychologist Robin Dunbar, breaks that number down into groups of friends that are on a spectrum of close to casual and hypothesizes that our inner circle usually comprises about five friends.[23] While the three to five number is an important consideration, unsurprisingly, friendship experts say that it's really about quality over quantity.

A great way of getting to the heart of the quality question comes from Arthur Brooks. Ask yourself this: Do you have real friends or deal friends? Deal friends are friends with whom your relationship is what Brooks calls *instrumental*—meaning that you both get something out of being friends. Usually, these friendships are all about context. Maybe it's the parents from playgroup who help you feel less alone in early parenting and give great tips on sleep training. Maybe it's the co-worker in the cubicle next to yours who helps the day go by faster. Maybe it's the neighbor who it's helpful to be friendly with for a number of reasons, from borrowing milk to having someone keep an eye on your house while you're gone. Maybe it's the well-connected friend of a friend who always lets you know about professional opportunities. If you're having a hard time discerning who's a deal friend and who is a real friend, a good question to ask is, would I be friends with this person if it weren't for [insert suspected transactional element]? If the answer is probably not, you've got yourself a deal friend. A real friend, on the other hand, is someone you enjoy being with on their own merits; there isn't a whole lot of expectation or obligation, but there is clear communication and boundaries. You make each other laugh, admire and respect each other, and maybe even share a similar philosophy on life. These are friends who you want to keep around and will go out of your way to spend time with. They see you and appreciate you as you are, and vice versa.

No matter what stage you're at in life, it's good to periodically reevaluate where you are with friendship. Take a look at the friends you have in your life now and ask yourself these questions: How many are a source of support, comfort, joy, and resilience? How many of them live within a fifty-mile radius? How many of them are your real friends versus your deal friends? That's your number. If you have at least two (your spouse can count as one), you're on the right track. If you only have one, that's okay, but it might be time to branch out. If you have ten, it might be a good idea to do a quality check. Even if you have five close friends, if two of them are not what you would consider particularly supportive or caring, you might want to reevaluate the health of the relationship. Remember that there are different stages of life when it's natural to have fewer friends—hello, early parenthood—and phases where you probably have so many you are slightly exhausted. And don't worry too much about the changing nature of friendship—there's no prize for who has held on to the most friends from kindergarten. Relationships change in nature; friendships come and go. It's all good, and it's all about making sure you have the friends you need *now*.

PARTNERSHIP

If you are in a happy, supportive marriage or partnership, a mountain of scientific evidence shows that you've got the golden ticket to well-being. In comparison with single people, happily-marrieds are healthier and more satisfied with their lives.[24] But for all the single readers out there, it's important to remember that what is at the root of these benefits is not a piece of paper signed by your local county clerk; it's a feeling of safety that you get from another person. Relationship experts like Marta Zaraska note that it's not even necessarily about cohabitation; it's about the commitment. She says, "Your HPA [hypothalamus-pituitary-adrenal] axis can really calm down because this person is there for you for better or for worse. No matter what happens to you, this person will be there."[25] If you compare that to someone in a failing marriage, where both partners have one foot out the door, there is of course not going to be a health and happiness benefit, because the safety net is frayed. This might be controversial, but we're going to say it anyway: you need a partner. Even if that partner is a beloved pet (yes, there is evidence that pets help you stay healthy).[26] You need a real-life, meaningful, loving, two-way relationship that deepens over time. It is just too important to your health and happiness not to make it a priority. Being alone with your thoughts and TikTok is not productive for your mental health or life span. And, again for the single folks, not to despair: if you have a best friend or sibling you consider to be your ride-or-die, that person can just as easily take the place of a partner in terms of being a stabilizing force in your life.

FAMILY AND COMMUNITY

For many of us, partners come and go, and those we can count on most are family, broadly defined. Sometimes people are able to connect with their blood relatives in ways that feel deep and nourishing. On the other hand, some family-of-origin relationships can be toxic, challenging, and riddled with problems. For that reason, many people create and cultivate a chosen family that feels healthier and more supportive. No matter what your family looks like, when those relationships are strong and safe, they can add years to your life, as we saw clearly in the stories of Blue Zone centenarians. All of the positive family and community relationships we have, like friendship or romantic partnership, are key components of health. This is not an all-or-nothing proposition. At different times in your life, different kinds of relationships can cycle through your life, lifting you up.

While friendships, partnerships, and family relationships all contribute to a feeling of safety that helps calm your stress response, another important aspect of well-being is your connection to a larger community. Whether it's a church group, a book club, a group of friends, a neighborhood, or an activist organization, naturally, people who are part of these networks feel much less socially isolated and alone. (Having just made a move to Miami, away from our beloved mindbodygreen office and all the colleagues whose lives we were so intimately involved in, we are deeply feeling this.) The Roseto study in particular showed us the power of social cohesion among a larger group of connected people. Being able to count on your neighbors, extended family, and fellow church congregants shouldn't be underestimated. One of the hardest parts of the pandemic was how the concept of social distance challenged these ties. When communities needed to move to Zoom to stay connected, it strained our ability to be with each other in the meaningful ways that soothe our hearts and bodies. It became clear quickly the toll this missing piece was taking on all of us, which is why mutual aid organizations flourished, and for a while it seemed like we were all finally understanding how important it is to be there for one another.

INTEGRATION TIPS FOR BUILDING AND MAINTAINING SOCIAL CONNECTION

No matter what kinds of relationships we have that bring us safety, joy, and meaning, it's not always easy to prioritize them. But now that we know what an amazing return on investment relationships are when it comes to health and happiness, how can we focus more of our energy on keeping them strong? The truth is that like anything connected to well-being, you've got to invest at least some time and energy. The following tips are things that you can do that don't cost money, maximize the time you've got, and can help you make the most of the relationships that you've already developed.

Integration Tip #1: *Double your fun.*

Why not combine physical activity with social connection? Go for a run or a walk with a friend instead of hitting the gym. If you want to act like a real Blue Zones centenarian, find a beautiful hill to walk up while you're at it.

Integration Tip # 2: *Put it in the calendar.*

Marta Zaraska has a great solution for the "making time" problem. Give social connection the same health priority as your personal training session by putting it in your calendar. Date night with your partner. A walk with your sister. An early morning bird-watching class. Whatever floats your boat, put it in the calendar.

Integration Tip #3. *Make it IRL.*

Eye contact, physical touch, body language—there are so many critical social inputs that we're missing by conducting our social lives online, staring into a camera. While we won't suggest you quit social media altogether (although it's not the worst idea), what about committing to more of your social interactions being in real life? Choose a phone call over a text message (especially if you know someone in your life is not doing well). Choose an outdoor picnic over a Zoom happy hour. Choose to go into the office when there is collaborative work even though you can technically work from home every day if you want. Whenever you have the choice between IRL and virtual, choose IRL—even if it's a little extra effort.

Integration Tip #4. *Be a helper.*

There is always someone in your social network who could use a boost. Be mindful of who that might be at any given time. Maybe it's a friend going through a divorce who could use an extra phone call this week. Maybe it's an elderly neighbor who could really use help shoveling their driveway. Kindness and empathy go a long way to strengthening the relationships that matter most. Sometimes it's as simple as putting yourself in someone else's shoes and showing them that while you might not be sharing their discomfort, frustration, or pain, you are here for them while they're in it.

Integration Tip #5: *Reach out and connect.*

This one comes to us from the inimitable psychotherapist and relationship guru Esther Perel. We know that reaching out to old friends that we've lost touch with can feel a little scary and awkward. Do we text? Call? Connect on Facebook? And what do we say? It's pretty easy to get so in your head about what that outreach will look like that we shy away from doing it at all. When we interviewed Perel on our podcast, she reminded us that it's actually easier than we think. It's as simple as picking up the phone or sending a voice text and, as she put it, saying, "I was sitting here and suddenly you came to my mind. I thought of you, it's been so long, whatever happened to us? I don't know where you're at, but I would love to share some news." Perel points out that you'll know pretty quickly whether or not someone is interested in reconnecting, and that you'll probably be surprised by just how resilient some relationships are.

FINAL THOUGHTS

In some ways, it feels so obvious that strong relationships lead to greater health and happiness. Humans need each other—of course we do. But it's one of those paradoxes where you know the importance of something, and yet you take it so fully for granted. Maybe it's because the inner workings of a happy reunion with an old friend are mysterious; we can't see the oxytocin squirting through our veins and boosting our mood. We can feel it, sure, but we don't understand that it has implications well beyond the moment of that first embrace. Each joyful interaction, each time you feel connected to someone you love, you are doing something good for your health. It's almost too good to be true—something that feels good, that you do naturally, that can increase your well-being and help you live longer? What's the catch? If science has shown us anything in the last few years about social connection, it's that there is no catch; there are only rewards. This is one of those health prescriptions that every doctor should love to give: you must hang out more with your friends, spend more time kissing your beloved, snuggle your kids, and rub your good dog's belly at least five times a day.

Rinse, repeat, and live a long and joyful life.

THAT EXTRA 20 PERCENT

GO ON A SOCIAL MEDIA DIET.

Take two weeks and commit to a digital minimalist plan (shout out to Cal Newport, author of *Digital Minimalism: Choosing a Focused Life*). We know that people need their phones to interact with the world, but set yourself up for mental success by uninstalling addictive apps like TikTok, Twitter, and Facebook. Get rid of all the time-wasters, even if it's your personal or work email—save those for your computer time when you don't have a choice but to plug in. We know for some people this can seem like a stretch given our hyper-online lives. In fact, it might make you feel even *more* lonely for a bit. But we'd argue that even that is a good thing, because it's showing you very clearly what is missing. If in those two weeks you don't have enough contact with the people in your life to keep your social engines firing on all cylinders, that's a big red flag. You want to weight your social engagements toward real-life interactions, not the other way around.

BRANCH OUT.

Instead of focusing on strengthening new relationships, what about—*gasp*—cultivating some new ones? Making friends as an adult can be scary, especially if you're not relying on existing social networks like school and work to help you meet people. The best place to start is with what you're already interested and excited in. If you're into hiking, join a local hiking group. If you're a book lover, why not reach out to your local library to see what book clubs they know about. When it comes to asking someone out on a friend date, there's bound to be a little vulnerability involved, so be gentle with yourself. Not every friendship is meant to be. Keep going and try to stay open.

JOIN A COLD-WATER SWIMMING CLUB.

You may recall from chapter 6 that there are cold-water swimming clubs all over the world. Why not combine the bonding experience of freezing your buns off and the healthy dose of hormetic stress to double your return on investment?

Chapter Nine

Something Bigger

It was December 7, 2013, at eight o'clock in the morning, and Jason was on a surgical table, shivering under a threadbare gown. Why was he there? Azoospermia. It sounds a lot cooler than it is, actually—which is the condition of having no sperm in your ejaculate. (That may be too much information, but if you've been with us for nine chapters, we consider you a friend. And we think it is time to start talking about how men account for 40 percent of fertility issues.) We were nearly a year into our fertility journey, which felt more like a slog through hell, when the doctors got around to testing Jason's sperm count. By then Colleen had already been through three cycles of Clomid hormone injections. And now it was Jason's turn to be manhandled by modern medicine in the hopes of ending up with the children that we so desperately wanted. By that time, the family we had dreamed about and hoped for since our first months of dating felt further away than ever.

The surgeon who would perform Jason's sperm extraction procedure had flown into Manhattan from St. Louis and showed up that morning gulping a Mountain Dew and displaying a horrible bedside manner. Before he put Jason under, he said something to the effect of "I hope it works out. Because adoption is just not a good option. You know, those kids have so many problems." As Jason counted backward from ten, he remembers thinking, *Well, that's not a good sign.* He was both vehemently opposed to this doctor's belief and completely appalled by his bedside manner. The sad part about that encounter was that it was par for the course. Up until that point, trying to get pregnant had been all struggle—pain, discomfort, and improbable, unexplained disappointments. No doctor could tell us why Jason couldn't get the proverbial team out of the locker room, despite the fact he was healthy and had no obvious problems that could explain the condition. They couldn't even tell us for sure that he had any sperm at all until they got in there. This was a make-it-or-break-it, sperm-or-no-sperm situation. It was terrifying, not to mention disorienting. This was not the plan! Not only was it not the plan, we found ourselves smack in the bowels of Western medicine. Countless doctors. Conflicting opinions. Medical fuck-ups. And worst of all, very little centering of our humanity. Here was one of the most important experiences in life and we were doing it in a way that was so *not us.* What would be us? Well, an original vision of the plan involved joyful sex, followed by a fulfilling pregnancy, and potentially a water birth at home with lots of candles. The reality? Not so much. Instead, when Colleen did finally get pregnant with our daughter Ellie two and a half years after Jason's surgery, it was a high-risk pregnancy because of her history of pulmonary embolism. And while, thankfully, mercifully, it was an easy pregnancy, Colleen still had to deliver in a hospital with lots of specialists waiting in the wings in case something went wrong.

In short, three years, three miscarriages, nine embryo transfers, and twelve vials of sperm (turns out surgery was a gold rush) later, we had one beautiful, healthy child and another one that would join us two and a half years later. In the end, we were lucky, but nonetheless, in the years since when we've told this story to various friends, we've gotten a lot of slack jaws and wide eyes. Partly, because in 2016, this wasn't something we felt like we could talk about openly—especially working in the wellness space where self-empowerment (*you can heal yourself*) can quickly tip into blame (*maybe you haven't done enough work to heal yourself*). Thankfully, sharing our personal traumas is more accepted now, and we're glad, because we want to. We know that when we see others survive and thrive after gut-wrenching times, we are all reminded of the resilience of the human spirit. Our children are reminders of our strength and how much we have endured personally and as a couple. In hindsight, we admit, we went through a lot to have kids. And we were fully ready to adopt if having our own biological child didn't work out. We wanted a family, full stop. But it was more than sheer desire and striving for a goal that got us through those dark nights of the soul—it was something bigger, something a little harder to define. And to completely embrace the "soul" of mindbodygreen, we just knew it was our path. We knew we were meant to have a family. So even at our lowest moments, we stayed the course, knowing that we were living in alignment with our values and our purpose. Even if it wasn't easy, that underlying faith is what buoyed us, or at the very least helped us put one foot in front of the other. This is not the only time our belief in something larger than ourselves, and our deep sense of purpose has kept us on an even keel during difficult times, and kept us open to opportunities that would enrich our lives. It has happened over and over again, from taking the risk of starting a business to moving across the country.

This final chapter is about the biggest, most mysterious part of health and happiness: purpose and belief in what we call Something Bigger.

While there is emerging research about how purpose and spirituality play a part in our health and happiness, so much is unknown. For thousands of years humans have relied on religious traditions and social structures to guide them to answers about the biggest, most important questions in life: What are we here for? Why do we get out of bed in the morning? What's the point of suffering? What is my purpose on earth? How do I make it through the hardest moments of my life? How do we make sense of the randomness of suffering and prosperity? What does it mean to live the good life? Most books about health (and even happiness) just don't want to go there; they'd rather leave it to religion and philosophy. Which is understandable— after all, this territory of the metaphysical and the spiritual is by definition unexplainable, hard to pin down, and nearly impossible to account for in a clinical trial. But we believe that if you ignore the bigger questions, if you only focus on the corporeal, you might find yourself in a moment of crisis with no life raft, or at the end of your life realizing that you have spent your previous days swimming in the wrong direction.

You can eat right, exercise, and do all the things, but if you don't have a sense of purpose and a belief in something bigger than yourself, you will miss out on a critical piece of well-being. We aren't theologians, and we aren't happiness experts. But beyond our own profound experiences, we have had the opportunity to talk to researchers and doctors who have witnessed firsthand the power of purpose or spirituality to act as a buffer for depression, to help cancer patients leap into spontaneous remission, and to help people not only live their lives, but live them well. And news flash: the metaphysical and the spiritual *do* have a measurable effect on the physical body, stress, mental health, and maybe even disease. So here we are, once again, and always, in the realm of *it's all connected*. You can't be healthy if you're not happy, and if you don't stop to examine your beliefs, your values, and your purpose, you won't be happy for long, because, as you already know, life happens, and you have to deal with it. How well we deal with the bad times, how much attention we pay to the big questions of which path to choose, and how hard we work to cultivate joy in the everyday can be made much easier by thinking more clearly about Something Bigger and acting in service to our life's purpose with more intention.

In this chapter we'll talk about purpose and Something Bigger separately, because while they are inextricably linked and intimately involved, they are slightly different conceptually and practically. Let's dive in.

WHAT WE TALK ABOUT WHEN WE TALK ABOUT PURPOSE

Here's our society's working definition of purpose: it's what drives you to be the best you can be at your job; it's what helps you spend decades climbing the corporate ladder or launching a company; it's what keeps your eyes on the prize as you claw your way to achieving fame, pleasure, money, power, or admiration. Purpose can be highly impacted by culture and circumstance. For instance, over the past few years, the pandemic has caused many of us to realign our purpose and priorities. From the Great Resignation to Quiet Quitting to all the folks who have relocated based on quality of life, people are reevaluating what they are striving for.

Everyone has something that drives them to do the things they do every day and make the choices that they make. One person's purpose in life might center on making enough money to be financially comfortable, so they get a job on Wall Street. Another person's purpose might be to gain the respect and admiration of their peers, so they wrestle their way to the top of the academic ladder. For others, it might be to live in pursuit of different experiences as a digital nomad, traveling the world, eating delicious food, meeting interesting people, and having lots of sex in Bali. There is nothing wrong with any of these life paths per se; the problem lies in centering purpose on any one pursuit or identity, particularly if these pursuits fall into certain categories. In an interview with Arthur Brooks, author of *From Strength to Strength: Finding Success, Happiness, and Deep Purpose in the Second Half of Life*, he describes what philosophers and theologians have long called the "idols that occupy us."[1] He describes them as pursuits that "overpromise and underdeliver" and turn us away from authentic happiness; they are money, power, pleasure, and fame. The reason that so many religious and philosophical traditions over the millennia have tagged these pursuits as problematic is that they are fleeting, unreliable, and characterized by diminishing returns. At some point in our lives, and definitely by the end of our days, these achievements fail to deliver meaning and contentment. If you've ever gambled in Vegas, you know what we're talking about—the high is great, but more likely than not you are walking out of the casino with empty pockets. What many happiness experts observe is that all too often, people anchor their life's purpose to one of these "idols" at the expense of doing things that would truly make them happy, like staying physically and mentally healthy, eating well, maintaining strong social connections, practicing gratitude, and being in service to something larger than yourself.

These earthly idols collide in a most spectacular way on the internet. For example, if you can position yourself as a social media influencer and get paid by corporations to advertise their wares to your hundreds of thousands or maybe millions of followers, well, by many people's standards, you've hit the jackpot: money (top influencers are rumored to make up to $1 million per post[2]), power (they call you an influencer for a reason), pleasure (so many likes—dopamine hit!), and fame (you might just get an invite to the Met Gala or the Oscars). In a 2019 *CBS News* report, the social media influencer economy was poised to be a $6.5 billion industry by the end of the decade.[3] Is it any wonder that a majority of kids in the United Kingdom and the United States want to be influencers when they grow up?[4] And it's not just the kids. As reported by *People*, in a survey of people between thirteen and thirty-eight years old, a market research firm found that 86 percent of them wanted to become a social media influencer.[5] We find this alarming on a lot of levels, but here are the two big ones: (1) Where will the people who actually make the world functional come from if everyone is aspiring for engagement on a social platform? (2) We have to be conscious of where we put our attention and thoughts, and one thing we know for sure is that children's attention on social media is not making kids happier. Considering the mental health crisis that today's youth are living through, we deeply question whether or not society's biggest and best idea of purpose is doing anything to help our kids understand what a happy, healthy life looks like.

Generation Z spans the spectrum of how this group thinks about goal versus well-being. We have seen Olympic gymnast Simone Biles prioritize her own mental well-being over achievement at the Olympics. Singer Shawn Mendes publicly canceled part of his tour to focus on mental health. On the other end, there are people still hyperfocused on climbing the ladder, hitting all their marks, and achieving wealth and success. Happiness expert and Yale professor Laurie Santos, PhD, relayed her concern about her students like this: "I'll have conversations with first-year students on campus who will ask what fourth class they should take to make sure they get that job at Google by the time they're 24. They come in planning this set of next steps, in part because that's how they got here in the first place… They develop this implicit belief that there is a path that's correct, and if you can figure out the Easter eggs, you can be on it."[6] She goes on to say that students frequently challenge her on the importance of money in cultivating happiness, even though studies clearly show that unless you are in poverty, making more money will not substantially move the needle on happiness. Once she has thoroughly disrupted her students' core beliefs about what will make them happy and what they should strive for, Santos says they often come to her exasperated and ask the question of all questions: "Then what's the purpose of life?"

This is not just a Gen Z or millennial problem. For eons, people have stumbled over this larger question about purpose, fulfillment, and what will make us truly happy. Boomers are not exempt. Arthur Brooks told us an amazing story about his experience on an airplane (which he also recounts in his book) overhearing a conversation between an elderly husband and wife who were sitting behind him. The man was clearly distressed, complaining about how irrelevant he felt in his life. He felt that no one cared about him, paid attention to him, or took him seriously anymore. His wife tried to comfort him, but Brooks could hear how unhappy the man was, how inconsolable. When the plane landed and the lights came up, Brooks was shocked to discover he was a rich, famous, and well-respected man, someone everyone would recognize and who has achieved great heights in his career and was now in his eighties. This was a watershed moment for Brooks, who was in his early fifties at the time and at the height of his own career; it made him think, "I wonder how long I can keep this party going…this guy had ten times the party I ever had. And he was pretty unhappy."[7]

Brooks would go on to write an entire book about how we have been working with what he calls the "misbegotten model of banking," one that tells us if we gather up enough success and achievements, we can die happy. Instead of fat savings accounts of Oscars, Pulitzers, and Nobels, Brooks thinks what we really need is a "happiness 401(k)," a plan for finding and cultivating ongoing, sustainable happiness, the kind that comes from understanding what truly brings enduring meaning to your life, not just the temporary states of being satisfied, full, proud, pleasured, or admired. There's nothing wrong with setting goals or having ambition as long as you understand that you won't find enduring happiness in reaching those goals. So many of us make the mistake of thinking that when we just do X, then we will be happy. When I finally buy a house, I'll be content. When I finally get tenure, I can relax. When I finally make a million dollars, life will be good.

There's a name for this tendency humans have to run from one pleasure or goal to the next: the hedonic treadmill. The problem with the hedonic treadmill is its fundamental principle: that you always return to your baseline happiness. You could become the top-paid influencer in the world, and that would feel really good for a while, but then you would go right back to being as happy or unhappy as you were before. Except now, you've gotten a little dopamine hit and you can't wait to jump right back on the treadmill and find another high. This happens with money, fame, success, admiration—all the idols. They give us a bump of happiness, but it never lasts. And we always want more. Nothing will kill your joy faster than chronic dissatisfaction.

So, what's the solution? Philosophers, theologians, social scientists, and happiness experts have been trying to answer this question for a very long time. The problem is part biology—we are built to "explore and exploit" our environment to gain bigger and bigger prizes like food, water, and shelter. Getting those things feels good, so we want more and more. But once you have satisfied those basic needs, it gets a lot trickier. The other problem is society—we are inundated by misleading images of what the good life looks like, whether that is a giant yacht or a splashy book review in the *New York Times* (I mean, we wouldn't turn that one down). And so, we want, want, want according to what we see all around us. Humans are wanting machines, after all.

The trick is to manage those wants, understand that they are not the path to enduring happiness, and spend your personal resources more wisely. Can you climb the corporate ladder like there's a rocket up your butt? Sure! But it means you are going to give up time with friends and loved ones, time in nature, time understanding yourself and the world, and time you could spend serving others and fostering connection with your fellow humans. If you choose the idols of earthly delights, instead of making those big deposits in your happiness 401(k), you're essentially spending all your money now. From where we stand, spending a little money now is great—life is also about enjoying the ice cream and the job well done, but it's not only about that. We're all for diversifying your happiness portfolio.

No one can tell you what your deeper purpose in life should be, nor should they. That's a personal journey of discovery. Personally, we define purpose as a higher calling (or callings) that pushes you through the hard times, and the belief that what you're doing is good and meaningful, and that it nourishes your body and your spirit. Our friend Dan Buettner told us that one strong association between longevity and people who lived in the Blue Zones was a deep sense of purpose in their lives. The way he described it, "people know why they wake up in the morning." This purpose is something that *throughout their lives* makes them feel relevant, needed, and connected to the world around them, which in turn has a powerful effect on health. In our interview with Dan, he mentioned that if you could put purpose in a capsule, it would be a blockbuster drug, and that the National Institute on Aging has even quantified it. In one study they found that people who had a well-defined sense of purpose lived eight years longer than those who did not.[8]

INTEGRATING PURPOSE

The big question now is, how do I find my purpose?

While purpose is something everyone should be in the market for, it's not exactly something you can go pick up at Target or work through in a few sessions with your therapist. You might need to spend some time searching for your purpose, reflecting on it, and committing to it. Your purpose might already be there in the background; you just haven't been paying enough attention. Or it might be something that shifts and morphs during the different phases of your life. Your purpose might be something that strikes you like a bolt of lightning. A major theme running throughout this book applies here: it's all personal. The best anyone can do is help guide you toward your own answers. Here are some ideas for how to find, cultivate, and live more closely in alignment with your purpose.

Reflect.

The practice of finding purpose and Something Bigger requires deep intentionality. It doesn't just happen. You make it happen by setting an intention to seek and act. So where do we start? Questions.

- What is your purpose right now?
- Why do you get out of bed in the morning?
- Is it about achieving, or is it about finding joy and helping others?
- What feels like a higher calling?
- Do you feel useful and relevant?
- Are you doing work that marries what you love with what you're good at?
- What parts of your life are devoted to caring for other people?
- What are the special ways that you can and want to contribute to bringing good things to the world?

A hot tip we got from Arthur Brooks: Write your "mission statement" and try to articulate what purpose means to you in terms of success for yourself and service to others.

Cultivate.

The Greater Good Science Center at the University of California Berkeley has some great evidence-based suggestions on their website for finding and cultivating purpose in life. They tout empirical studies that suggest that reading widely can help connect people with their purpose by exposing the reader to diverse peoples (both real and fictional), new ideas, and a greater understanding of the world.[9] Another suggestion from the center is to "turn hurts into healing for others" in order to connect to yourself and others in a way that is deep, meaningful, and motivating. For instance, if you are someone who struggled with substance abuse in the past, you might find yourself in a position to help others, whether as a sponsor or a mentor. There is great power and healing in turning your pain into something positive for someone else.

Prioritize.

After reflecting on what your purpose might be today or what you want it to be in the future, it's important to center that purpose in your life. If you find yourself wanting to spend more time fulfilling that purpose but keep getting stymied by a lack of time, it could be time to reorient. Not everyone has the flexibility and capacity to combine the way they make money and their purpose. If you do have that ability, seriously consider the ways in which your life would be better if you were spending more of your workday in alignment with your values and purpose. If that's not possible, perhaps spend some time thinking about how you can center your purpose more effectively in your non-working hours. The goal for everyone should be to keep in close contact with purpose, the thing that brings joy, meaning, and motivation.

CONNECTING TO SOMETHING BIGGER

Spirituality. Religion. Faith. Belief. These are loaded words. Whether or not the baggage they carry for you is good, bad, or just a gaping hole, you have to admit these words pack some serious heat. Which is why we personally prefer to tuck them all under a large, friendly, multicolored umbrella that we call Something Bigger. We can't just look out for our physical and mental health, we've got to keep an eye on our metaphysical health as well, because—you guessed it—it's all connected. To us, this means believing in, experiencing, and leaning on something bigger than ourselves, something bigger than the world we can see with our eyes, something bigger than our immediate concerns and problems, something that helps us stay the course, and something that helps us maintain the perspective we need to be resilient and strong in tough times. Something Bigger, like purpose, is something you must discover and define for yourself. For some people it might be the understanding that we are all deeply connected on a cellular, vibrational, and spiritual level. For others it might be the belief that the highest calling of anyone is to love other people. For many, Something Bigger is God. For us it is believing that there is some larger force at work guiding us on our path, whether that path is creating a business, cultivating our relationships, or working toward the greater good, even if we can't fully grasp it in every moment. Our Something Bigger helps us keep the faith that we are making positive ripples in the world that extend far beyond our line of sight.

There is a strong argument to be made for having both purpose and Something Bigger guiding that purpose. If you're uncomfortable with anything resembling spirituality, we get it, but hear us out. You could just focus on purpose, sure. But what happens when your purpose is shaken by traumatizing events beyond your control that make you question everything? What determines how you treat other people in the world? What underpins your own personal moral code? What happens when people you love are hurt or die? What happens when you yourself are hurt or are dying? The last two questions especially are things we don't want to think about, and yet, as we have learned from the last few years of the pandemic, they are things we will all experience. Having a strong connection to Something Bigger, in whatever form that takes, helps us answer those deeply important questions. In those low moments of our lives, nothing could be more important. We all know that. But what about the everyday?

Many people view Something Bigger as what we need to call on only in case of emergency—kind of like the oxygen masks on a plane. Does spirituality really matter that much in the day-to-day? For a long time, we weren't sure about this ourselves. Colleen grew up in a "completely secular but celebrates Christian holidays" kind of household, and she has been pretty wary of organized religion all her life. Jason, on the other hand, was raised Christian and even taught Sunday school as a teenager, but as an adult his spiritual practice evolved to meditation and the occasional Joel Osteen podcast. To him spirituality is personal, and he was excited when he began to see science emerge in support of a faith-based practice. After a lot of digging and reading and deep conversations, we have both come to a much different resting place with spirituality than we had before.

Our answer to the question about whether Something Bigger is important in the day-to-day is unequivocal. One of the experts who really blew our minds, and changed them, about the importance of Something Bigger to our well-being is Lisa Miller, PhD, author of *The Awakened Brain: The New Science of Spirituality and Our Quest for the Inspired Life*. Her body of research and contributions to the field of clinical psychology have revolved around the idea that there is science behind spirituality, and that everyone can use it to make better decisions, be healthier, and live what Miller calls an "inspired life."

As a postdoctoral researcher at Columbia University Medical School, Miller began looking into what factors in childhood are protective against depression. Using data from another researcher who had conducted a massive fifteen-year longitudinal study, she combed through the intersecting data points, trying to find the relationships between them that might give her insight into whether or not spiritual experiences played into resilience against depression. Her own personal experience up to that point had piqued her curiosity, but she never expected to discover just how hugely impactful spirituality would be. With valuable answers to questions about spirituality ("How personally important is religion or spirituality to you? How frequently do you attend religious services?") in the data sets, Miller was able to use a complex equation to connect the dots between the participant's experience of spirituality and their mother's experiences of spirituality.[10] What she found was that "when mother and child were both high in spirituality, the child was 80 percent protected against depression, compared with mothers and children who were not concordant for spirituality, or mothers and children who were not high in spirituality. In other words, a child was five times less likely to be depressed when spiritual life was shared with a mother."[11] For context, her research showed that spirituality not only was a hugely protective factor, but it was the *biggest* protective factor over the course of an entire lifetime.

We know the question you're asking yourself now: What exactly is the definition of spirituality? Is it praying daily? Is it going to church? Is it more of a mindset? In our conversation with Miller, and in her book, she defines it as a "capacity for transcendent awareness and in particular, a transcendent relationship."[12] Neither of these things need happen in the form of organized religion or belief in a specific god. The transcendent relationship piece might be feeling loved and embraced by something bigger than ourselves, whether that is a higher being or nature. Whereas transcendent awareness might be the belief or experience of there being something bigger that we are intimately connected to and that "we matter, belong, and are never alone."[13] Miller uses the metaphor of a point and a wave to describe what it means to have transcendent awareness—you understand that you are one distinct individual (a point), but also that you are an inextricable part of something larger that moves together and is connected (a wave). Anything you do that enhances and foregrounds those types of awareness is exercising what Miller calls your "spiritual muscles." There are plenty of ways to tap into deeper meaning and connection in your life, whether it is through prayer, a walk in the woods, or volunteering to pick up trash on the side of the road—whatever helps you feel clarity and connection beyond your individual material experience and brings you closer to what feel like universal truths and experiences that we all share.

The benefits of deepening your ability to connect with Something Bigger go well beyond fostering resilience to depression. It's also about well-being, contentment, and finding enduring satisfaction in your life. And it makes sense, right? If you are convinced that you are alone in the world, just a physical body that is born alone and dies alone, that's going to make you feel isolated, especially at the low moments. And if you can't connect to something deeper, something more meaningful at the core of your existence, something that buoys you on its wave of collective experience—it is so much easier to fall into the trap of chasing money, fame, and power. Laurie Santos, in her *New York Times Magazine* interview says, "There's a lot of evidence that religious people, for example, are happier in a sense of life satisfaction and positive emotion in the moment." But she is quick to point out that it seems to be less about the belief part of religion and more about what you do within that "cultural apparatus" and how being part of it motivates you to action in the first place. She notes that "what it tells us is, if you can get yourself to do it—to meditate, to volunteer, to engage with social connection—you will be happier."[14] We know that many belief systems are flawed and inspire people to engage in harmful behavior—which we don't condone in any way—but we also think Santos is right, and that creating your own container or "apparatus" for engaging with purpose and community is critical.

As committed members of the It's All Connected Club, we would be shocked if cultivating a spiritual practice conferred all these psychological benefits (stronger brain, less depression and anxiety, more resilience and creativity) and *didn't* also help our physical bodies in some way.[15] We're only scratching the surface on how spirituality can affect your health, but the limited data we do have makes a clear connection: individuals with some sense of spirituality have enhanced mental health, immune function, and longevity.[16] So it's worth it to strengthen your spiritual muscles.

How, exactly?

This is going to depend a little on your background, your core beliefs, and what your values are. There are going to be questions— so many questions. What if you have grown up in a religion and rejected it? What if you have been harmed by religion? What if you were raised atheist and just don't even know where to begin? What if you're just highly skeptical of all of this?

Before you start listing the reasons why this health and happiness practice isn't for you—and it's okay if it's not—consider that you are built for Something Bigger. In fact, there's a whole part of the brain that is designed for your spiritual life. In her research using MRI scanners, Lisa Miller discovered that the brain has what she calls a "natural docking station for spiritual awareness."[17] In concert with research partners from Yale, Miller put people in an fMRI machine and scanned their brains while they recounted a spiritual experience. They located two brain networks that light up during these experiences—the ventral attention network and the frontotemporal network. The former is a neural network that allows us to focus on perceptions beyond our current experience, allowing us to let in information that tells us, as Miller puts it, that "the world is alive and talking to us"; the latter network she describes as "where we feel the warm, loving embrace of others and of life itself."[18] And then finally, there is the parietal lobe of the brain, which deals with meaning and belonging. This study revealed that no matter whether the participants had had a spiritual experience in nature or in church, the same neural pathways lit up. This tells us that we all have the innate ability to tap into transcendence. There are actual parts of the brain built for this! And just as with exercising different muscle groups or different cognitive modes, you can strengthen your spiritual neural pathways by engaging them.[19] Miller says, "spiritual awakening is a choice we can make at every moment—a choice of how we perceive the world and ourselves."

INTEGRATING SOMETHING BIGGER

It's important to understand that we don't have to start going to church to cash in on the benefits of Something Bigger and spiritual awakening. We simply have to turn toward some intentional practices to help support and cultivate this awareness. One helpful construct that Miller offers is from a study that she did in 2016 that sought to research the universal dimensions of spirituality. They gathered information on spiritual practices from 5,500 participants, including people from major religions—Christianity, Islam, Hinduism, Buddhism—and people who considered themselves nonreligious or secular. The participants hailed from China, India, and the United States, demonstrating unified underlying aspects of their spiritual lives.[20] Miller and her team decided to call these aspects the "five common spiritual phenotypes": Altruism, Love of Neighbor as Self, Sense of Oneness, Practice of a Sacred Transcendence, and Adherence to a Moral Code. Across religions and geography, these phenotypes persisted as the way spiritually people expressed their engagement with the transcendent. Because we aren't writing an academic paper, we're going to call these five by slightly different monikers in hopes it will help you remember them. These are some simple access points to the divine, all of them entirely free, and most of them requiring very little time. Strengthening muscles is a long game, so don't be afraid to start slow, and keep it consistent.

Do Good

This one is pretty straightforward. By helping other people, you widen your gaze beyond yourself, in essence acknowledging and deepening the somatic understanding that we are all connected. Showing care (in many ways) for others in your community feels good. And by volunteering, engaging in mutual aid, participating in climate activism, or baking cookies for the church bake sale, you are practicing "relational spirituality," which, according to Miller, helps connect us not only to each other but also to the divine.

INTEGRATION TIPS:

Start simple by asking a friend or neighbor how you can help. Be there fully for a friend who is going through a difficult transition. Find a group that speaks to your soul and volunteer your time. Offer to mow your elderly neighbor's lawn, buy groceries for the person ahead of you in line at the store, volunteer at your local animal shelter, or volunteer to hand out brown-bagged meals to the unhoused. Doing Good in the world doesn't need to be flashy—you don't need a million dollars to give to charity, you just need to show up for people. However, if you *do* give money to charity, that's great, and you'll get a bigger benefit if you see the good it's doing by engaging actively in that organization.

Remember the Golden Rule

This is a popular intersection of many religions: treating others as you'd want to be treated. Similar to doing good for others, this is important because it helps connect you with your neighbor by attempting to walk a mile in their shoes. In order to act on the Golden Rule, you have to do some role playing first. It demands that you stop, decenter yourself, and take another perspective. When you acknowledge another person's sacred humanity and make a choice to treat them with respect, you are tapping into that relational spirituality once again.

INTEGRATION TIPS:

This one you've been aware of since you were a kid, so it's not a new idea, but it should become a more intentional practice. Start with one difficult interaction or moment of friction and give yourself a beat.

Think about the person you are in front of, or across the internet from, and think about all you don't know about their situation, intentions, and needs. Then think about how you want to be treated in the vacuum of knowledge. Do you want others to assume bad intent? If you are late responding to an email, would you want that person to think you just don't care, or that you're disrespectful and bad at your job? Or would you want them to give you the benefit of the doubt and wait to find out what the real reason is for your tardiness? Think of how many times a day these little banal irritations with each other rub us the wrong way. Sometimes we can shrug them off, and other times they can derail us emotionally for hours. When you consider it from that perspective, this is not a purely selfless practice. By giving others some grace, you improve your own emotional state as well.

Seek Connection

Connection comes in many forms, but the kind we're talking about here isn't purely about friendship or love. It's about all of those things *and* Something Bigger, or a sense of oneness with other people, nature, God, and the universe.

INTEGRATION TIPS:

- *Be Open.* There are many ways to feel more connected and more in sync with the universe, but most of them begin with a mindset of openness. You have to be open to connection before you can experience it. Tune in to this in whatever way feels natural to you—whether it's meditation, breathing or starting your day with some mantras.
- *Smile.* Smile at the first five people you encounter every morning on your walk to coffee or grocery store run. It might seem benign, but it's powerful. On our podcast Stephen Trzeciak, MD, MPH, recounted a story about how a smile could literally

save someone's life: When a leading suicide expert, Thomas Joiner, PhD, was conducting research, he found in a suicide note this sentence: "I'm going to walk to the bridge and if one person smiles at me, I will not jump."[21]

■ *Learn from the past.* A good place to start is by thinking about what connection and oneness means to you. Have you ever had a moment where you experienced the vast interconnectedness of life? What frame of mind were you in? What was the circumstance?

■ *Ritual.* Many find connection in tradition and rituals, both new rituals that you have created and ones that have been passed down religiously, culturally, or intergenerationally. Rituals—ceremonies where there are prescribed actions performed in the same order—help us sink into the fundamental truth that we are part of a long lineage of people who have struggled, rejoiced, and lived in the same ways that we are now.

Ride the Wave

Riding the wave to us means seeking out experiences that encourage us to recognize that we are not merely a single point bobbing in the sea, but we are also always part of a wave. As waves do, they rise and fall, become more or less noticeable to us, but we always should strive to hang on to the awareness that we are moving in concert with every other thing in the living world. Once we recognize that more readily, we can ride the wave with ease, knowing that we are not alone, that our actions matter, and that there are larger forces propelling us.

INTEGRATION TIPS:

■ *Consider synchronicity.* The dictionary definition of synchronicity is "the simultaneous occurrence of events which appear significantly related but have no discernible causal connection." If you've experienced this phenomenon before, you know it is powerful. It's impossible not to feel like there is some larger path being revealed, or some meaning that you can't comprehend but that you simply trust. The tip here is simply to pay attention to moments of synchronicity: be aware of how they make you feel and what they could mean if you looked at them in a slightly different way. Instead of brushing off these collisions of meaning and circumstance as mere coincidences, ask yourself, *What if I'm seeing the wave?*

▪ *Immerse yourself in art.* Music, poetry, dance, painting. Thousands of years of human achievement are at our disposal when it comes to connecting to Something Greater. Great artists like Leonardo da Vinci, Emily Dickinson, and James Baldwin reveal the interconnectedness of the human experience and the transcendence of creativity. Humans have been poking around and peeking at the divine for as long as we've been writing on cave walls. So why not experience the wave from someone else's point of view? Like ritual, absorbing and meditating on art can help us feel connected to a lineage of seekers of meaning. So head to the local art museum when they have free admission days or stop by the library and check out the poetry section. We promise you'll find a new perspective.

▪ *Mindfulness.* We'd be pretty remiss not to mention mindfulness and meditation in a chapter about spirituality. We all know that the health benefits of mindfulness are increasingly confirmed by science, but another reason to meditate might just be the original one: spiritual awakening. The same holds true for prayer, which is another way to come into contact with oneness and set aside the ego. If you haven't meditated or prayed before and are at all interested, this can be a beautiful way to amplify awareness and perception, clear your mind, and maybe even connect with Something Bigger.

Be Ethical

This one is simple, so simple you might think it's not even worth mentioning. But unless you have never lied, stolen, cheated, or hurt anyone, you should probably consider it. So we say, have a moral code and do your best to live by it. By now you should be sensing the theme that what contributes to the development of our own spiritual awareness is acting in accordance with the understanding that we are all connected, and thus, living like what we do has implications for the whole. If you act like you're in it just for yourself, then in a real way you are reinforcing that worldview and contributing to your own isolation as a result.

INTEGRATION TIPS:

We'll skip over the biggies like don't hurt people or steal, because that should be obvious. Basically, try to be a good person, as often as possible. Maybe it's as simple as a concerted effort to take back your grocery cart every single time, no matter how late you're running. Maybe it is calling your mom every weekend. Maybe it's keeping your cool with the frustrating customer service representative. We all have room for improvement on this front, so don't overthink it; just try to do the right thing.

FINAL THOUGHTS

Faith and purpose have played a huge role in our lives, and we hope you'll think deeply about how they might intersect with yours. Life is mysterious. We don't always get to have all the answers. Jason still has no idea why he had azoospermia—there was no medical reason given. And that's okay, if you let it be. In a world where so much is unexplained, cultivating the ability to let go and let the wave of life carry you in times of need, is critical. It's what keeps many people clear of crippling anxiety, substance abuse, and mental health collapse.

While we had a happy ending with our fertility struggles, unhappy endings are a reality for everyone at one point or another.

Sometimes bad things happen to good people, and there are simply no explanations to offer any comfort. When Jason lost his dad suddenly at nineteen and one of his closest friends at twenty-seven, what got him through those losses was faith in Something Bigger.

Sometimes the future is uncertain and tenuous, and we have no idea how things will turn out. Colleen spends more time than she likes to admit worrying about the world that our girls are inheriting and what that means for the future of all children. Between the youth mental health crisis and the cultural obsession with achievement, it's hard to embrace the inevitable letting go that comes with parenthood. For her the fears of the parenting journey to come are balanced by leaning into the decisions we are making now, knowing that we're being purposeful and intentional about how we raise our girls and knowing that the rest is out of our hands.

Sometimes you just have no idea what to do. We all face decision points in our lives that could go either way but we know they are deeply consequential. Should I move across the country and take my dream job but leave friends and family behind? Should I say yes to that promotion that I worry will burn me out? When we were first talking to people about writing this book, many advised us to come up with a catchy finite protocol or solution—something with *ten days* or *five steps* in it—and build the book around that. We understood the wisdom of it (those books sell like crazy), but we knew we couldn't write something like that with integrity. We couldn't pretend that we had some ultimate solution when in fact we know it to be a journey. What kept us on our path was faith in our purpose. All we had to really do was ask whether or not that kind of book would be honest and grounded in our values.

Purpose and faith are not only for tough or uncertain times; they deepen our experience of living in the good times. It's very easy to live on the surface of this life, make small talk, do the bare minimum for others, and spend all your time hustling. But if you want to make it to 80 percent of your maximum health and happiness, you've got to put real money in the happiness 401(k), consistently, over time. What's beautiful about where this metaphor breaks down is that the investments you make are not all for the future—they are also doing double duty by connecting you to the now. When you carve out time to deepen your connection with others, when you spend a solitary and nourishing afternoon hiking, when you devote yourself to raising money for cancer, when you eat a bowl of perfectly ripe strawberries, and when you give yourself a minute to soak up the beauty of a bright red cardinal balancing on your birdfeeder, you are living more fully in the now, which is of course its own reward. Most importantly, remember: you were meant for Something Bigger.

THAT EXTRA 20 PERCENT

JOIN A FAITH OR SPIRITUAL COMMUNITY.

This one won't be for everyone, but there's no denying that having the traditional structure of a spiritual community that comes ready-made with its own rituals, ceremonies, and community is beneficial when it comes to deepening your spiritual life. It can help you stay on track with your commitment to Something Bigger and connect you to people who may be on the same path.

READ WIDELY.

There are so many books out there about faith and spirituality and Something Bigger. Especially if you grew up in a household with no faith tradition or have actively rejected religion, getting your spiritual feet wet with a smorgasbord of beliefs and practices will help you find your footing. For a big, soulful list of our favorite books in this realm, check out thejoyofwellbeing.com/spirituality.

ASK THE TIME-MACHINE QUESTION.

There is one question that we find gives us the perspective we need from time to time. Here it is: *Are you looking forward, or are you looking backward?* Are you at the stage in your life when you're constantly reminiscing, or are you looking forward and thinking about the future? How are you spending your time? Are you planning for your future, or are you spending your time looking at old yearbooks and photos of your teenage daughter when she was a baby? Checking in with where you are in time and space can help you see where you are putting your energy so you can get down to the important business of putting it where you really want it.

Conclusion:
Be Water, My Friend

Be like water making its way through cracks. Do not be assertive, but adjust to the object, and you shall find a way around or through it. If nothing within you stays rigid, outward things will disclose themselves...Be water, my friend.

—BRUCE LEE

While Bruce Lee's famous quote can be interpreted a number of ways, we can't help but look at it through a well-being lens as a call to be open, flexible, and patient. One of the biggest problems with the wellness world is how dogmatic it is; for many, it can be ideology. This creates an inflexibility and a vulnerability to your own biases that can cut you off from important growth and learning. And while there is value in structure and in holding yourself accountable, this approach to life often bumps up against the fact that the world is always changing—and so are wellness and lifestyle trends. If we are the water, the world is all of this...stuff. These trends, best practices, and new scientific findings are in our path, and we must respond to them, move around them, or crash against them. If you are rigid about how you engage with your well-being, you are going to break when you run into the million things that are confusing, contradictory, and transactional. If you are like water, you can eddy softly next to them or flow past them altogether—you get to choose. So, we'll say this: if you're going to be rigid about anything, we hope you are rigid about being flexible in your journey. When you are water, it is much easier to stay whole while also staying true to what you know to be the best decision for your health and your happiness.

Please know that we are on the journey with you. We have good days and bad days, but we know that we are always evolving in the right direction. We react to life stressors far better than we did ten years ago, we feel stronger in our bodies and our hearts, *and* we still need to be intentional and open to learning new lessons.

We have given you nine chapters of ideas, practices, and ways of being that in any number of configurations can help you live *your* good life. There is no one right way. You are water; adjust as necessary. Be flexible about your routine, your practices, your relationships. Remember that consistency beats perfectionism every day of the week and twice on Sundays. Don't let wellness frustrate you—it should be a sanctuary, it should bring you joy, and it should pull you away from your phone. Do what feels good and makes you happy, and understand that living the good life is the ultimate alchemy: true well-being. You have to experiment, mix and match, learn and try and fail and try again. Like all good alchemy, there is always a part of the equation that is a little bit magical and mysterious—we can't emphasize this point enough. Numbers might be important when we talk about things like biological markers, grams of fiber we're consuming, or the number of flights of stairs we're running up, but if your family and friends don't like you and you have no purpose in life, all those numbers are meaningless. In fact, we'd argue you have a higher mortality risk than someone whose numbers are much worse on paper but who is likable, joyful, and purpose driven. Connection, purpose, and the spontaneity and the synchronicity of life are the magic and the mystery that makes this life joyful. What is the joy of well-being? This is a question that no one can answer definitively because we can only answer it individually. Consider the practices and guidance we have shared to be a little like a recipe passed down through the generations, one that's a little faded on the paper and includes all kinds of ingredients that you might not have or aren't quite sure how to use. Don't be dissuaded—this is the fun part. Get in there and make some joy of your own.

Acknowledgments

Thank you to our incredibly supportive family, especially our loving parents—Nana, Grandpa George, and Grandma Alyse for always being there for us.

Thank you to our amazing team at mindbodygreen—we are extremely grateful for all of you. Special shout-out to our co-founder and CTO, Tim Glenister, for being on this entrepreneurial journey with us.

We are eternally grateful to the mindbodygreen community of readers, listeners, contributors, instructors, podcast guests, and partners.

Thank you to the Benvolio Group, Lew Frankfort and Ernest Odinec, and all of our investors for believing in and supporting our vision.

Thank you to all of our friends past and present, from Palos Verdes Estates and Manhasset to Northfield Mount Hermon, Columbia, Stanford, Dumbo, and now Miami—and from all the various teams and jobs along the way. Thank you to all the great coaches we've had—you all know who you are. Thank you!

Thank you to Celeste, Mia, John, Sarah, and the entire team at Park & Fine for helping steer the editorial ship. Thank you to our partner on this project, Lauren Hamlin; we couldn't have done this without you. Thank you to Nana K. Twumasi and the team at Balance for believing in *The Joy of Well-Being* and bringing it to life.

Thank you to all of the healers and practitioners that we work with to ensure that we're going to be living joyfully for a long, long time.

Endnotes

Chapter One. What Well-Being Looks Like

1. Dan Buettner, *The Blue Zones: 9 Power Lessons for Living Longer from the People Who've Lived the Longest* (Washington, DC: National Geographic, 2012), 1–50.
2. James Nestor, *Breath: The New Science of a Lost Art* (New York: Riverhead Books, 2020), 5.
3. Ibid., 32.
4. Centers for Disease Control and Prevention, "CDC—Sleep Home Page—Sleep and Sleep Disorders," Centers for Disease Control and Prevention, 2019, https://www.cdc.gov/sleep/index.html.
5. "Sleep Deprivation Described as a Serious Public Health Problem," American Association for the Advancement of Science, 2014, https://www.aaas.org/news/sleep-deprivation-described-serious-public-health-problem.
6. Alana Rhone, "USDA ERS—Documentation," USDA, 2018, https://www.ers.usda.gov/data-products/food-access-research-atlas/documentation.
7. Andrew DePietro, "U.S. Poverty Rate by State in 2021," *Forbes*, November 4, 2021, https://www.forbes.com/sites/andrewdepietro/2021/11/04/us-poverty-rate-by-state-in-2021.
8. "How Consumers Purchase Food Is Changing," American Farm Bureau Federation, March 19, 2020, https://www.fb.org/market-intel/how-consumers-purchase-food-is-changing.
9. Rebecca Heaton, "Cooking at Home Is Cool," Live Naturally Magazine, December 28, 2016, https://livenaturallymagazine.com/blog/cooking-home-cool/#:~:text=But %20 according%20to%20a%20recent.
10. Peter Dockrill, "Some Foods Really Are Linked with a Higher Rate of Death, Study Finds," ScienceAlert, February 13, 2019, https://www.sciencealert.com/ultraprocessed-foods-are-linked-with-a-higher-rate-of-death-study-finds.
11. "Highly Processed Foods Form Bulk of U.S. Youths' Diets," National Institutes of Health, August 23, 2021, https://www.nih.gov/news-events/nih-research-matters/highly-processed-foods-form-bulk-us-youths-diets.
12. "Congress Finally Passed a New Farm Bill and It Continues to Pay Homage to the Cult of Corn and Soy," Modern Farmer, January 7, 2019,

https://modernfarmer.com/2019/01/congress-finally-passed-a-new-farm-bill
-and-it-continues-to-pay-homage-to-the-cult-of-corn-and-soy.

13. Emily N. Ussery et al., "Joint Prevalence of Sitting Time and Leisure-Time
Physical Activity among US Adults, 2015–2016." *JAMA* 320, no. 19 (November 20, 2018): 2036, https://doi.org/10.1001/jama.2018.17797.

14. Mary MacVean, " 'Get Up!' or Lose Hours of Your Life Every Day, Scientist
Says," *Los Angeles Times*, July 31, 2014, https://www.latimes.com/science
/sciencenow/la-sci-sn-get-up-20140731-story.html.

15. "Stress in America 2020: A National Mental Health Crisis," American Psychological Association, October 2020, https://www.apa.org/news/press/releases
/stress/2020/report-october#.

16. Selin Kesebir and Pelin Kesebir, "How Modern Life Became Disconnected from
Nature," Greater Good, September 20, 2017, https://greatergood.berkeley.edu
/article/item/how_modern_life_became_disconnected_from_nature.

17. Kay S. Hymowitz, "Alone: The Decline of Family Has Unleashed an Epidemic of
Loneliness," *City Journal*, Spring 2019, https://www.city-journal.org/decline-of
-family-loneliness-epidemic.

18. "How Finding Your Purpose Can Improve Your Health and Life," Blue Zones,
August 22, 2011, https://www.bluezones.com/2011/08/the-right-outlook-how
-finding-your-purpose-can-improve-your-life.

19. Dhruv Khullar, "Finding Purpose for a Good Life. But Also a Healthy One,"
New York Times, January 1, 2018, https://www.nytimes.com/2018/01/01/upshot
/finding-purpose-for-a-good-life-but-also-a-healthy-one.html.

20. Christine E. Cherpak, "Mindful Eating: A Review of How the Stress-Digestion-
Mindfulness Triad May Modulate and Improve Gastrointestinal and Digestive
Function," *Integrative Medicine: A Clinician's Journal* 18, no. 4 (August 1,
2019): 48–53, https://www.ncbi.nlm.nih.gov/pmc/articles/PMC7219460.

Chapter Two. Breathe

1. "4 Breathing Techniques for Better Health," Northwestern Medicine, https://
www.nm.org/healthbeat/healthy-tips/4-breathing-techniques-for-better-health.

2. Kyle Kiesel et al., "Development of a Screening Protocol to Identify Individuals
with Dysfunctional Breathing," *International Journal of Sports Physical Therapy*
12, no. 5 (October 2017): 774–86, https://doi.org/10.26603/ijspt20170774.

3. Ibid.

4. Teresa Hale and Leo Galland, *Breathing Free: The Revolutionary 5-Day Program
to Heal Asthma, Emphysema, Bronchitis, and Other Respiratory Ailments*
(New York: Three Rivers Press, 2000).

5. Ibid.

6. Jason Wachob interview with Patrick McKeown, *mindbodygreen* podcast, June
23, 2021, https://podcasts.apple.com/us/podcast/how-to-actually-tell-if-youre
-breathing-right-patrick/id1246494475?i=1000526590632.

7. Ibid.

8. James Nestor, *Breath: The New Science of a Lost Art* (New York: Riverhead Books, 2020), 115.
9. Ibid., 47.
10. Ibid.
11. Jason Wachob interview with James Nestor, *mindbodygreen* podcast, August 26, 2021, https://podcasts.apple.com/us/podcast/how-to-actually-tell-if-youre -breathing-right-patrick/id1246494475?i=1000526590632.
12. Nestor, *Breath*, 51.
13. Wachob interview with Nestor.
14. Nestor, *Breath*, 72.
15. Melissa Dahl, " 'Mouth-Breathing' Gross, Harmful to Your Health," NBC News, January 11, 2011, https://www.nbcnews.com/healthmain/mouth-breathing -gross-harmful-your-health-1c6437430.
16. Jan Martel et al., "Could Nasal Nitric Oxide Help to Mitigate the Severity of COVID-19?" *Microbes and Infection* 22, no. 4–5 (May 2020), https://doi.org /10.1016/j.micinf.2020.05.002.
17. Wachob interview with McKeown.
18. "Rhinitis," www.hopkinsmedicine.org, https://www.hopkinsmedicine.org/health /conditions-and-diseases/rhinitis.
19. Brian Mackenzie in conversation with the authors, January 12, 2022.
20. "Why Nose Hairs Grow So Long," Cleveland Clinic, May 3, 2022, https:// health.clevelandclinic.org/nose-hair.
21. "Facts & Statistics," Anxiety and Depression Association of America, April 21, 2021, https://adaa.org/understanding-anxiety/facts-statistics.
22. Ibid.
23. Kira Newman, "Is the Way You Breathe Making You Anxious?" Greater Good, November 10, 2020, https://greatergood.berkeley.edu/article/item/is_the_way _you_breathe_making_you_anxious.
24. Ibid.
25. Michael Flanell, "The Athlete's Secret Ingredient: The Power of Nasal Breathing," *EC Pulmonology and Respiratory Medicine* 8, no. 6 (June 2019): 471–75.
26. Ibid.
27. Wachob interview with McKeown.
28. Ibid.
29. Tanya Bentley, in conversation with the authors, January 12, 2022.
30. Ibid.
31. Emails with Tanya Bentley.
32. Wachob interview with McKeown.
33. Ibid.; Aida Bairam et al., "An Overview on the Respiratory Stimulant Effects of Caffeine and Progesterone on Response to Hypoxia and Apnea Frequency in Developing Rats," *Advances in Experimental Medicine and Biology* 860 (2015): 211–20, https://doi.org/10.1007/978-3-319-18440-1_23.

34. Afton Vechery, "Commentary: Why Is Women's Health Still So Under-Researched?" *Fortune*, March 9, 2021, https://fortune.com/2021/03/09/womens-health-research-fda-trials.

35. Wachob interview with Nestor.

Chapter Three. Sleep: A Vital Sign

1. Barry Krakow and Antonio Zadra, "Clinical Management of Chronic Nightmares: Imagery Rehearsal Therapy," *Behavioral Sleep Medicine* 4, no. 1 (February 2006): 45–70, https://doi.org/10.1207/s15402010bsm0401_4.

2. Shelby Harris, in conversation with the authors, February 11, 2022.

3. Yong Liu et al., "Prevalence of Healthy Sleep Duration among Adults—United States, 2014," *Morbidity and Mortality Weekly Report* 65, no. 6 (February 19, 2016): 137–41, https://doi.org/10.15585/mmwr.mm6506a1.

4. Paula Alhola and Päivi Polo-Kantola, "Sleep Deprivation: Impact on Cognitive Performance," *Neuropsychiatric Disease and Treatment* 3, no. 5 (October 2007): 553–67, https://www.ncbi.nlm.nih.gov/pmc/articles/PMC2656292.

5. Ashley Jordan Ferira, "The mindbodygreen Guide to a Good Night's Sleep," https://res.mindbodygreen.com/doc/sleep/mindbodygreen_sleep_guide.pdf.

6. Ibid.

7. Oliver Cameron Reddy and Ysbrand D. van der Werf, "The Sleeping Brain: Harnessing the Power of the Glymphatic System through Lifestyle Choices," *Brain Sciences* 10, no. 11 (November 17, 2020): 868, https://doi.org/10.3390/brainsci10110868.

8. National Sleep Foundation, "What Is REM Sleep?" National Sleep Foundation, November 1, 2020, https://www.thensf.org/what-is-rem-sleep.

9. Ferira, "The mindbodygreen Guide to a Good Night's Sleep."

10. Joel Shurkin, "Camping Resets Your Internal Clock, Say Researchers," *Christian Science Monitor*, August 1, 2013, https://www.csmonitor.com/Science/2013/0801/Camping-resets-your-internal-clock-say-researchers.

11. Andrew Huberman, PhD, Twitter post, June 23, 2022, 3:30 p.m., https://twitter.com/hubermanlab/status/1540054616963878912.

12. Gianluca Tosini, Ian Ferguson, and Kazuo Tsubota, "Effects of Blue Light on the Circadian System and Eye Physiology," *Molecular Vision* 22 (2016): 61–72, https://www.ncbi.nlm.nih.gov/labs/pmc/articles/PMC4734149.

13. Jason Wachob interview with Michael Breus, *mindbodygreen* podcast, January 8, 2021.

14. Danielle Pacheco, "Exercise and Sleep," Sleep Foundation, January 22, 2021, https://www.sleepfoundation.org/physical-activity/exercise-and-sleep.

15. Wei-Li Wang et al., "The Effect of Yoga on Sleep Quality and Insomnia in Women with Sleep Problems: A Systematic Review and Meta-Analysis," *BMC Psychiatry* 20, no. 1 (May 1, 2020), https://doi.org/10.1186/s12888-020-02566-4.

16. Christopher E. Kline et al., "The Effect of Exercise Training on Obstructive Sleep Apnea and Sleep Quality: A Randomized Controlled Trial," *Sleep* 34, no. 12 (December 2011): 1631–40, https://doi.org/10.5665/sleep.1422.

17. Wachob interview with Breus.
18. Sarah M, Inkelis, "Sleep and Alcohol Use in Women," *Alcohol Research: Current Reviews* 40, no. 2 (2020), https://doi.org/10.35946/arcr.v40.2.13.
19. Ibid.
20. Nicole K.Y. Tang, D. Anne Schmidt, and Allison G. Harvey, "Sleeping with the Enemy: Clock Monitoring in the Maintenance of Insomnia," Journal of Behavior Therapy and Experimental Psychiatry 38, no. 1 (March 2007): 40–55, https://doi.org/10.1016/j.jbtep.2005.07.004.
21. Wachob interview with Breus.

Chapter Four. Eat Real Food
1. Mark Schatzker, *The End of Craving: Recovering the Lost Wisdom of Eating Well* (New York: Avid Reader Press, 2021), 16–23.
2. Ibid., 25–27.
3. Kristin Baird Rattini, "The American South's Deadly Diet," *Discover Magazine*, July 18, 2018, https://www.discovermagazine.com/health/the-american-souths-deadly-diet.
4. Schatzker, *The End of Craving*, 20–23.
5. Ibid., 25.
6. Ibid., 33.
7. Ibid.
8. Julia Belluz, "The Problem with Diet Books Written by Doctors.," *Vox*, March 24, 2016, https://www.vox.com/2016/3/24/11296168/down-with-diet-books.
9. Scott Galloway, *Adrift* (Penguin, 2022), 124.
10. Dariush Mozaffarian, Irwin Rosenberg, and Ricardo Uauy, "History of Modern Nutrition Science—Implications for Current Research, Dietary Guidelines, and Food Policy," *BMJ* 361 (June 13, 2018): k2392, https://doi.org/10.1136/bmj.k2392.
11. "21 Reasons to Eat Real Food," Healthline, May 19, 2021, https://www.healthline.com/nutrition/21-reasons-to-eat-real-food#TOC_TITLE_HDR_13.
12. Ibid.
13. Robert H. Lustig, *Metabolical: The Lure and the Lies of Processed Food, Nutrition, and Modern Medicine* (New York: Harperwave, 2021), 2.
14. Charlotte Debras et al., "Artificial Sweeteners and Cancer Risk: Results from the NutriNet-Santé Population-Based Cohort Study," *PLOS Medicine* 19, no. 3 (March 24, 2022): e1003950, https://doi.org/10.1371/journal.pmed.1003950.
15. Schatzker, *The End of Craving*, 125.
16. Ibid., 129.
17. Jason Wachob interview with Mark Schatzker, *mindbodygreen* podcast, January 7, 2022, https://www.stitcher.com/show/the-mindbodygreen-podcast/episode/365-brain-fooling-foods-how-to-control-your-cravings-award-winning-food-writer-mark-schatzker-89526351.
18. Paul A. S. Breslin, "An Evolutionary Perspective on Food and Human Taste," *Current Biology* 23, no. 9 (May 2013): R409–18, https://doi.org/10.1016/j.cub.2013.04.010; Wachob interview with Schatzker.

19. Wachob interview with Schatzker.
20. Schatzker, *The End of Craving*, 87–91.
21. Ibid.
22. Wachob interview with Schatzker.
23. Ibid.
24. "Fiber," Nutrition Source, Harvard School of Public Health, June 6, 2018, https://www.hsph.harvard.edu/nutritionsource/carbohydrates/fiber.
25. Jason Wachob interview with Robert Lustig, *mindbodygreen* podcast, May 12, 2021, https://podcasts.apple.com/us/podcast/what-were-getting-wrong-about -metabolic-health-weight/id1246494475?i=1000521431249.
26. "Only 12% of Americans Are Metabolically Healthy," Healthline, December 6, 2018, https://www.healthline.com/health-news/what-does-it-mean-to-be-meta bolically-healthy#Explaining-the-low-rates-of-metabolic-health.
27. Ibid.
28. Diane Quagliani and Patricia Felt-Gunderson, "Closing America's Fiber Intake Gap," *American Journal of Lifestyle Medicine* 11, no. 1 (July 7, 2016): 80–85, https://doi.org/10.1177/1559827615588079.
29. Jason Wachob interview with Will Bulsiewicz, *mindbodygreen* podcast, June 9, 2022, https://open.spotify.com/episode/0relTeRUixvHUakPdFIXpL.
30. Christine N. Spencer et al., "Dietary Fiber and Probiotics Influence the Gut Microbiome and Melanoma Immunotherapy Response," *Science* 374, no. 6575 (December 24, 2021): 1632–40, https://doi.org/10.1126/science.aaz7015.; Wachob, interview with Will Bulsiewicz, *the mindbodygreen* podcast, podcast audio, June 9, 2022, https://open.spotify.com/episode/0relTeRUixvHUakPdFIXpL.
31. Lustig, *Metabolical*, 261.
32. Stephanie Eckelkamp, "Your Definitive Guide to Intermittent Fasting," mind-bodygreen, January 12, 2018, https://www.mindbodygreen.com/articles/your-definitive-guide-to-intermittent-fasting.
33. Réda Adafer et al., "Food Timing, Circadian Rhythm and Chrononutrition: A Systematic Review of Time-Restricted Eating's Effects on Human Health," *Nutrients* 12, no. 12 (December 8, 2020): 3770, https://doi.org/10.3390/nu12123770.
34. Humaira Jamshed et al., "Early Time-Restricted Feeding Improves 24-Hour Glucose Levels and Affects Markers of the Circadian Clock, Aging, and Autophagy in Humans," *Nutrients* 11, no. 6 (May 30, 2019): 1234, https://doi .org/10.3390/nu11061234; Elizabeth F. Sutton et al., "Early Time-Restricted Feeding Improves Insulin Sensitivity, Blood Pressure, and Oxidative Stress Even without Weight Loss in Men with Prediabetes," *Cell Metabolism* 27, no. 6 (June 2018): 1212–1221.e3, https://doi.org/10.1016/j.cmet.2018.04.010.
35. Lindsay Boyers, "Achieve Your Healthy Weight by Syncing Meals with Your Internal Clock," mindbodygreen, July 20, 2020, https://www.mindbodygreen.com /articles/what-is-circadian-rhythm-fasting.
36. Priya Crosby et al., "Insulin/IGF-1 Drives PERIOD Synthesis to Entrain Circadian Rhythms with Feeding Time," *Cell* 177, no. 4 (May 2, 2019): 896–909. e20, https://doi.org/10.1016/j.cell.2019.02.017.

37. Eckelkamp, "Your Definitive Guide to Intermittent Fasting."
38. "Why We Aren't Anti-Aging, We Are Pro-Healthy Aging," mindbodygreen, December 8, 2019, https://www.mindbodygreen.com/articles/why-we-arent-anti-aging-we-are-pro-healthy-aging.
39. Jason Wachob interview with Kristen Willeumier, *mindbodygreen* podcast, May 21, 2021, https://podcasts.apple.com/us/podcast/sneaky-things-affecting-your-brain-health-kristen-willeumier/id1246494475?i=1000522630950.
40. Ibid.
41. Jodi D. Stookey et al., "Underhydration Is Associated with Obesity, Chronic Diseases, and Death within 3 to 6 Years in the U.S. Population Aged 51–70 Years," *Nutrients* 12, no. 4 (March 26, 2020): 905, https://doi.org/10.3390/nu12040905.
42. Abby Moore, "The 8 Most Unhealthy Vegetable Oils to Eat & Why This MD Avoids Them," mindbodygreen, January 29, 2021, https://www.mindbodygreen.com/articles/unhealthy-vegetable-oils#:~:text=%22For%20all%20foods%2C%20we%20have.
43. Abby Moore, "The 8 Most Unhealthy Vegetable Oils to Eat & Why This MD Avoids Them," mindbodygreen, January 29, 2021, https://www.mindbodygreen.com/articles/unhealthy-vegetable-oils.
44. Eliza Sullivan, "11 Things to Know If You Want to Try Eating a Mediterranean Diet," mindbodygreen, January 8, 2020, https://www.mindbodygreen.com/articles/tk-tips-for-people-trying-mediterranean-diet.
45. Michael Pollan, *In Defense of Food: An Eater's Manifesto*. (Turtleback Books, 2009).
46. "New Heart Risk Factor Could Be the Key to Preventing Heart Disease," Project Baseline, https://www.projectbaseline.com/heart-disease-risk-factor.
47. George Thanassoulis, "Screening for High Lipoprotein(A)," *Circulation* 139, no. 12 (March 19, 2019): 1493–96, https://doi.org/10.1161/circulationaha.119.038989.
48. "Homocysteine: Levels, Tests, High Homocysteine Levels," Cleveland Clinic, https://my.clevelandclinic.org/health/articles/21527-homocysteine.
49. Jennifer G. Robinson et al., "Eradicating the Burden of Atherosclerotic Cardiovascular Disease by Lowering Apolipoprotein B Lipoproteins Earlier in Life," *Journal of the American Heart Association* 7, no. 20 (October 16, 2018), https://doi.org/10.1161/jaha.118.009778.

Chapter Five. Just ~~Do~~ Move It

1. "7 Great Reasons Why Exercise Matters," Mayo Clinic, October 8, 2021, https://www.mayoclinic.org/healthy-lifestyle/fitness/in-depth/exercise/art-20048389.
2. Jennifer Heisz, *Move the Body, Heal the Mind: Overcome Anxiety, Depression, and Dementia and Improve Focus, Creativity, and Sleep* (Boston: Mariner Books, 2022), 102.
3. Heart Essentials, "80% of Americans Don't Get Enough Exercise—and Here's How Much You Actually Need," Cleveland Clinic, November 20, 2018, https://health.clevelandclinic.org/80-of-americans-dont-get-enough-exercise-and-heres-how-much-you-actually-need.

4. "New Ministries for Millennials," Harvard Divinity School, April 13, 2016, https:// news-archive.hds.harvard.edu/news/2016/04/13/new-ministries-millennials.

5. Heisz, *Move the Body, Heal the Mind*, 3.

6. Michelle Segar et al., "Rethinking Physical Activity Communication: Using Focus Groups to Understand Women's Goals, Values, and Beliefs to Improve Public Health," *BMC Public Health* 17, no. 1 (May 18, 2017), https://doi.org/10 .1186/s12889-017-4361-1.

7. Borja del Pozo Cruz et al., "Association of Daily Step Count and Intensity with Incident Dementia in 78 430 Adults Living in the UK," *JAMA Neurology*, September 6, 2022, https://doi.org/10.1001/jamaneurol.2022.2672.

8. Grant W. Ralston et al., "Weekly Training Frequency Effects on Strength Gain: A Meta-Analysis," *Sports Medicine—Open* 4, no. 1 (August 3, 2018), https://doi .org/10.1186/s40798-018-0149-9.

9. Brian J. Fogg, *Tiny Habits: The Small Changes That Change Everything* (New York: Mariner Books, 2020), 26.

10. Annabel Streets, *52 Ways to Walk: The Surprising Science of Walking for Wellness and Joy, One Week at a Time* (New York: G. P. Putnam's Sons, 2022), xv.

11. Streets, *52 Ways to Walk*, xviii–xix.

12. Streets, *52 Ways to Walk*, xviii.

13. Heisz, *Move the Body, Heal the Mind*, 149.

14. Jason Wachob interview with Jennifer Heisz, *mindbodygreen* podcast, April 1, 2022, https://www.stitcher.com/show/the-mindbodygreen-podcast/episode /389-the-best-worst-types-of-exercise-for-anxiety-neuroscientist-jennifer-heisz -ph-d-201955459.

15. Jason Wachob interview with Annabel Streets, *mindbodygreen* podcast, March 23, 2022, https://www.stitcher.com/show/the-mindbodygreen-podcast /episode/386-are-you-actually-walking-correctly-award-winning-writer-author -annabel-streets-201637584.

16. Streets, *52 Ways to Walk*, 68–69.

17. Ibid., 129.

18. Ibid., 76.

19. Ibid.

20. Ibid., 77.

21. Ibid., 208–209.

22. Ibid., 170–71.

23. Ibid., 170.

24. "London Transport Workers Study," University of Minnesota, http://www .epi.umn.edu/cvdepi/study-synopsis/london-transport-workers-study.

25. Bente Klarlund Pedersen, "Which Type of Exercise Keeps You Young?" *Current Opinion in Clinical Nutrition and Metabolic Care* 22, no. 2 (March 2019): 167–73, https://doi.org/10.1097/mco.0000000000000546.

26. Jason Wachob interview with Dan Buettner, *mindbodygreen* podcast, March 12, 2019, https://podcasts.apple.com/us/podcast/the-daily-habits-of-people-who -live-longer-with/id1246494475?i=1000458501937.

27. Valter Santilli et al., "Clinical Definition of Sarcopenia," *Clinical Cases in Mineral and Bone Metabolism* 11, no. 3 (2014): 177–80, https://www.ncbi.nlm .nih.gov/pmc/articles/PMC4269139.

28. "Muscle Mass Percentage Averages and How to Calculate It," Healthline, https://www.healthline.com/health/muscle-mass-percentage#high-muscle-mass -benefits.

29. Mark Sisson, "Sarcopenia: What to Do for Age Related Muscle Loss," Mark's Daily Apple, July 15, 2020, https://www.marksdailyapple.com/sarcopenia-age -related-muscle-loss/.

30. Ibid.

31. Ibid.

32. Jane E. Brody, "Preventing Muscle Loss as We Age," *New York Times*, September 3, 2018, https://www.nytimes.com/2018/09/03/well/live/preventing-muscle-loss -among-the-elderly.html.

33. Peter Attia, Twitter post, June 5, 2022, 10:51 a.m., https://twitter.com /peterattiamd/status/1533461602787381248.
    CDC, "Facts about Falls," www.cdc.gov, September 30, 2020, https:// www.cdc.gov/ falls/facts.html.

34. "Strength Training Builds More than Muscles," Harvard Health, October 13, 2021, https://www.health.harvard.edu/staying-healthy/strength-training-builds -more-than-muscles.

35. Sisson, "Sarcopenia."

36. Peter Attia, "The Importance of Muscle Mass, Strength, and Cardiorespiratory Fitness for Longevity," Drive podcast, episode 176, September 20, 2021, https://peterattiamd.com/ama27.

37. Gretchen Reynolds, "Stronger Muscles in 3 Seconds a Day," *New York Times*, March 2, 2022, https://www.nytimes.com/2022/03/02/well/move/stronger -muscles-health.html.

38. Wachob interview with Heisz.

39. Ibid.

40. Gretchen Reynolds, "Can Moving the Body Heal the Mind?" *New York Times*, March 30, 2022, https://www.nytimes.com/2022/03/30/well/move/exercise -mental-health.html; Felipe B. Schuch et al., "Exercise as a Treatment for Depression: A Meta-Analysis Adjusting for Publication Bias," *Journal of Psychiatric Research* 77 (June 2016): 42–51, https://doi.org/10.1016/j.jpsychires.2016 .02.023.

41. "Facts about Falls," Centers for Disease Control and Prevention, September 30, 2020, https://www.cdc.gov/falls/facts.html.

42. Attia, "The Importance of Muscle Mass."

Chapter Six. Stress

1. "Hormesis: The Good Type of Stress," Ice Barrel, January 18, 2022, https:// icebarrel.com/hormesis-the-good-type-of-stress/.

2. Elissa S. Epel, "The Geroscience Agenda: Toxic Stress, Hormetic Stress, and the Rate of Aging," *Ageing Research Reviews* 63 (November 2020): 101167, https://doi.org/10.1016/j.arr.2020.101167.

3. "Hormesis."

4. Max G. Levy, "Could Being Cold Actually Be Good for You?" *Wired*, January 3, 2022, https://www.wired.com/story/could-being-cold-actually-be-good-for-you.

5. "The Founder of Twitter Has Revealed His Bizarre Eating Habits," *Independent*, April 11, 2019, https://www.independent.co.uk/life-style/jack-dorsey-daily -routine-mediation-ben-greenfield-podcast-a8864651.html.

6. Katherine May, *Wintering: The Power of Rest and Retreat in Difficult Times* (New York: Riverhead, 2020), 180.

7. P. Sramek et al., "Human Physiological Responses to Immersion into Water of Different Temperatures," *European Journal of Applied Physiology* 81, no. 5 (February 11, 2000): 436–42, https://doi.org/10.1007/s004210050065.

8. "Drug Abuse, Dopamine, and the Brain's Reward System," Hazelden Betty Ford Foundation, September 1, 2015, https://www.hazeldenbettyford.org/education /bcr/addiction-research/drug-abuse-brain-ru-915.

9. Andrew Huberman in conversation with Susanna Soeberg, "Cold and Heat Protocols," Instagram video, November 21, 2021, https://www.instagram.com /tv/CWjRRlnBG9S.

10. Matt Fuchs, "Perspective | Are Ice-Cold Showers Good for You? I Tried It for Two Months.," Washington Post, March 10, 2022, https://www.washingtonpost.com /wellness/2022/03/10/benefits-of-cold-water-immersion/.

11. Levy, "Could Being Cold Actually Be Good for You?"

12. Ibid.

13. Timothy Huzar, "Scientists Reveal Link between Brown Fat and Health Benefits," Medical News Today, January 9, 2021, https://www.medicalnewstoday.com /articles/scientists-reveal-link-between-brown-fat-and-health-benefits.

14. Ibid.

15. Steven Leckart, "Hot Trend: Tapping the Power of Cold to Lose Weight," *Wired*, February 12, 2013, https://www.wired.com/2013/02/ff-cold-weight-loss.

16. M. Chondronikola et al., "Brown Adipose Tissue Improves Whole-Body Glucose Homeostasis and Insulin Sensitivity in Humans," *Diabetes* 63, no. 12 (July 23, 2014): 4089–99, https://doi.org/10.2337/db14-0746.

17. "How Stress Can Boost Immune System," *Science Daily*, June 21, 2012, https://www.sciencedaily.com/releases/2012/06/120621223525.htm.

18. "These Are the Health Benefits of Showering in Cold Water," World Economic Forum, October 1, 2021, https://www.weforum.org/agenda/2021/10/cold-showers -health-benefits-immune-system-depression.

19. "Cold Exposure," Found My Fitness, https://www.foundmyfitness.com/topics /cold-exposure-therapy.

20. Huberman in conversation with Søberg, "Cold and Heat Protocols."

21. "Cold Water Therapy: Benefits of Cold Showers, Baths, Immersion Therapy," *Healthline*, July 8, 2020, https://www.healthline.com/health/cold-water-therapy.

22. Huberman in conversation with Søberg, "Cold and Heat Protocols."
23. "Cold Exposure."
24. Huberman in conversation with Soeberg, "Cold and Heat Protocols."
25. Andrew Huberman, "The Best Time to Do Deliberate Cold (or Heat) Exposure," Instagram video, April 7, 2022, https://www.instagram.com/reel/CcEJ0TMgpsy.
26. Susanna Søberg et al., "Altered Brown Fat Thermoregulation and Enhanced Cold-Induced Thermogenesis in Young, Healthy, Winter-Swimming Men," *Cell Reports Medicine* 2, no. 10 (October 19, 2021), https://doi.org/10.1016/j .xcrm.2021.100408.
27. Susanna Søberg, "Is the Soeberg et al. Method the Sweet Spot?" Instagram post, March 15, 2022, https://www.instagram.com/p/CbI2HQIMi9r.
28. "The Healing Madness of Sea Swimming by Dr. Mark Harper," YouTube, May 4, 2017, https://www.youtube.com/watch?v=0pXLF0sucDU.
29. Jason Wachob interview with Ben Greenfield, *mindbodygreen* podcast, February 9, 2022, https://www.stitcher.com/show/the-mindbodygreen-podcast /episode/374-how-to-use-cold-therapy-to-optimize-your-blood-sugar-brain -health-sleep-exercise-physiologist-ben-greenfield-90346623.
30. Søberg, "Is the Soeberg et al. Method the Sweet Spot?"

Chapter Seven. Regenerate

1. Caitlin Andrews, "Forever Chemicals Ruined His Farm. It Took Years for Maine to See a Bigger Problem," *Bangor Daily News*, April 18, 2022, https://bangordaily news.com/2022/04/18/politics/pfas-ruined-arundel-farm-joam40zk0w.
2. "PFAS Chemicals Overview," Agency for Toxic Substances and Disease Registry, June 24, 2020, https://www.atsdr.cdc.gov/pfas/health-effects/overview.html.
3. "Mitchell Center Researchers Examine Options for Managing PFAS," *UMaine News*, June 2, 2021, https://umaine.edu/news/blog/2021/06/02/mitchell-center -researchers-examine-options-for-managing-pfas.
4. "State Wildlife Officials to Expand PFAS Testing of Deer," *News Center Maine*, 2021, https://www.newscentermaine.com/article/tech/science/environment/pfas /state-wildlife-officials-to-expand-pfas-testing-of-deer/97-5bbb3bf3-62e2-4f37 -9734-f550ac478d11.
5. Andrews, "Forever Chemicals Ruined His Farm."
6. "Mitchell Center Researchers Examine Options for Managing PFAS."
7. Michele Marill, " 'Forever Chemicals' Are in Your Popcorn—and Your Blood," *Wired*, October 10, 2009, https://www.wired.com/story/pfas-forever-chemicals -are-in-your-popcornand-your-blood.
8. Ibid.
9. Richard Grant, "Do Trees Talk to Each Other?" *Smithsonian*, February 21, 2018, https://www.smithsonianmag.com/science-nature/the-whispering-trees -180968084.
10. Hannah Ritchie, "How Essential Are Pollinators for Global Food Security?" World Economic Forum, August 9, 2021, https://www.weforum.org/agenda /2021/08/how-essential-are-pollinators-for-global-food-security.

11. Francisco Sánchez-Bayo and Kris A. G. Wyckhuys, "Worldwide Decline of the Entomofauna: A Review of Its Drivers," *Biological Conservation* 232, no. 232 (April 2019): 8–27, https://doi.org/10.1016/j.biocon.2019.01.020; Philip Donkersley, "Bees: How Important Are They and What Would Happen If They Went Extinct?" *The Conversation*, August 19, 2019, https://theconversation.com/bees -how-important-are-they-and-what-would-happen-if-they-went-extinct-121272.

12. Christian Lindmeier, "Stop Using Antibiotics in Healthy Animals to Preserve Their Effectiveness," World Health Organization, November 7, 2017, https:// www.who.int/news-room/detail/07-11-2017-stop-using-antibiotics-in-healthy -animals-to-prevent-the-spread-of-antibiotic-resistance.

13. Margaret Osborne, "Microplastics Detected in Human Blood in New Study," *Smithsonian*, March 28, 2022, https://www.smithsonianmag.com/smart-news /microplastics-detected-in-human-blood-180979826.

14. Roland Geyer, Jenna R. Jambeck, and Kara Lavender Law, "Production, Use, and Fate of All Plastics Ever Made," *Science Advances* 3, no. 7 (July 19, 2017), https://doi.org/10.1126/sciadv.1700782; Rebecca Altman, "How Bad Are Plastics, Really?" *The Atlantic*, January 3, 2022, https://www.theatlantic.com /science/archive/2022/01/plastic-history-climate-change/621033.

15. Neeti Rustagi, Ritesh Singh, and S .K. Pradhan, "Public Health Impact of Plastics: An Overview," *Indian Journal of Occupational and Environmental Medicine* 15, no. 3 (2011): 100, https://doi.org/10.4103/0019-5278.93198.

16. Jason Wachob interview with Shanna Swan, *mindbodygreen* podcast, August 11, 2021, https://podcasts.apple.com/us/podcast/sperm-count-is-declining-everyone -should-care-shanna/id1246494475?i=1000531688279.

17. Ibid.

18. Shanna H. Swan and Stacey Colino, Count Down: How Our Modern World Is Threatening Sperm Counts, Altering Male and Female Reproductive Development, and Imperiling the Future of the Human Race (New York: Scribner, 2021), 112.

19. Julia Moskin et al., "Your Questions about Food and Climate Change, Answered," *New York Times*, April 30, 2019, https://www.nytimes.com /interactive/2022/dining/climate-change-food-eating-habits.html.

20. Ibid.

21. Jason Wachob interview with Paul Hawken, *mindbodygreen* podcast, August 23, 2021, https://podcasts.apple.com/lt/podcast/are-electric-cars-plant-based -meat-really-the-answer/id1246494475?i=1000534674780.

22. Emma Newburger and Amelia Lucas, "Beyond Meat Uses Climate Change to Market Fake Meat Substitutes. Scientists Are Cautious," CNBC (September 2, 2019), https://www.cnbc.com/2019/09/02/beyond-meat-uses-climate-change -to-market-fake-meat-substitutes-scientists-are-cautious.html.

Olivia Roos, "Is Fake Meat Better for You, or the Environment?" NBC News (NBC News, October 13, 2019), https://www.nbcnews.com/news/us-news /fake-meat-better-you-or-environment-n1065231.

23. Wachob interview with Hawken, *mindbodygreen* podcast, August 23, 2021, https://podcasts.apple.com/lt/podcast/are-electric-cars-plant-based-meat-really-the-answer/id1246494475?i=1000534674780.

24. Katherine Kornei, "This Antioxidant May Provide a Key Link between Regenerative Agriculture and Human Health," *Civil Eats*, May 10, 2022, https://civileats.com/2022/05/10/ergothioneine-regenerative-agriculture-longetive-soil-health-bionutrients-crops-producing-farming-human-health.

25. Virginia Gewin, "As Carbon Markets Reward New Efforts, Will Regenerative Farming Pioneers Be Left in the Dirt?" *Civil Eats*, July 27, 2021, https://civileats.com/2021/07/27/as-carbon-markets-reward-new-efforts-will-regenerative-farming-pioneers-be-left-in-the.dirt.

26. "Fight Climate Change by Preventing Food Waste," World Wildlife Fund, https://www.worldwildlife.org/stories/fight-climate-change-by-preventing-food-waste.

27. Wachob interview with Hawken.

28. Rachael Dottle and Jackie Gu, "The Global Glut of Clothing Is an Environmental Crisis," Bloomberg, February 23, 2022, https://www.bloomberg.com/graphics/2022-fashion-industry-environmental-impact.

29. Ibid.

30. Swan and Colino, *Count Down*, 185.

31. Scott Galloway, *Adrift* (Penguin, 2022), 118.

32. Wachob interview with Hawken.

33. Jim Robbins, "Ecopsychology: How Immersion in Nature Benefits Your Health," *Yale Environment 360*, January 9, 2020, https://e360.yale.edu/features/ecopsychology-how-immersion-in-nature-benefits-your-health.

Chapter Eight. In It Together

1. Brenda Egolf, Judith Lasker, and Louise Potvin, "The Roseto Effect: A 50-Year Comparison of Mortality Rates," August 1992, https://www.ncbi.nlm.nih.gov/pmc/articles/PMC1695733/pdf/amjph00545-0027.pdf.

2. Ibid.

3. "The Italian Americans," PBS, February 15, 2015, https://www.pbs.org/video/italian-americans-introduction.

4. Ashley Abramson, "Substance Use during the Pandemic," *Monitor on Psychology* 52, no. 2 (March 1, 2021), https://www.apa.org/monitor/2021/03/substance-use-pandemic.

5. Ibid.

6. Julianne Holt-Lunstad, Timothy B. Smith, and J. Bradley Layton, "Social Relationships and Mortality Risk: A Meta-Analytic Review," *PLoS Medicine* 7, no. 7 (July 27, 2010), https://doi.org/10.1371/journal.pmed.1000316.

7. "Understanding the Stress Response," Harvard Health Publishing, July 6, 2020, https://www.health.harvard.edu/staying-healthy/understanding-the-stress-response.

8. Christopher Bergl, "Face-to-Face Connectedness, Oxytocin, and Your Vagus Nerve," *Psychology Today*, May 19, 2017, https://www.psychologytoday.com/us /blog/the-athletes-way/201705/face-face-connectedness-oxytocin-and-your -vagus-nerve.

9. Sigrid Breit et al., "Vagus Nerve as Modulator of the Brain–Gut Axis in Psychiatric and Inflammatory Disorders," *Frontiers in Psychiatry* 9, no. 44 (March 13, 2018), https://doi.org/10.3389/fpsyt.2018.00044.

10. "Understanding the Stress Response"; Fatih Ozbay et al., "Social Support and Resilience to Stress: From Neurobiology to Clinical Practice," *Psychiatry (Edgmont)* 4, no. 5 (2007): 35–40, https://www.ncbi.nlm.nih.gov/pmc/articles /PMC2921311.

11. David Furman et al., "Chronic Inflammation in the Etiology of Disease across the Life Span," *Nature Medicine* 25, no. 12 (December 2019): 1822–32, https://doi.org/10.1038/s41591-019-0675-0.

12. Jason Wachob, "3 Underrated Ways Social Interactions Can Affect Your Longevity," mindbodygreen, December 9, 2020, https://www.mindbodygreen.com /articles/how-social-interactions-can-impact-your-longevity.

13. Emma Seppälä, "Social Connection Boosts Health, Even When You're Isolated," *Psychology Today*, March 23, 2020, https://www.psychologytoday.com/us/blog /feeling-it/202003/social-connection-boosts-health-even-when-youre-isolated.

14. Ralph S. Paffenbarger et al., "The Association of Changes in Physical-Activity Level and Other Lifestyle Characteristics with Mortality among Men," *New England Journal of Medicine* 328, no. 8 (February 25, 1993): 538–45, https:// doi.org/10.1056/nejm199302253280804; Marc Nocon et al., "Association of Physical Activity with All-Cause and Cardiovascular Mortality: A Systematic Review and Meta-Analysis," *European Journal of Cardiovascular Prevention and Rehabilitation* 15, no. 3 (2008): 239–46, https://doi.org/10.1097/HJR .0b013e3282f55e09; X. Wang et al., "Fruit and Vegetable Consumption and Mortality from All Causes, Cardiovascular Disease, and Cancer: Systematic Review and Dose-Response Meta-Analysis of Prospective Cohort Studies," *BMJ* 349 (July 29, 2014), https://doi.org/10.1136/bmj.g4490.

15. Julianne Holt-Lunstad, Theodore F. Robles, and David A. Sbarra, "Advancing Social Connection as a Public Health Priority in the United States.," *American Psychologist* 72, no. 6 (September 2017): 517–30, https://doi.org/10.1037 /amp0000103; Julianne Holt-Lunstad, Timothy B. Smith, and J. Bradley Layton, "Social Relationships and Mortality Risk: A Meta-Analytic Review," *PLoS Medicine* 7, no. 7 (July 27, 2010), https://doi.org/10.1371/journal.pmed.1000316.

16. Holt-Lunstad, Smith, and Layton, "Social Relationships and Mortality Risk."

17. Jonathan Haidt, "The Dangerous Experiment on Teen Girls," *The Atlantic*, November 21, 2021, https://www.theatlantic.com/ideas/archive/2021/11 /facebooks-dangerous-experiment-teen-girls/620767.

18. Ibid.

19. Kate Fagan, *What Made Maddy Run: The Secret Struggles and Tragic Death of an All-American Teen* (New York: Little Brown & Company, 2018) 241.

20. Fagan, *What Made Maddy Run*, 147; Leslie J. Seltzer et al., "Instant Messages vs. Speech: Hormones and Why We Still Need to Hear Each Other," *Evolution and Human Behavior* 33, no. 1 (January 1, 2012): 42–45, https://www.ncbi.nlm.nih.gov/pmc/articles/PMC3277914.

21. Daniel A. Cox, "Men's Social Circles Are Shrinking," Survey Center on American Life, June 29, 2021, https://www.americansurveycenter.org/why-mens-social-circles-are-shrinking.

22. Catherine Pearson, "How Many Friends Do You Really Need?" *New York Times*, May 7, 2022, https://www.nytimes.com/2022/05/07/well/live/adult-friendships-number.html.

23. Ibid.

24. Robert H. Shmerling, "The Health Advantages of Marriage," Harvard Health Blog, November 30, 2016, https://www.health.harvard.edu/blog/the-health-advantages-of-marriage-2016113010667.

25. Jason Wachob, "3 Underrated Ways Social Interactions Can Affect Your Longevity," mindbodygreen, December 9, 2020, https://www.mindbodygreen.com/articles/how-social-interactions-can-impact-your-longevity.

26. "5 Ways Pets Help with Stress and Mental Health," American Heart Association, https://www.heart.org/en/healthy-living/healthy-bond-for-life-pets/pets-and-mental-health.

Chapter Nine. Something Bigger

1. Jason Wachob interview with Arthur Brooks, *mindbodygreen* podcast, March 30, 2022, https://podcasts.apple.com/us/podcast/overcoming-success-addiction-why-you-should-have-a/id1246494475?i=1000555688368.

2. "How Much Do Influencers Make?—Everything You Need to Know," Nashville Film Institute, January 7, 2022, https://www.nfi.edu/how-much-do-influencers-make.

3. Sarah Min, "86% of Young Americans Want to Become a Social Media Influencer," CBS News, November 8, 2019, https://www.cbsnews.com/news/social-media-influencers-86-of-young-americans-want-to-become-one.

4. "LEGO Group Kicks Off Global Program to Inspire the Next Generation of Space Explorers as NASA Celebrates 50 Years of Moon Landing," PR Newswire, July 16, 2019, https://www.prnewswire.com/news-releases/lego-group-kicks-off-global-program-to-inspire-the-next-generation-of-space-explorers-as-nasa-celebrates-50-years-of-moon-landing-300885423.html.

5. "The Influencer Report: Engaging Gen Z and Millennials," Morning Consult, November 2019, https://morningconsult.com/wp-content/uploads/2019/11/The-Influencer-Report-Engaging-Gen-Z-and-Millennials.pdf.

6. David Marchese, "Yale's Happiness Professor Says Anxiety Is Destroying Her Students," *New York Times*, February 21, 2022, https://www.nytimes.com/interactive/2022/02/21/magazine/laurie-santos-interview.html.

7. Wachob interview with Brooks.

8. Wachob interview with Buettner.

9. Jeremy Adam Smith, "How to Find Your Purpose in Life," Greater Good, January 10, 2018, https://greatergood.berkeley.edu/article/item/how_to_find _your_purpose_in_life.

10. Lisa Miller, *The Awakened Brain: The New Science of Spirituality and the Quest for an Inspired Life* (New York: Random House, 2021), 47.

11. Ibid., 51–52.

12. Jason Wachob interview with Lisa Miller, *mindbodygreen* podcast, October 22, 2021, https://podcasts.apple.com/pt/podcast/this-is-your-brain-on-spirituality -lisa-miller-ph-d/id1246494475?i=1000539377627.

13. Miller, *The Awakened Brain*, 162.

14. Marchese, "Yale's Happiness Professor Says Anxiety Is Destroying Her Students."

15. Miller, *The Awakened Brain*, 9.

16. Harold G. Koenig, "Religion, Spirituality, and Health: The Research and Clinical Implications," *ISRN Psychiatry* 2012 (December 6, 2012): 1–33, https://doi.org/10.5402/2012/278730.

17. Miller, *The Awakened Brain*, 8.

18. Ibid., 162.

19. Ibid., 164.

20. Ibid., 202.

21. Jason Wachob interview with Stephen Trzeciak, *mindbodygreen* podcast, August 18, 2022, https://podcasts.apple.com/us/podcast/the-antidote-to-burnout -icu-surgeon-stephen-trzeciak-m-d/id1246494475?i=1000576467313.

Index

About the Authors

JASON WACHOB is the founder and co-CEO of mindbodygreen, the leading independent media brand dedicated to well-being with 15 million monthly unique visitors. He is also the host of the popular *mindbodygreen* podcast and the bestselling author of *Wellth: How I Learned to Build a Life, Not a Resume.* He has been featured in the *New York Times, Entrepreneur, Forbes, Fast Company, Business Insider, BoF,* and *Vogue,* and has a BA in history from Columbia University, where he played varsity basketball for four years. He lives with his wife, co-founder and co-CEO Colleen, in Miami with their daughters, Ellie and Grace. In his spare time he loves walking to get hot black coffee. You can find him on Instagram at @jasonwachob.

COLLEEN WACHOB is the co-founder and co-CEO at mindbodygreen, the leading independent media brand dedicated to well-being with 15 million monthly unique visitors. She lives in Miami, Florida, with her husband, mindbodygreen founder and co-CEO Jason Wachob and their two girls, Ellie and Grace. She graduated from Stanford University with degrees in international relations and Spanish. She spent ten years working at Fortune 500 companies including Gap, Walmart, and Amazon before devoting her life's work to mindbodygreen. Colleen has been a speaker at Fortune 500 companies and numerous trade conferences on well-being trends. Her new passion that brings her joy is pickleball. You can find her on Instagram at @colleenwachob.